PENCILLERS
MIKE WIERINGO
ED McGUINNESS
DOUG MAHNKE
KANO
RON GARNEY
LEONARD KIRK

INKERS
JOSÉ MARZÁN, JR.
CAM SMITH
MARLO ALQUIZA
MARK MORALES
ROBIN RIGGS
LARY STUCKER
TOM NGUYEN

ROB SCHWAGER
GENE D'ANGELO

LETTERERS
RICHARD STARKINGS
& COMICRAFT
BILL OAKLEY
KEN LOPEZ

SUPERMAN CREATED BY JERRY SIEGEL AND JOE SHUSTER

PERMAN: WORLDS WAR

BOOK ONE

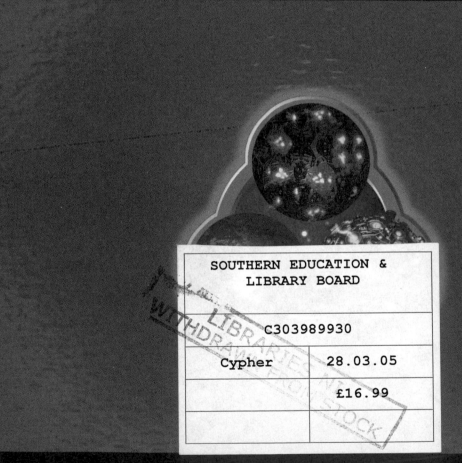

SUPERMAN: OUR WORLDS AT WAR BOOK ONE.
PUBLISHED BY DC COMICS. COVER AND COMPILATION COPYRIGHT © 2002 DC COMICS. ALL RIGHTS RESERVED.
ORIGINALLY PUBLISHED IN SINGLE MAGAZINE FORM AS SUPERMAN 171, ADVENTURES OF SUPERMAN 593, SUPERMAN: THE MAN OF
STEEL 115, ACTION COMICS 780, SUPERGIRL 59, SUPERMAN 172, JLA: OUR WORLDS AT WAR 1, ADVENTURES OF SUPERMAN 594,
SUPERMAN: THE MAN OF STEEL 116, ACTION COMICS 781. COPYRIGHT © 2001 DC COMICS. ALL RIGHTS RESERVED.
ALL CHARACTERS, THEIR DISTINCTIVE LIKENESSES AND RELATED INDICIA FEATURED IN THIS PUBLICATION ARE TRADEMARKS
OF DC COMICS. THE STORIES, CHARACTERS, AND INCIDENTS FEATURED IN THIS PUBLICATION ARE ENTIRELY FICTIONAL.
DC COMICS DOES NOT READ OR ACCEPT UNSOLICITED SUBMISSIONS OF IDEAS, STORIES OR ARTWORK.

DC COMICS, 1700 BROADWAY, NEW YORK, NY 10019 · A DIVISION OF WARNER BROS. — AN AOL TIME WARNER COMPANY
PRINTED IN CANADA. FIRST PRINTING.
ISBN: 1-56389-915-9
COVER ILLUSTRATION BY ED McGUINNESS & CAM SMITH · COVER COLOR BY RICHARD & TANYA HORIE

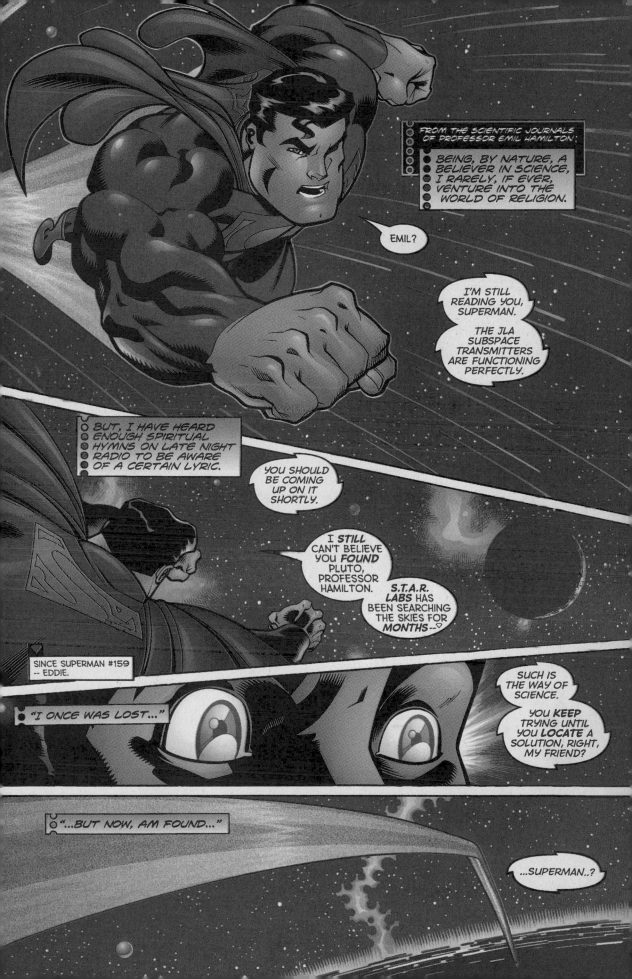

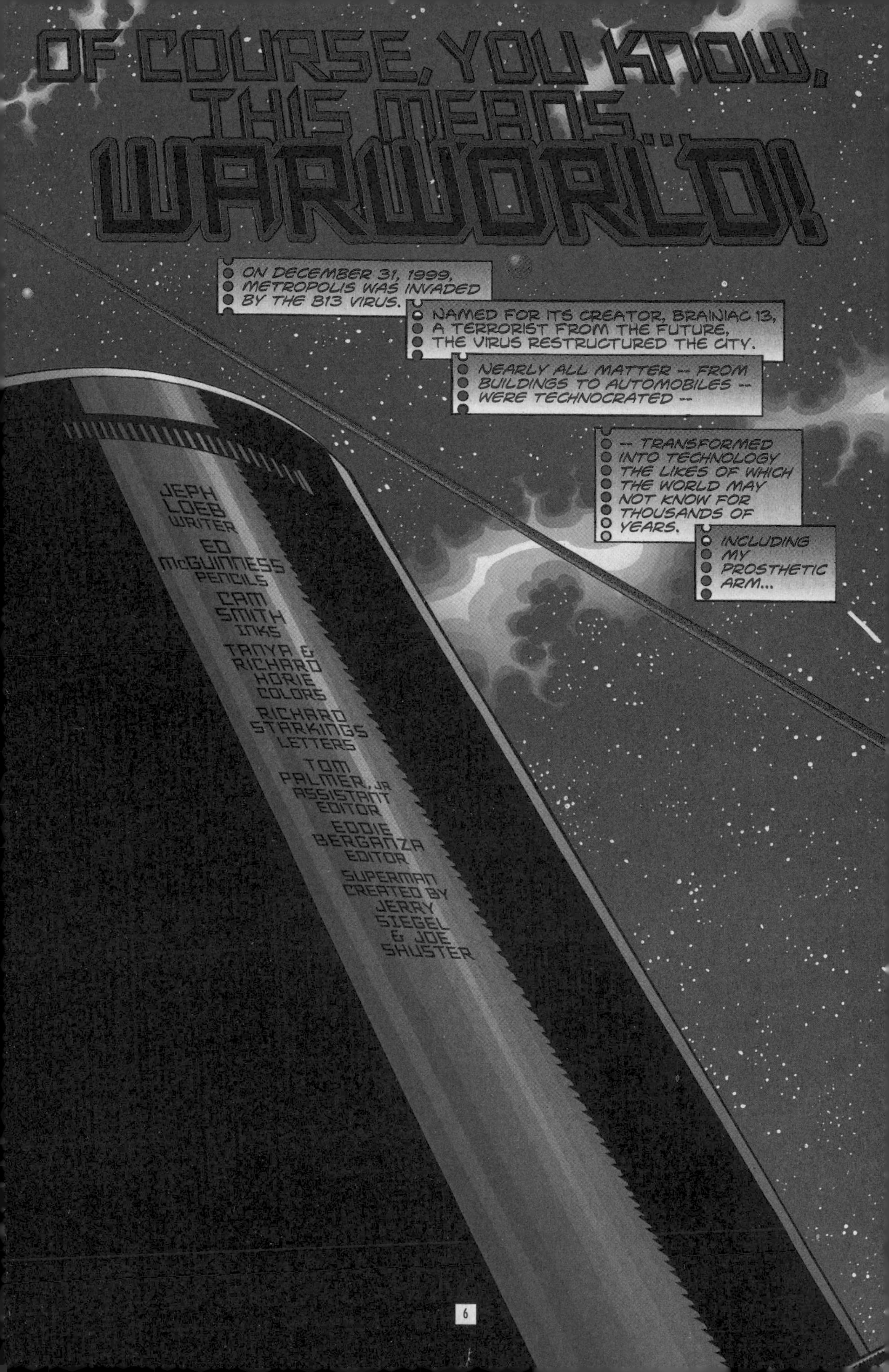
OF COURSE, YOU KNOW, THIS MEANS... WARWORLD!
ON DECEMBER 31, 1999, METROPOLIS WAS INVADED BY THE B13 VIRUS.
NAMED FOR ITS CREATOR, BRAINIAC 13, A TERRORIST FROM THE FUTURE, THE VIRUS RESTRUCTURED THE CITY.
NEARLY ALL MATTER -- FROM BUILDINGS TO AUTOMOBILES -- WERE TECHNOCRATED --
-- TRANSFORMED INTO TECHNOLOGY THE LIKES OF WHICH THE WORLD MAY NOT KNOW FOR THOUSANDS OF YEARS.
INCLUDING MY PROSTHETIC ARM...
JEPH LOEB WRITER
ED McGUINNESS PENCILS
CAM SMITH INKS
TANYA & RICHARD HORIE COLORS
RICHARD STARKINGS LETTERS
TOM PALMER, JR ASSISTANT EDITOR
EDDIE BERGANZA EDITOR
SUPERMAN CREATED BY JERRY SIEGEL & JOE SHUSTER

PROFESSOR HAMILTON.
THIS ISN'T PLUTO..!
IN THE RESULTING UPHEAVAL, I FELL AND WAS SWALLOWED BY THE EARTH.
I WANDERED FOR MONTHS IN THE LOWER LEVELS OF THE CITY, LOST IN SOMETHING BOTH MIRACULOUS AND CHILLING.
WHEN I RETURNED, MUCH HAD CHANGED. SOME THINGS... I WILL NEVER GET USED TO...

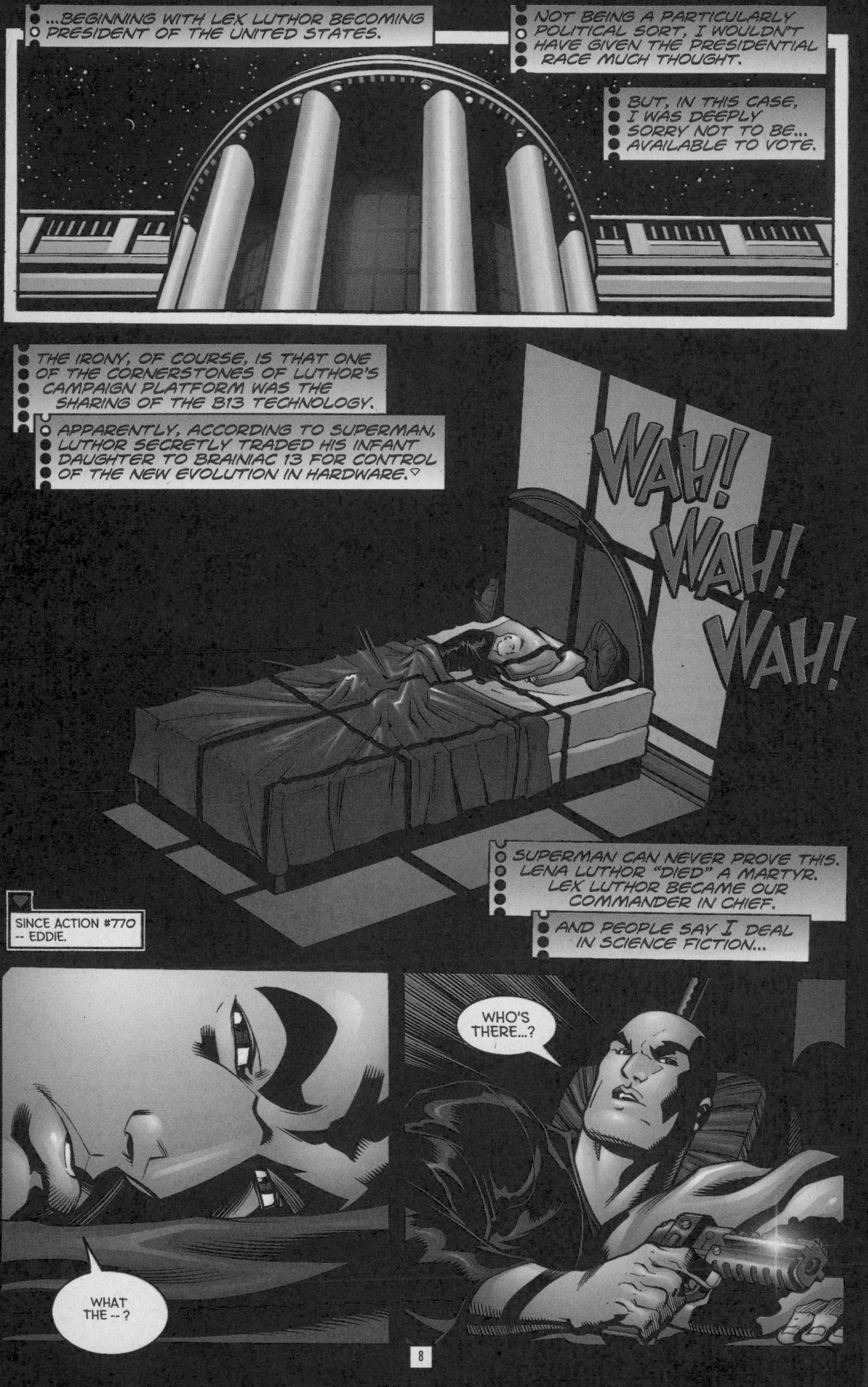
...BEGINNING WITH LEX LUTHOR BECOMING PRESIDENT OF THE UNITED STATES.
NOT BEING A PARTICULARLY POLITICAL SORT, I WOULDN'T HAVE GIVEN THE PRESIDENTIAL RACE MUCH THOUGHT.
BUT, IN THIS CASE, I WAS DEEPLY SORRY NOT TO BE... AVAILABLE TO VOTE.
THE IRONY, OF COURSE, IS THAT ONE OF THE CORNERSTONES OF LUTHOR'S CAMPAIGN PLATFORM WAS THE SHARING OF THE B13 TECHNOLOGY.
APPARENTLY, ACCORDING TO SUPERMAN, LUTHOR SECRETLY TRADED HIS INFANT DAUGHTER TO BRAINIAC 13 FOR CONTROL OF THE NEW EVOLUTION IN HARDWARE.
WAH! WAH! WAH!
SUPERMAN CAN NEVER PROVE THIS. LENA LUTHOR "DIED" A MARTYR. LEX LUTHOR BECAME OUR COMMANDER IN CHIEF.
SINCE ACTION #770 -- EDDIE.
AND PEOPLE SAY I DEAL IN SCIENCE FICTION...
WHAT THE --?
WHO'S THERE...?

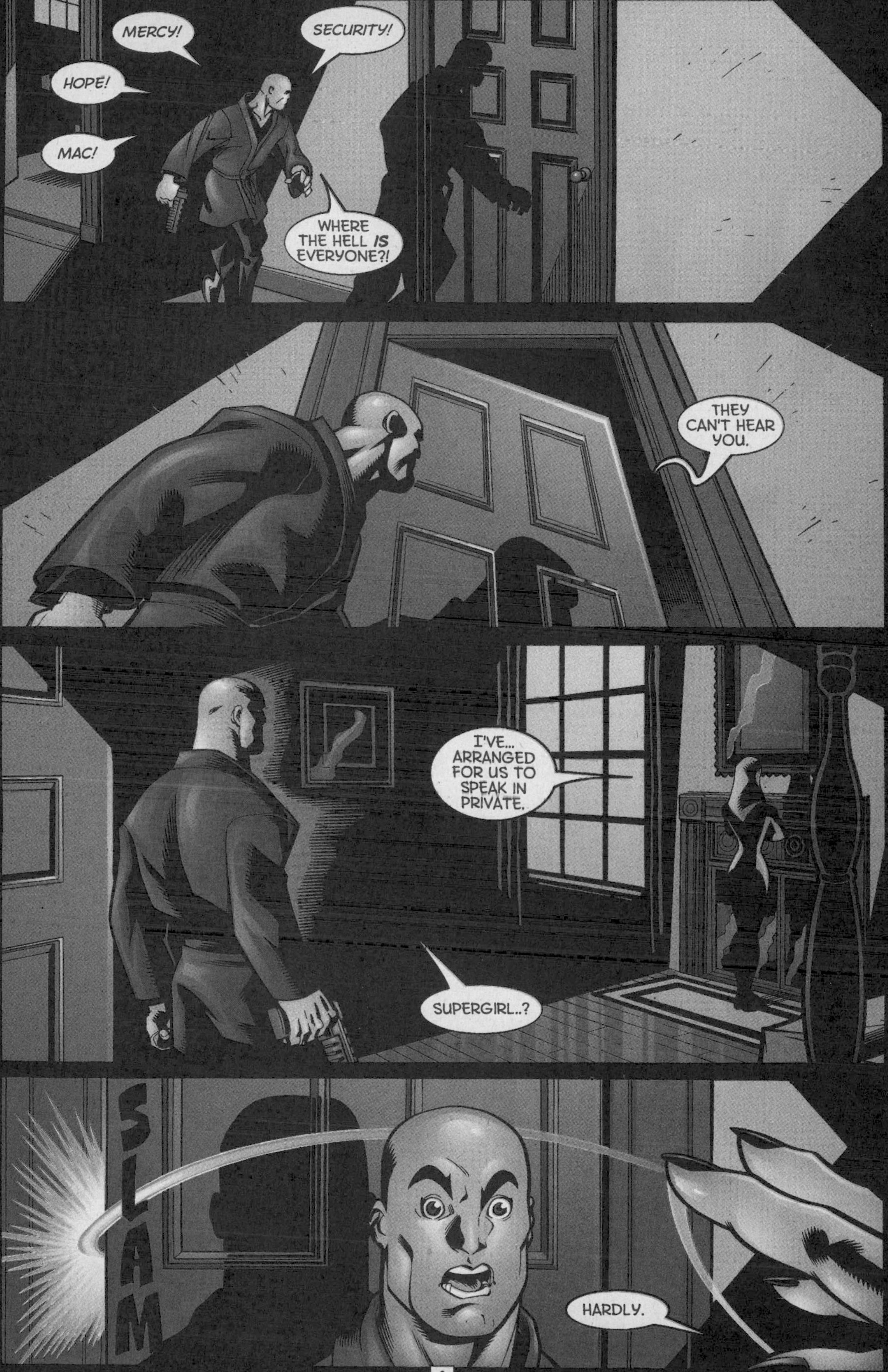
MERCY!
HOPE!
MAC!
SECURITY!
WHERE THE HELL IS EVERYONE?!
THEY CAN'T HEAR YOU.
I'VE... ARRANGED FOR US TO SPEAK IN PRIVATE.
SUPERGIRL..?
SLAM
HARDLY.

DO YOU HAVE ANY IDEA WHO YOU ARE DEALING WITH?
I AM THE PRESIDENT OF THE UNITED STATES!
BLAM BLAM BLAM
YES, YOU ARE.
AND WITH MY HELP, YOU MAY BECOME ONE OF THE MOST LEGENDARY AND INFLUENTIAL FIGURES IN HISTORY.
WASHINGTON.
LINCOLN.
ROOSEVELT.
ALL THE GREATEST PRESIDENTS HAD A SINGLE THING IN COMMON.
WHICH IS...?
A WAR.

WHILE I WAS MISSING, AT FIRST, I ADMIT I DID FIND IT... DISAPPOINTING... THAT SUPERMAN DID NOT COME TO MY RESCUE.
...WELL, IT MAY HAVE THE SIZE, DENSITY AND CIRCUMFERENCE OF PLUTO, EMIL...
...BUT SOMETHING OR SOMEONE HAS TRANSFORMED THIS ENTIRE PLANET INTO A NEW WARWORLD.
WARWORLD? THE WEAPONS PLANET?
SOMETHING THIS LARGE HAS TO HAVE A POWER SOURCE.
YOU'RE NOT PICKING UP ANYTHING?!
GRANTED, MY SCANNERS HAVE LIMITATIONS AT THIS DISTANCE, BUT NO -- YOU'RE ALL ALONE OUT THERE.
AN ENTIRE PLANET THAT IS A WEAPON, YES.
BUT, FROM WHAT I WAS TOLD BY MONGUL, IT HAD BEEN DESTROYED.
WHICH MAY ACCOUNT FOR YOUR RECENT BATTLE WITH HIM AND HIS SISTER.
I'M BEGINNING TO WISH I HAD BROUGHT KRYPTO ALONG...
ALONE. WANDERING. EACH TURN BRINGING ME ONLY FURTHER AWAY FROM WHERE I WANTED TO BE.

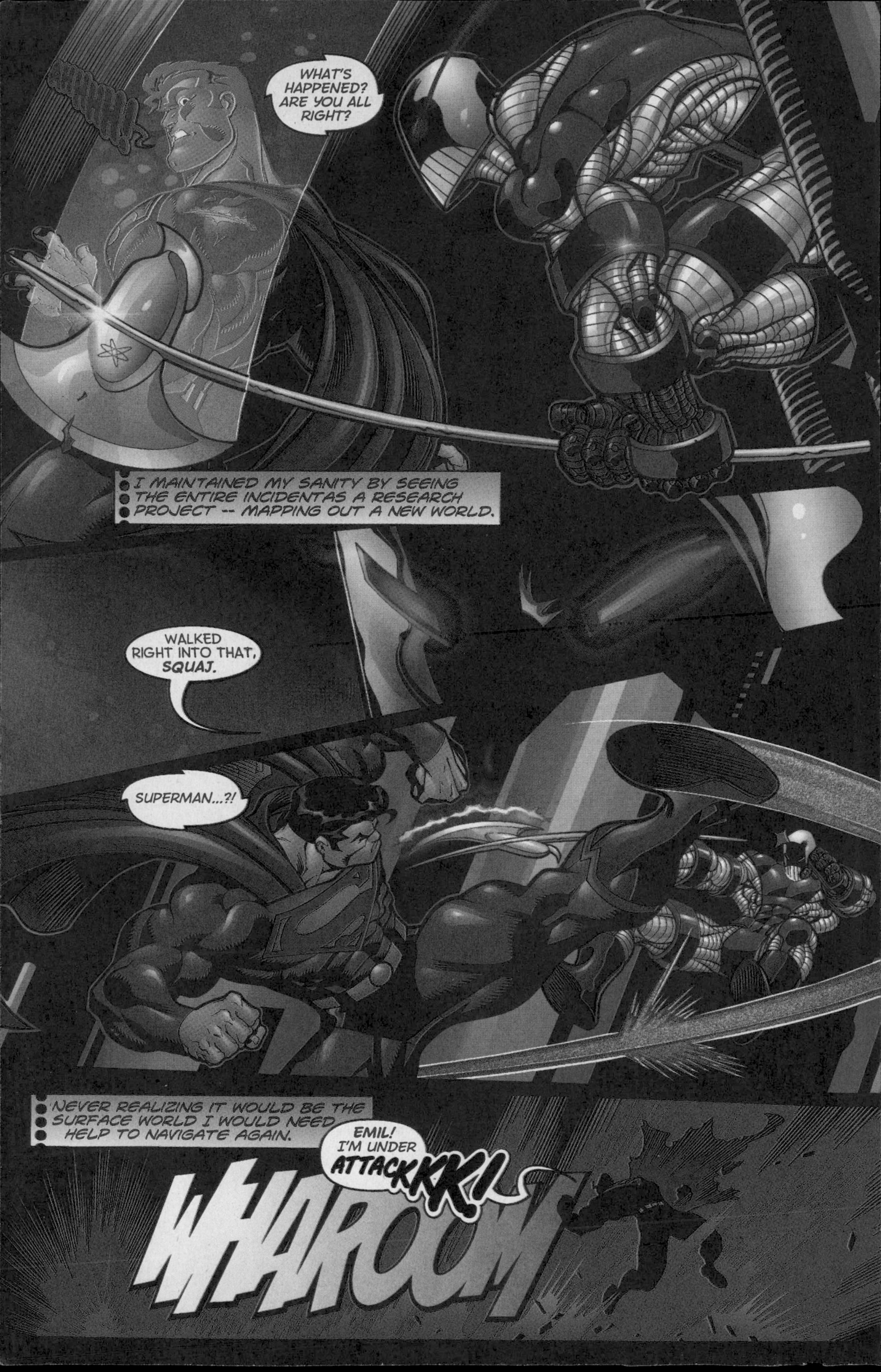

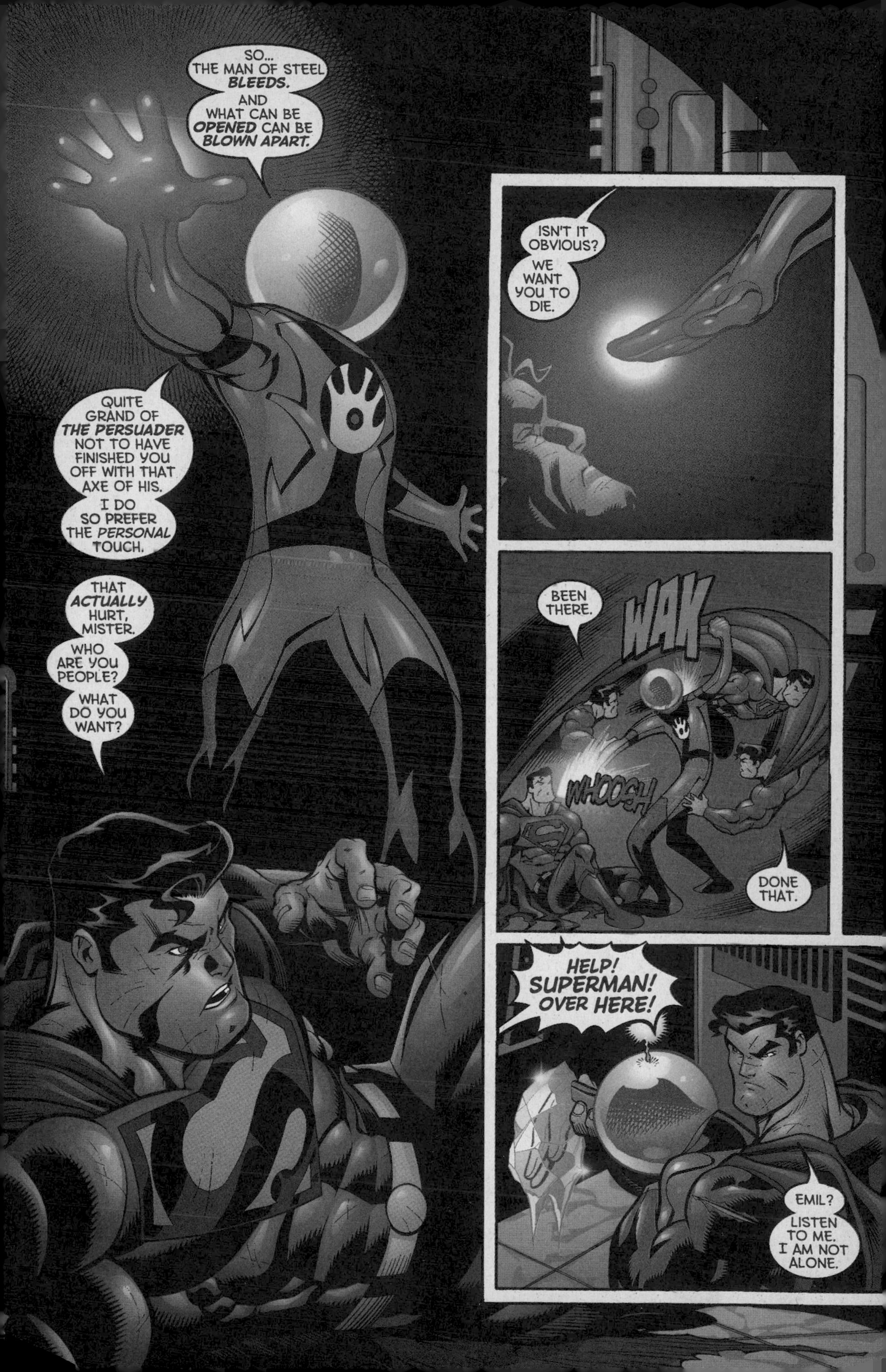
SO... THE MAN OF STEEL BLEEDS.
AND WHAT CAN BE OPENED CAN BE BLOWN APART.
QUITE GRAND OF THE PERSUADER NOT TO HAVE FINISHED YOU OFF WITH THAT AXE OF HIS.
I DO SO PREFER THE PERSONAL TOUCH.
THAT ACTUALLY HURT, MISTER.
WHO ARE YOU PEOPLE?
WHAT DO YOU WANT?
ISN'T IT OBVIOUS?
WE WANT YOU TO DIE.
BEEN THERE.
WAK
WHOOSH
DONE THAT.
HELP! SUPERMAN! OVER HERE!
EMIL?
LISTEN TO ME. I AM NOT ALONE.

-- PRESS...!
SWOOSH
I WANT ANSWERS! WHAT'S HAPPENED TO THIS PLANET?!
THE EYE! DON'T YOU DARE TOUCH IT! GIVE IT TO ME! NOW!
I COMMAND YOU!
WRONG ANSWER.
SUPERMAN, IF YOU ARE SPEAKING TO SOMEONE ELSE --
VZZZZZT
-- I CAN'T HEAR THEIR HALF OF THE CONVERSATION.

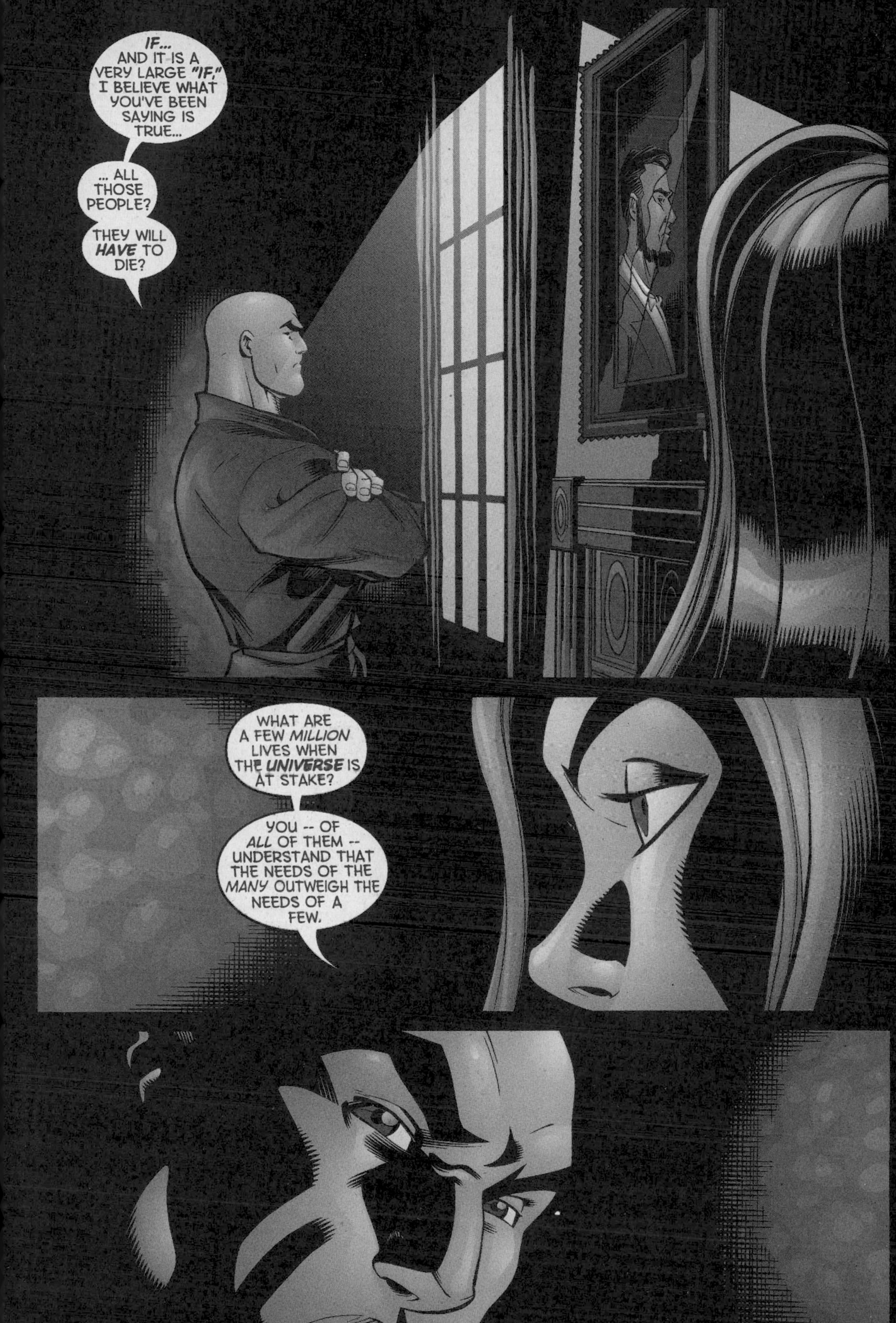
IF... AND IT IS A VERY LARGE "IF," I BELIEVE WHAT YOU'VE BEEN SAYING IS TRUE...
... ALL THOSE PEOPLE?
THEY WILL HAVE TO DIE?
WHAT ARE A FEW MILLION LIVES WHEN THE UNIVERSE IS AT STAKE?
YOU -- OF ALL OF THEM -- UNDERSTAND THAT THE NEEDS OF THE MANY OUTWEIGH THE NEEDS OF A FEW.

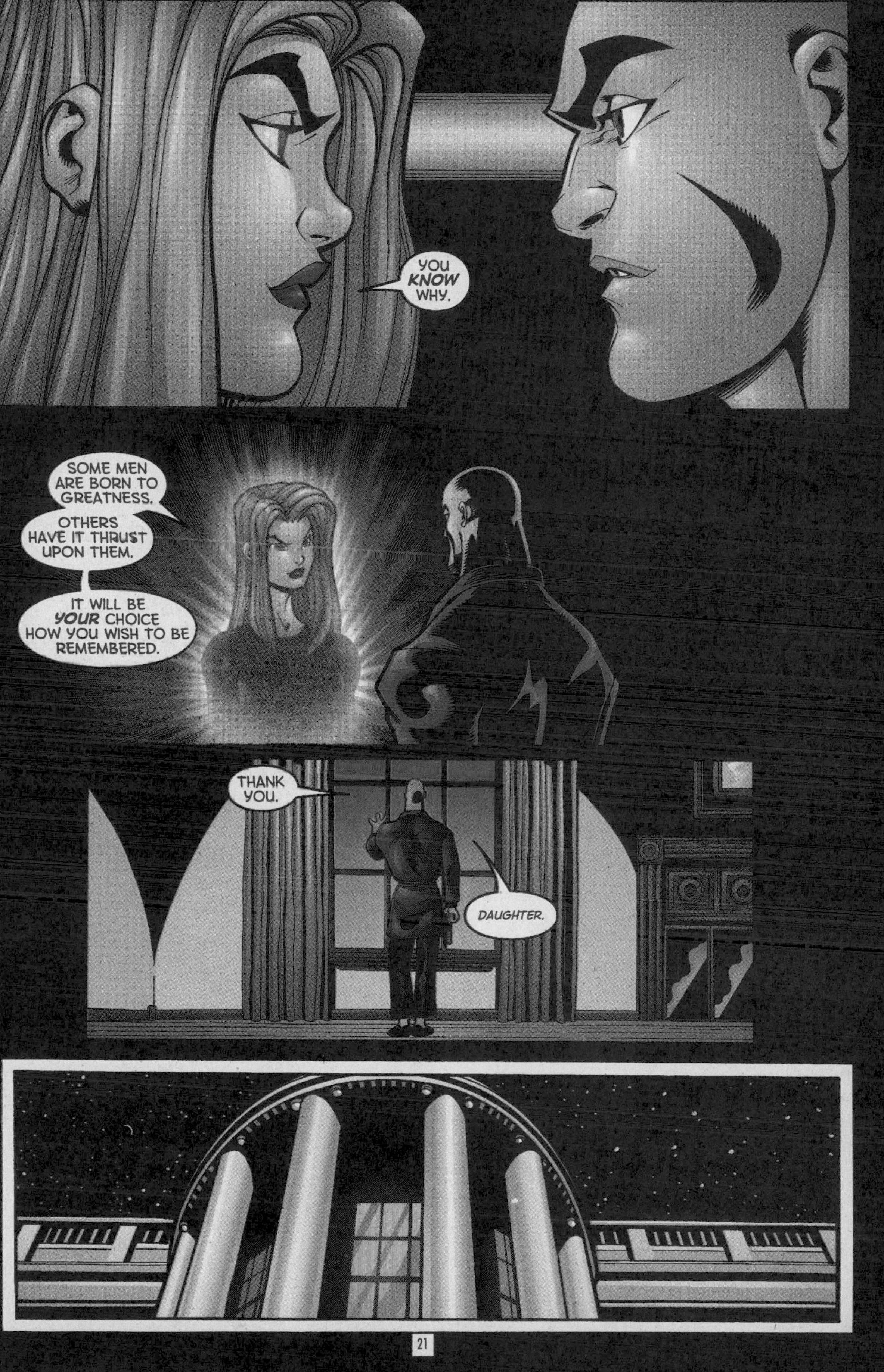
YOU KNOW WHY.
SOME MEN ARE BORN TO GREATNESS.
OTHERS HAVE IT THRUST UPON THEM.
IT WILL BE YOUR CHOICE HOW YOU WISH TO BE REMEMBERED.
THANK YOU.
DAUGHTER.

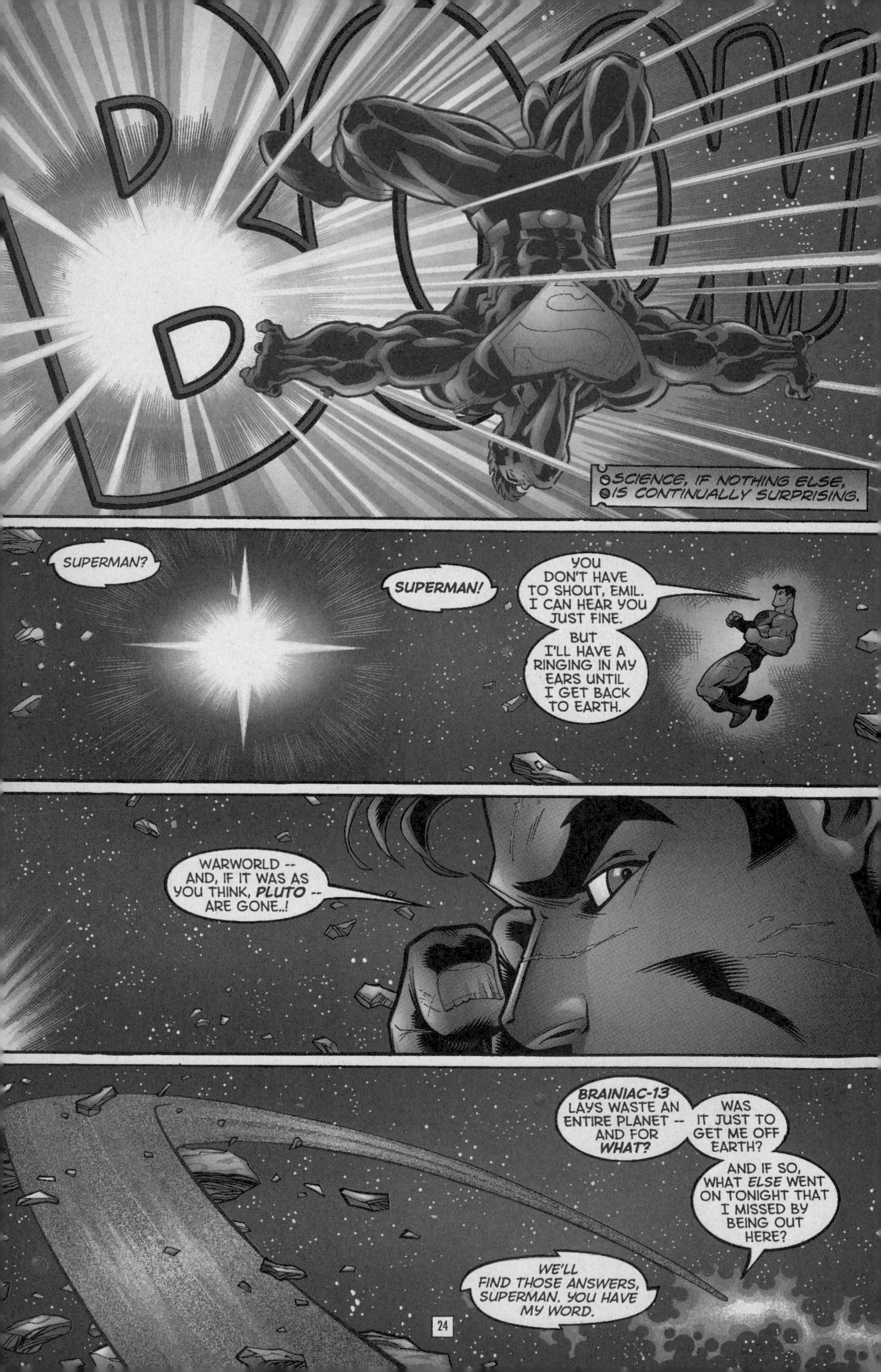

DOOM
SCIENCE, IF NOTHING ELSE, IS CONTINUALLY SURPRISING.
SUPERMAN?
SUPERMAN!
YOU DON'T HAVE TO SHOUT, EMIL. I CAN HEAR YOU JUST FINE.
BUT I'LL HAVE A RINGING IN MY EARS UNTIL I GET BACK TO EARTH.
WARWORLD -- AND, IF IT WAS AS YOU THINK, PLUTO -- ARE GONE..!
BRAINIAC-13 LAYS WASTE AN ENTIRE PLANET -- AND FOR WHAT?
WAS IT JUST TO GET ME OFF EARTH?
AND IF SO, WHAT ELSE WENT ON TONIGHT THAT I MISSED BY BEING OUT HERE?
WE'LL FIND THOSE ANSWERS, SUPERMAN. YOU HAVE MY WORD.

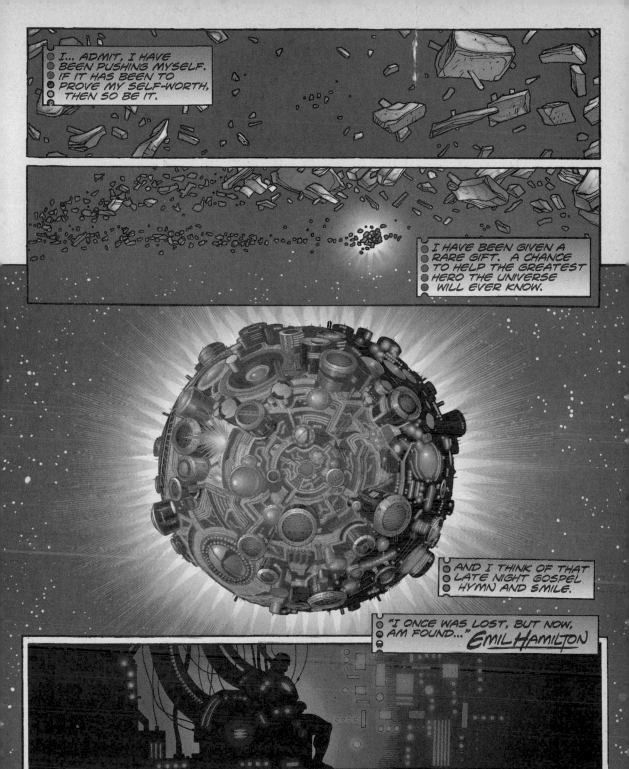

I... ADMIT, I HAVE BEEN PUSHING MYSELF. IF IT HAS BEEN TO PROVE MY SELF-WORTH, THEN SO BE IT.

I HAVE BEEN GIVEN A RARE GIFT. A CHANCE TO HELP THE GREATEST HERO THE UNIVERSE WILL EVER KNOW.

AND I THINK OF THAT LATE NIGHT GOSPEL HYMN AND SMILE.

"I ONCE WAS LOST, BUT NOW, AM FOUND..." *EMIL HAMILTON*

HMM...

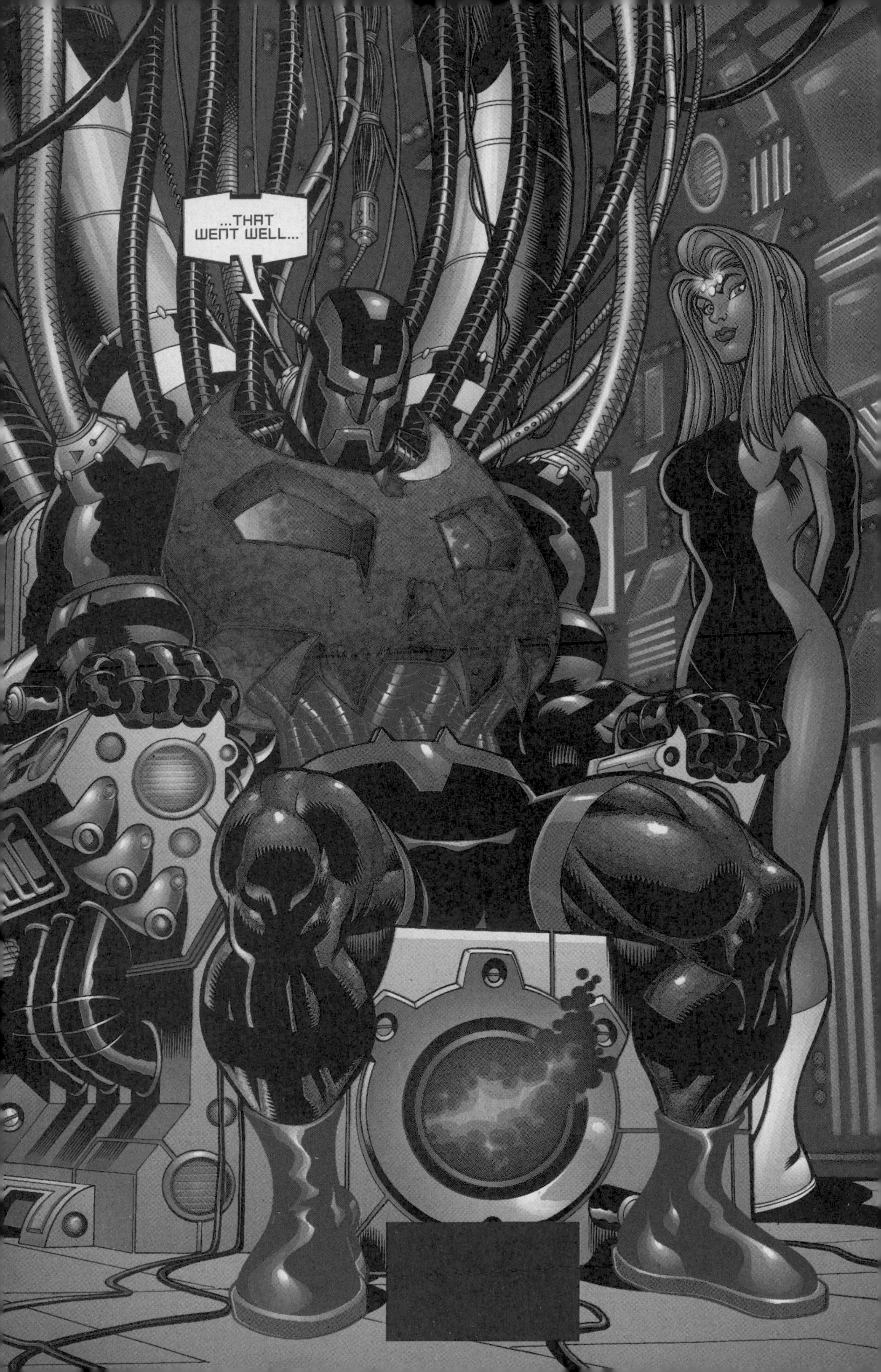
...THAT WENT WELL...

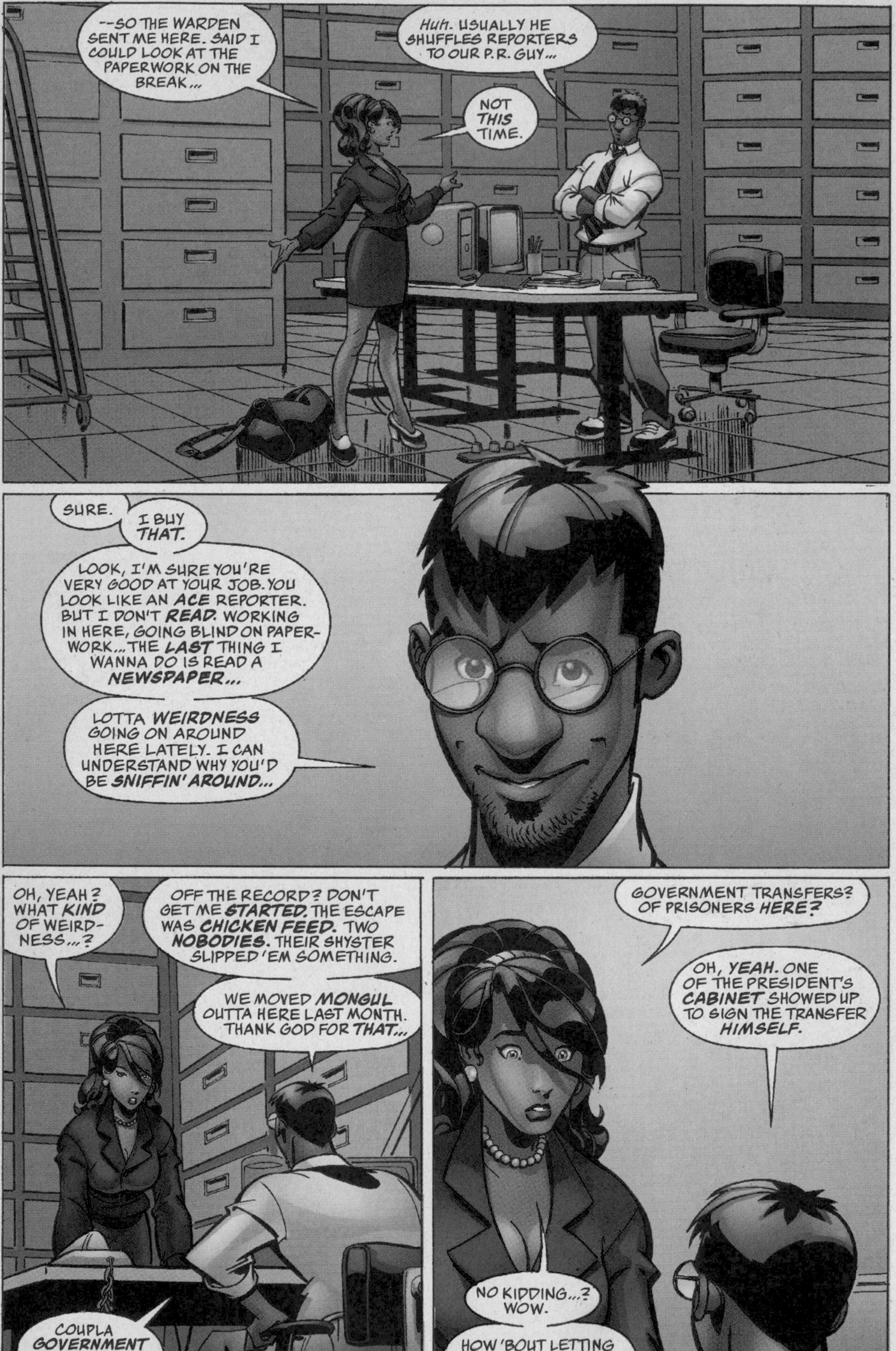
--SO THE WARDEN SENT ME HERE. SAID I COULD LOOK AT THE PAPERWORK ON THE BREAK...
HUH. USUALLY HE SHUFFLES REPORTERS TO OUR P.R. GUY...
NOT THIS TIME.
SURE.
I BUY THAT.
LOOK, I'M SURE YOU'RE VERY GOOD AT YOUR JOB. YOU LOOK LIKE AN ACE REPORTER. BUT I DON'T READ. WORKING IN HERE, GOING BLIND ON PAPERWORK... THE LAST THING I WANNA DO IS READ A NEWSPAPER...
LOTTA WEIRDNESS GOING ON AROUND HERE LATELY. I CAN UNDERSTAND WHY YOU'D BE SNIFFIN' AROUND...
OH, YEAH? WHAT KIND OF WEIRD-NESS...?
OFF THE RECORD? DON'T GET ME STARTED. THE ESCAPE WAS CHICKEN FEED. TWO NOBODIES. THEIR SHYSTER SLIPPED 'EM SOMETHING.
WE MOVED MONGUL OUTTA HERE LAST MONTH. THANK GOD FOR THAT...
COUPLA GOVERNMENT TRANSFERS LAST WEEK...
GOVERNMENT TRANSFERS? OF PRISONERS HERE?
OH, YEAH. ONE OF THE PRESIDENT'S CABINET SHOWED UP TO SIGN THE TRANSFER HIMSELF.
NO KIDDING...? WOW.
HOW 'BOUT LETTING ME TAKE A LOOK AT THAT TRANSFER?

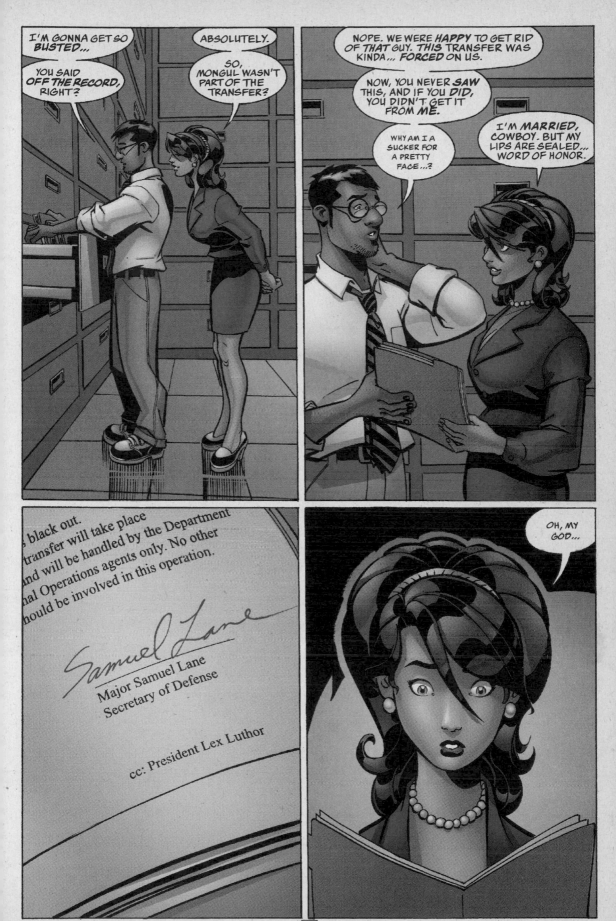

SUICIDE MISSION

JOE CASEY writer · **MIKE WIERINGO** pencils · **JOSE MARZAN, JR.** inks · **BILL OAKLEY** letters · **WILDSTORM FX** colors · **TOM PALMER, JR.** asst. ed. · **EDDIE BERGANZA** editor

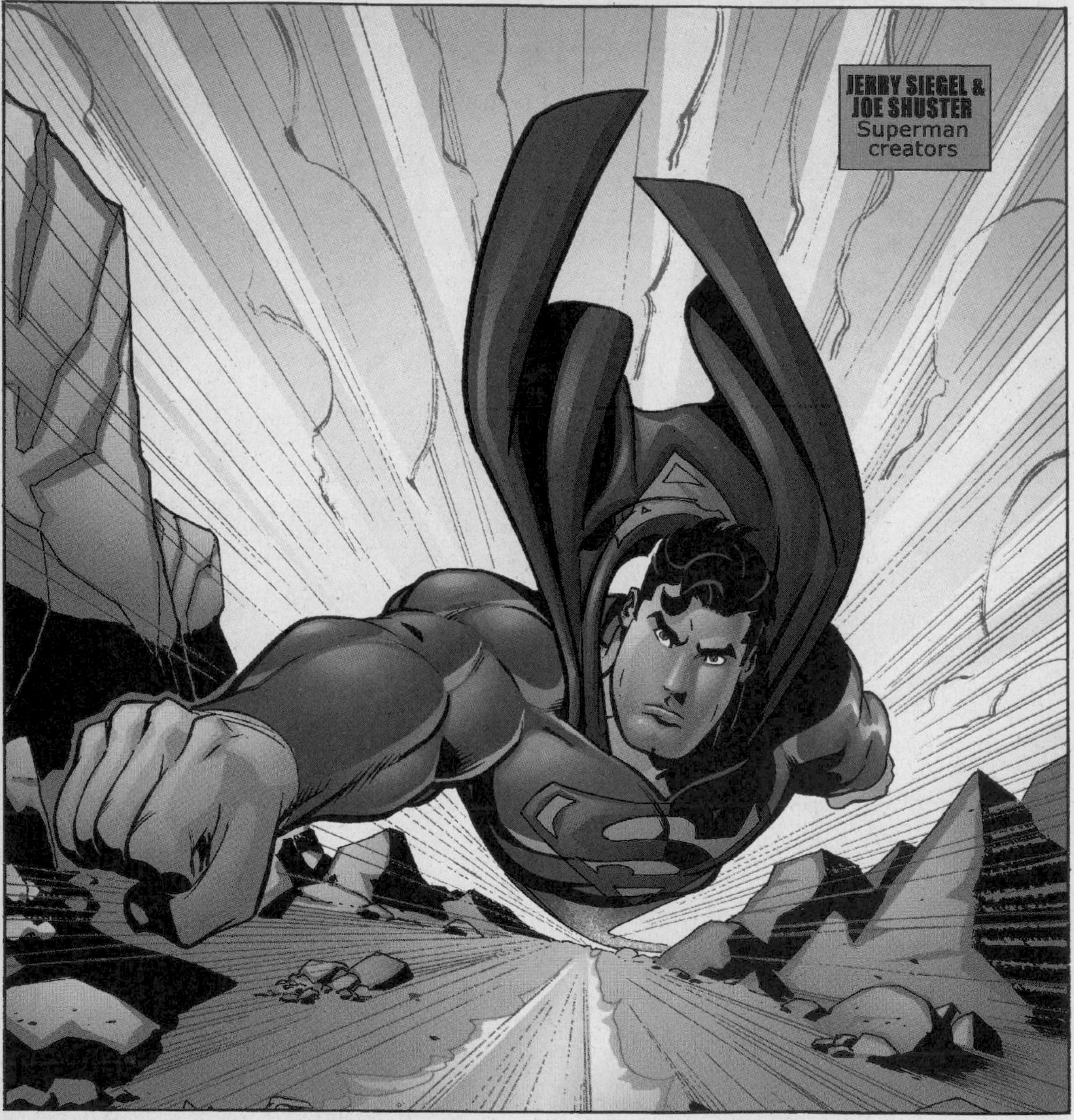
JERRY SIEGEL & JOE SHUSTER
Superman creators

AREA 8...

...ABANDONED **YEARS** AGO, DUE TO MILITARY CUTBACKS.

AND THERE IT **IS**...

A RADIO **TRANSMITTER**, SENDING A HYPERSONIC SIGNAL ALL THE WAY ACROSS THE COUNTRY, TO METROPOLIS.

ASIDE FROM THE OCCASIONAL **DOG**, I'M PROBABLY THE ONLY ONE **HEARING** IT.

SO WHO'S **RESPONSIBLE**... AND WHY DID THEY WANT TO LEAD ME **HERE**... OUT TO THE MIDDLE OF NOWHERE--?

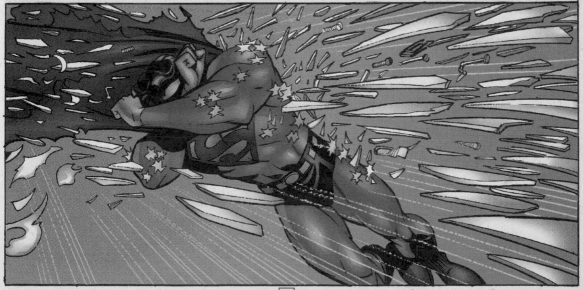

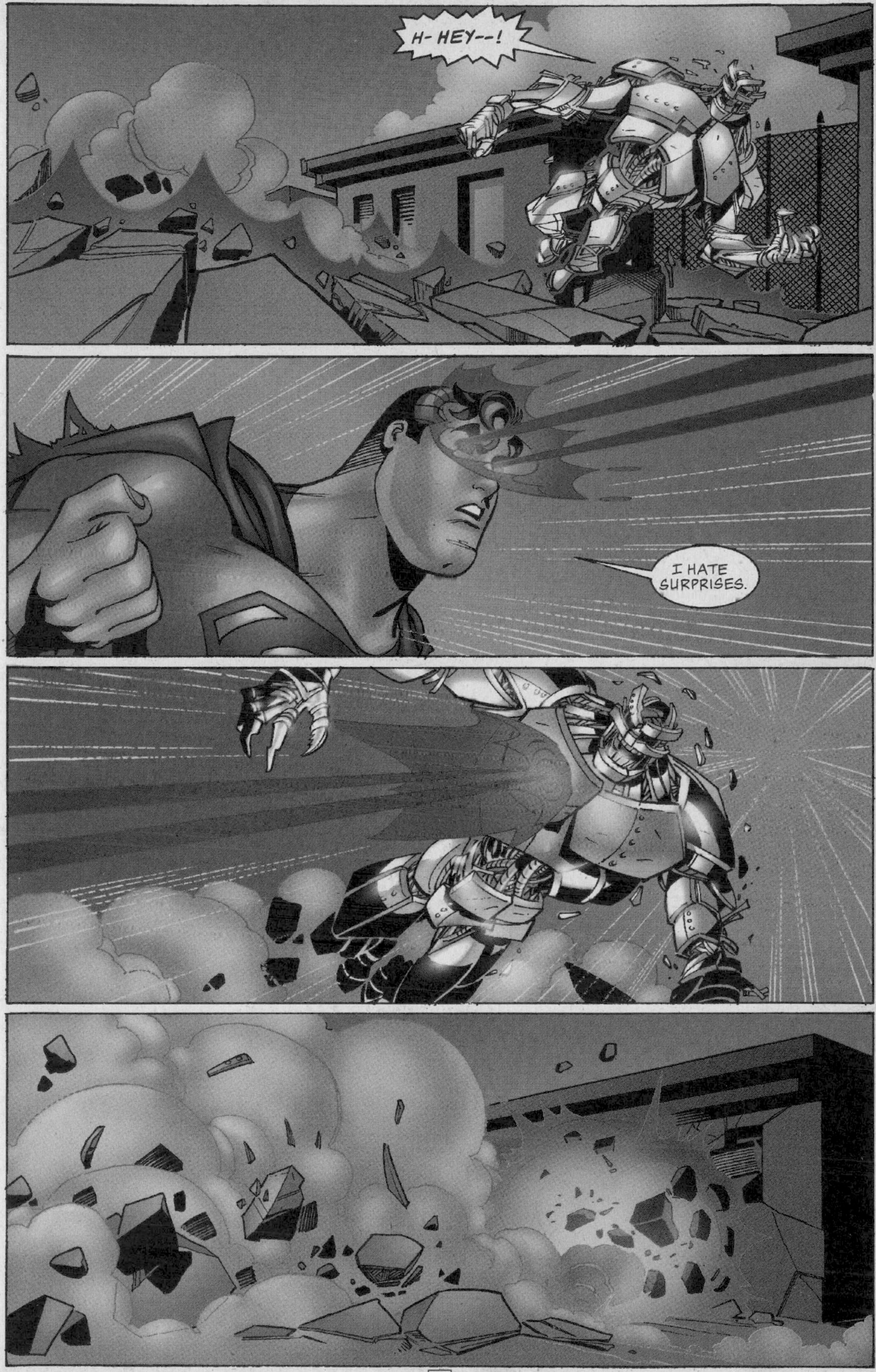
H- HEY--!
I HATE SURPRISES.

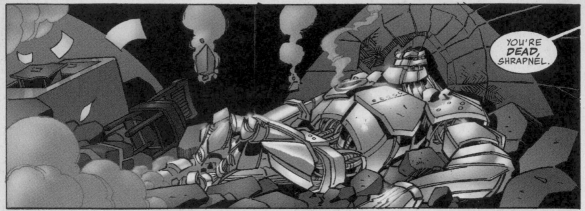

YOU'RE *DEAD*, SHRAPNEL.

WHY'D WE PULL YOU OUTTA STRYKER'S, SQUIRE?

GIMME ANOTHER *SHOT* AT HIM.

WE CLEAN THE *RUST* OFFA YOU AND *HE* SHOVES YER KNICKERS UP YER BUM...

I SHOULDN'T *DO* THIS. I'M BREAKING THE *RULES* FOR YA, MATE. I'M GETTIN' BLEEDIN' *SOFT* IN MY OLD AGE...

THIS ISN'T LIKE TAG ON THE SCHOOLYARD. HE'S THE TOUGHEST NUT ON THE BLOCK. YOU GOTTA BE *TOUGHER*.

GO.

WELL, I THINK I'VE GOT MY ANSWER.

ALTHOUGH I'M SURE IT'S NOT OVER YET...

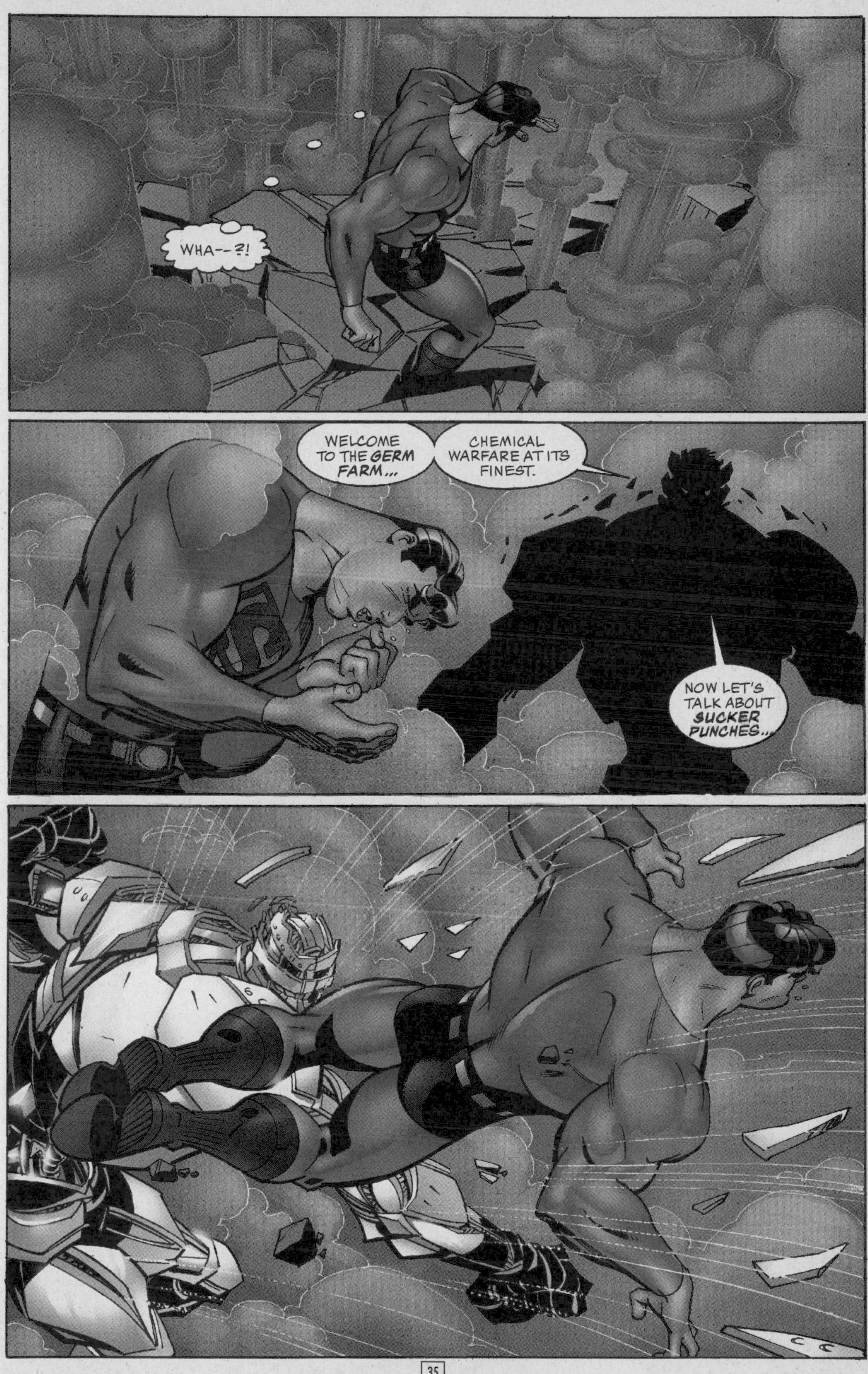
WHA--?!
WELCOME TO THE GERM FARM...
CHEMICAL WARFARE AT ITS FINEST.
NOW LET'S TALK ABOUT SUCKER PUNCHES...

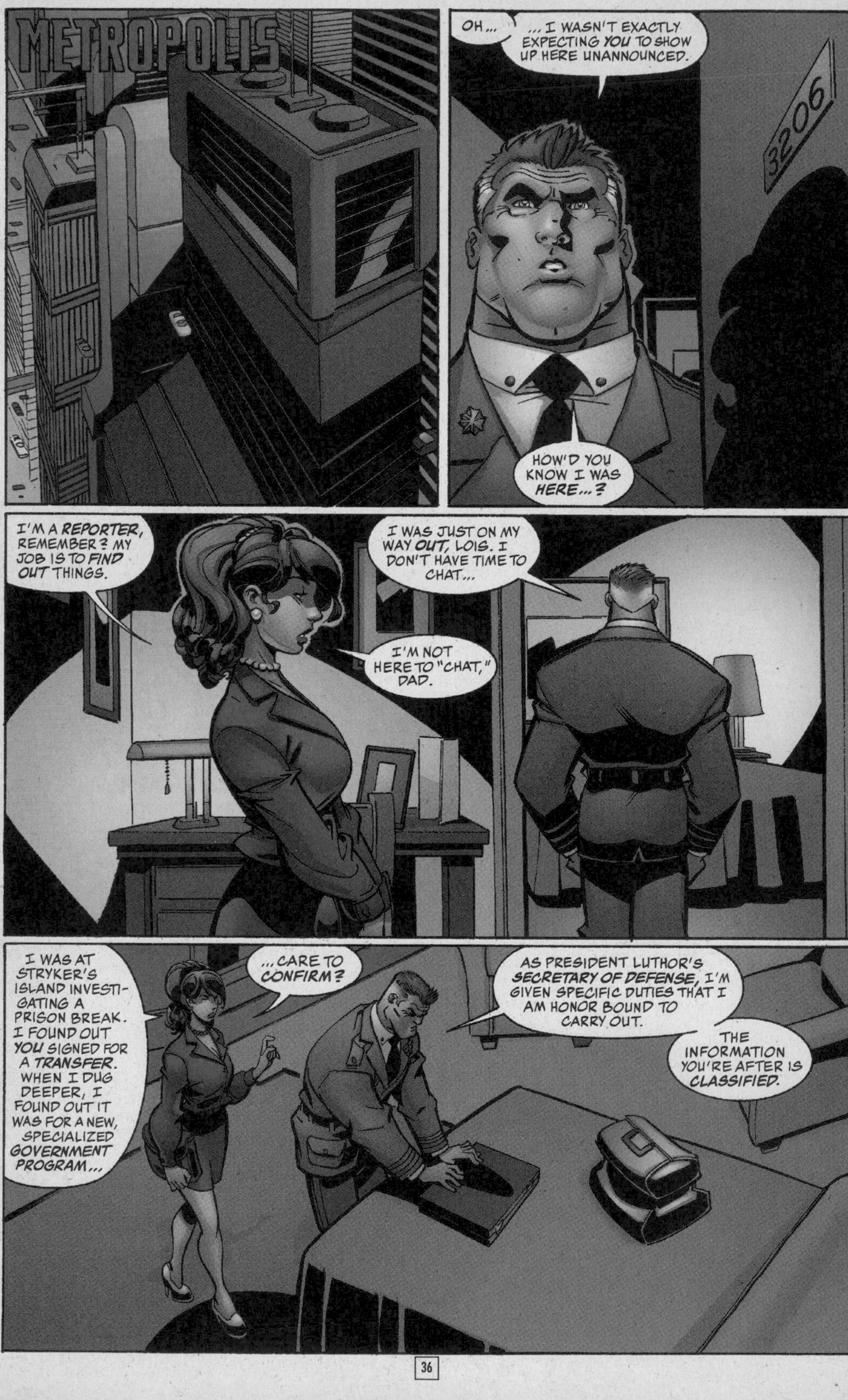
METROPOLIS
OH...
...I WASN'T EXACTLY EXPECTING YOU TO SHOW UP HERE UNANNOUNCED.
3206
HOW'D YOU KNOW I WAS HERE...?
I'M A REPORTER, REMEMBER? MY JOB IS TO FIND OUT THINGS.
I WAS JUST ON MY WAY OUT, LOIS. I DON'T HAVE TIME TO CHAT...
I'M NOT HERE TO "CHAT," DAD.
I WAS AT STRYKER'S ISLAND INVESTIGATING A PRISON BREAK. I FOUND OUT YOU SIGNED FOR A TRANSFER. WHEN I DUG DEEPER, I FOUND OUT IT WAS FOR A NEW, SPECIALIZED GOVERNMENT PROGRAM...
...CARE TO CONFIRM?
AS PRESIDENT LUTHOR'S SECRETARY OF DEFENSE, I'M GIVEN SPECIFIC DUTIES THAT I AM HONOR BOUND TO CARRY OUT.
THE INFORMATION YOU'RE AFTER IS CLASSIFIED.

I'M IMPRESSED BY YOUR TENACITY, THOUGH...

I'M GOOD AT WHAT I DO. THE QUESTION IS...

...HOW AM I GOING TO GET *YOU* TO TALK? STRYKER'S IS A *METAHUMAN* FACILITY. WHY ARE *YOU* AUTHORIZING TRANSFERS? IS LUTHOR GIVING *PARDONS*--?

DON'T BE RIDICULOUS.

NOW, I'M REALLY IN A RUSH, SO IF YOU'LL *EXCUSE* ME--

YOU'RE NOT GETTING OFF *THAT* EASY, "MISTER SECRETARY"...

...IF I SMELL A *RAT*, I HAVE NO CHOICE BUT TO COME AT YOU *AND* LUTHOR WITH ALL I'VE GOT--

HOW *DARE* YOU, YOUNG LADY?! HOW DARE YOU *QUESTION MY LOYALTY* TO MY COUNTRY?!

IF YOU HAD ANY *INKLING* AS TO WHAT MAY BE COMING, YOU'D GET RIGHT IN LINE BEHIND YOUR GOVERNING EXECUTIVE AND PLEDGE YOUR UNDYING SUPPORT, AS I HAVE!

THIS IS MAJOR SAM LANE IN SUITE 3206. COULD YOU ALERT THE CAR THAT I'M COMING DOWN...?

THANK YOU.

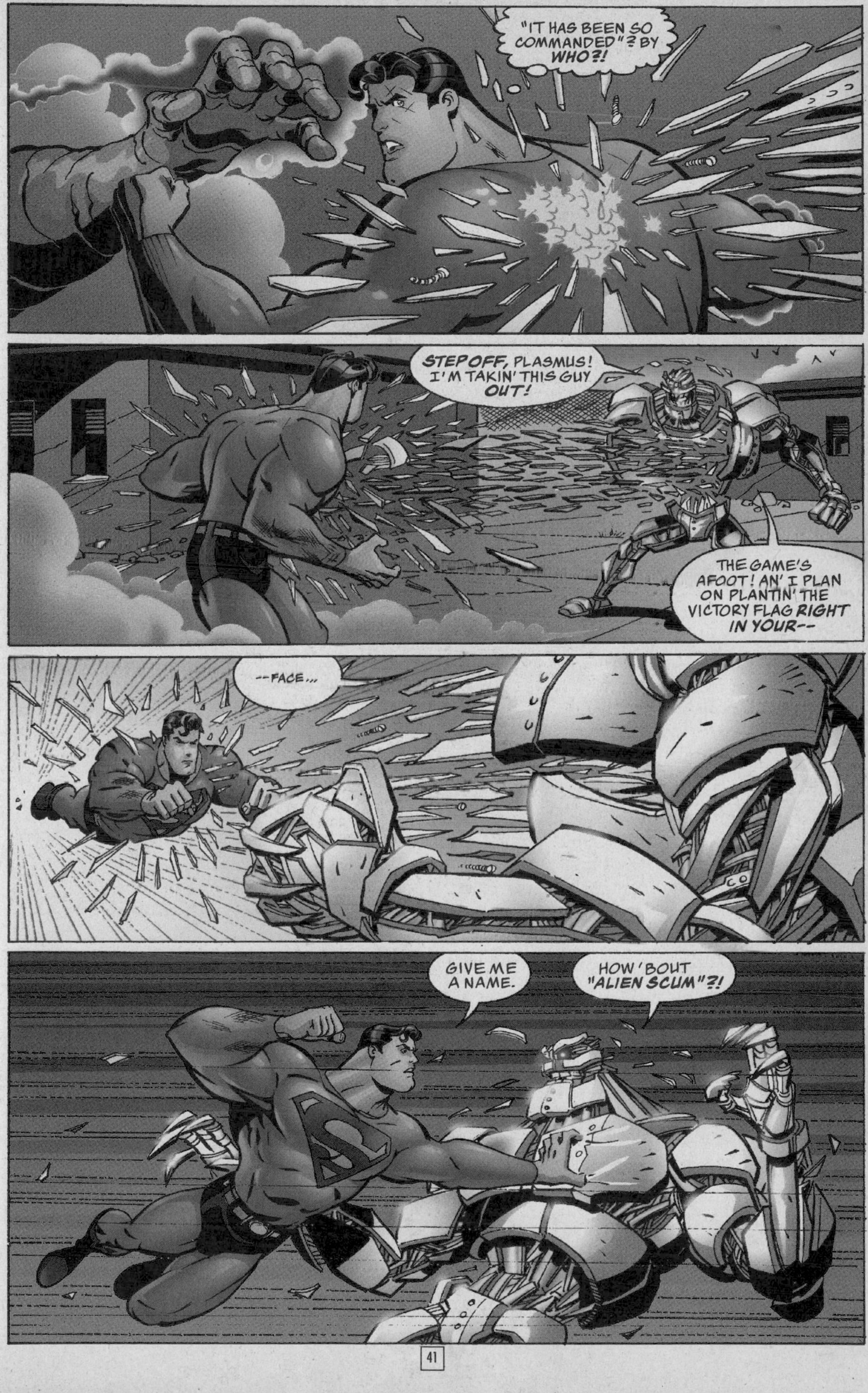
"IT HAS BEEN SO COMMANDED"? BY WHO?!
STEP OFF, PLASMUS! I'M TAKIN' THIS GUY OUT!
THE GAME'S AFOOT! AN' I PLAN ON PLANTIN' THE VICTORY FLAG RIGHT IN YOUR--
--FACE...
GIVE ME A NAME.
HOW 'BOUT "ALIEN SCUM"?!

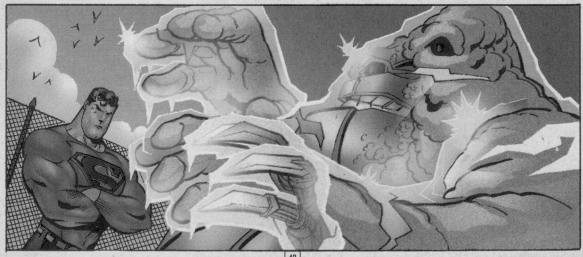

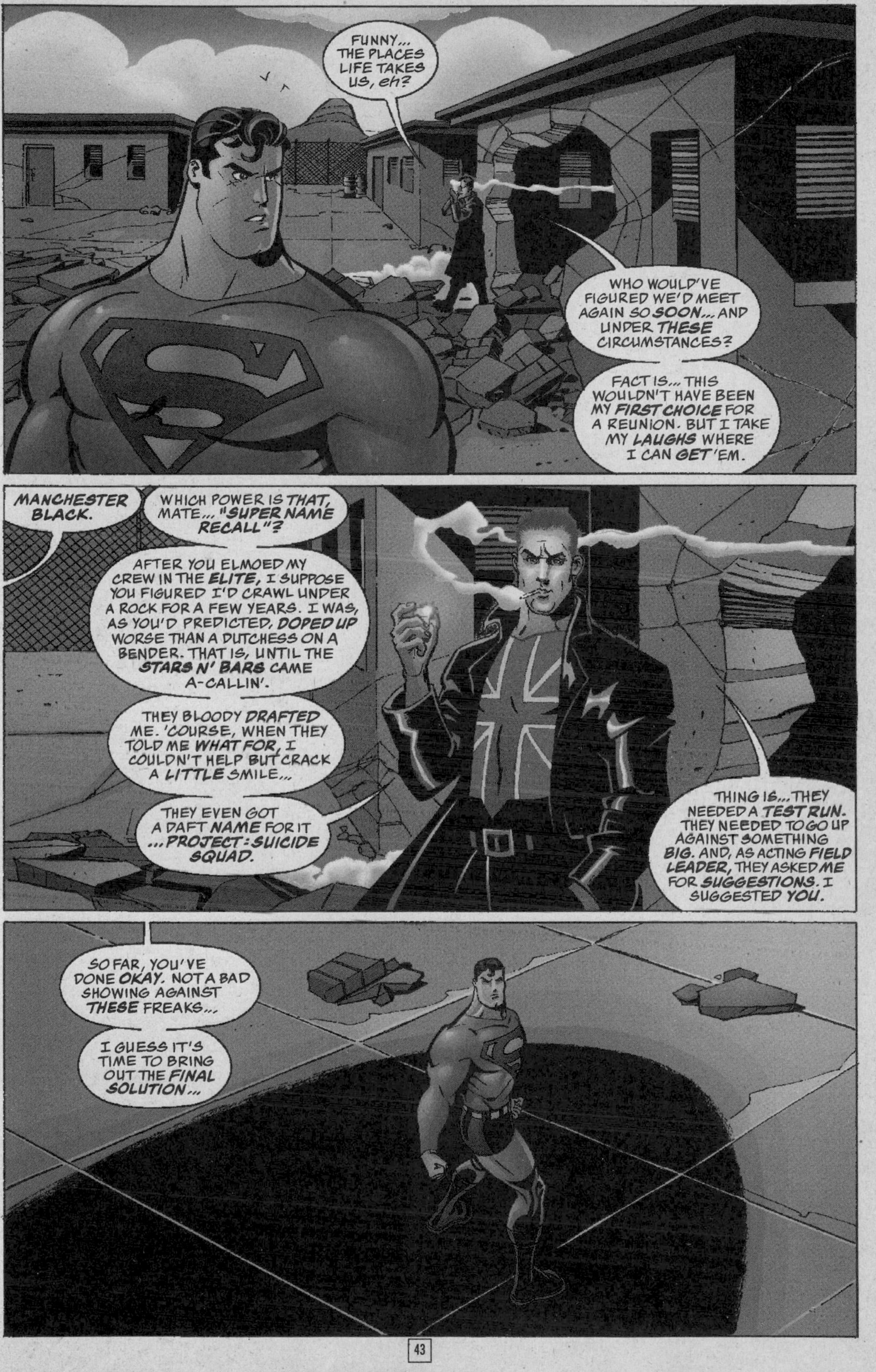
FUNNY... THE PLACES LIFE TAKES US, eh?
WHO WOULD'VE FIGURED WE'D MEET AGAIN SO SOON... AND UNDER THESE CIRCUMSTANCES?
FACT IS... THIS WOULDN'T HAVE BEEN MY FIRST CHOICE FOR A REUNION. BUT I TAKE MY LAUGHS WHERE I CAN GET 'EM.
MANCHESTER BLACK.
WHICH POWER IS THAT, MATE... "SUPER NAME RECALL"?
AFTER YOU ELMOED MY CREW IN THE ELITE, I SUPPOSE YOU FIGURED I'D CRAWL UNDER A ROCK FOR A FEW YEARS. I WAS, AS YOU'D PREDICTED, DOPED UP WORSE THAN A DUTCHESS ON A BENDER. THAT IS, UNTIL THE STARS N' BARS CAME A-CALLIN'.
THEY BLOODY DRAFTED ME. 'COURSE, WHEN THEY TOLD ME WHAT FOR, I COULDN'T HELP BUT CRACK A LITTLE SMILE...
THEY EVEN GOT A DAFT NAME FOR IT ...PROJECT: SUICIDE SQUAD.
THING IS... THEY NEEDED A TEST RUN. THEY NEEDED TO GO UP AGAINST SOMETHING BIG. AND, AS ACTING FIELD LEADER, THEY ASKED ME FOR SUGGESTIONS. I SUGGESTED YOU.
SO FAR, YOU'VE DONE OKAY. NOT A BAD SHOWING AGAINST THESE FREAKS...
I GUESS IT'S TIME TO BRING OUT THE FINAL SOLUTION...

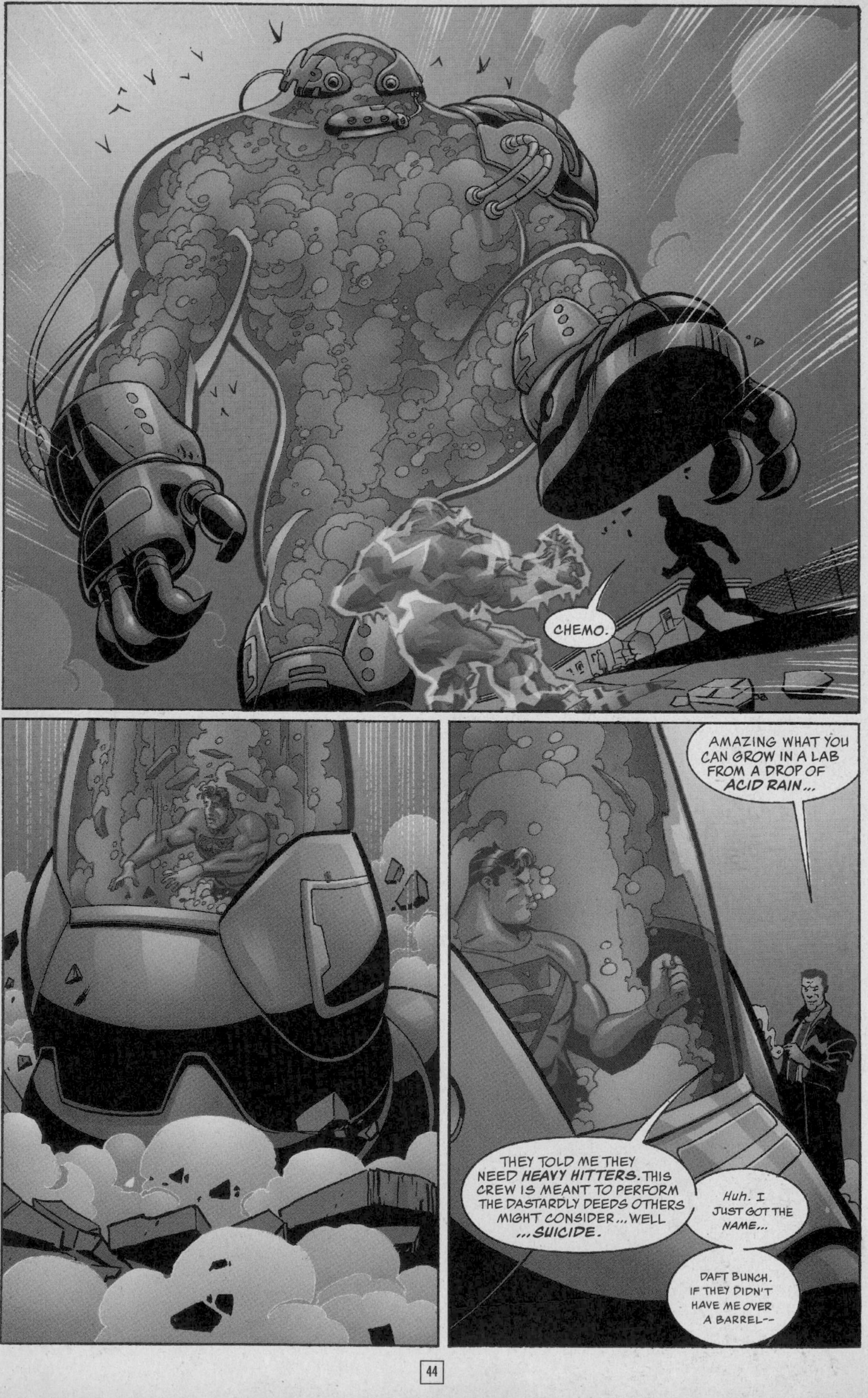
CHEMO.
AMAZING WHAT YOU CAN GROW IN A LAB FROM A DROP OF ACID RAIN...
THEY TOLD ME THEY NEED HEAVY HITTERS. THIS CREW IS MEANT TO PERFORM THE DASTARDLY DEEDS OTHERS MIGHT CONSIDER... WELL ...SUICIDE.
Huh. I JUST GOT THE NAME...
DAFT BUNCH. IF THEY DIDN'T HAVE ME OVER A BARREL--

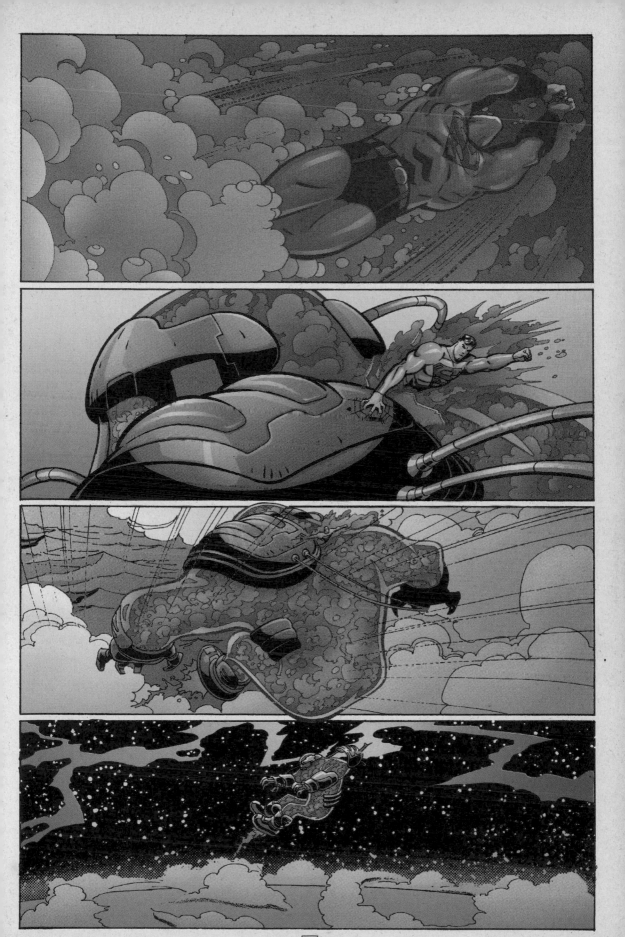

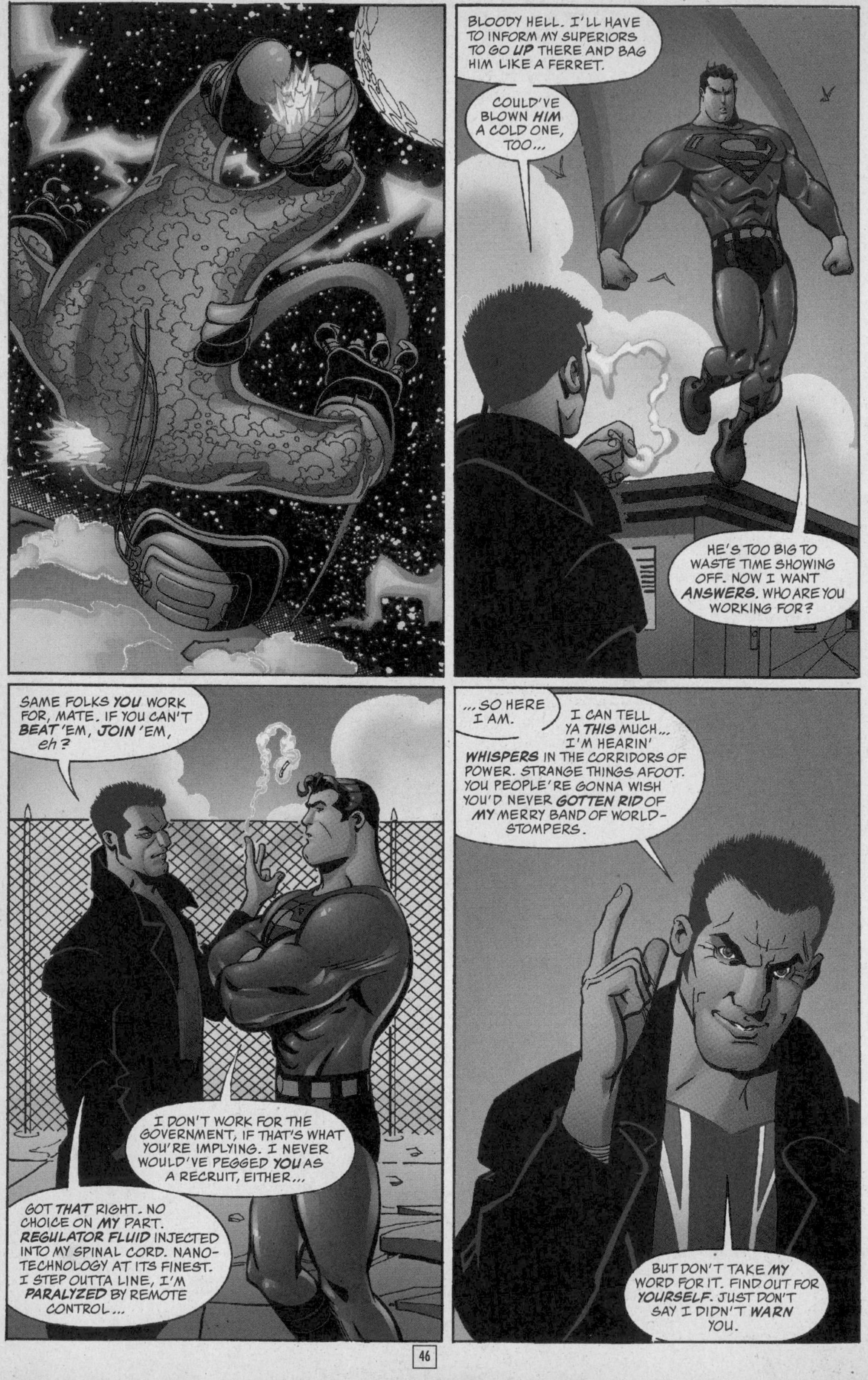
BLOODY HELL. I'LL HAVE TO INFORM MY SUPERIORS TO GO UP THERE AND BAG HIM LIKE A FERRET.
COULD'VE BLOWN HIM A COLD ONE, TOO...
HE'S TOO BIG TO WASTE TIME SHOWING OFF. NOW I WANT ANSWERS. WHO ARE YOU WORKING FOR?
SAME FOLKS YOU WORK FOR, MATE. IF YOU CAN'T BEAT 'EM, JOIN 'EM, eh?
I DON'T WORK FOR THE GOVERNMENT, IF THAT'S WHAT YOU'RE IMPLYING. I NEVER WOULD'VE PEGGED YOU AS A RECRUIT, EITHER...
GOT THAT RIGHT. NO CHOICE ON MY PART. REGULATOR FLUID INJECTED INTO MY SPINAL CORD. NANO-TECHNOLOGY AT ITS FINEST. I STEP OUTTA LINE, I'M PARALYZED BY REMOTE CONTROL...
...SO HERE I AM.
I CAN TELL YA THIS MUCH... I'M HEARIN' WHISPERS IN THE CORRIDORS OF POWER. STRANGE THINGS AFOOT. YOU PEOPLE'RE GONNA WISH YOU'D NEVER GOTTEN RID OF MY MERRY BAND OF WORLD-STOMPERS.
BUT DON'T TAKE MY WORD FOR IT. FIND OUT FOR YOURSELF. JUST DON'T SAY I DIDN'T WARN YOU.

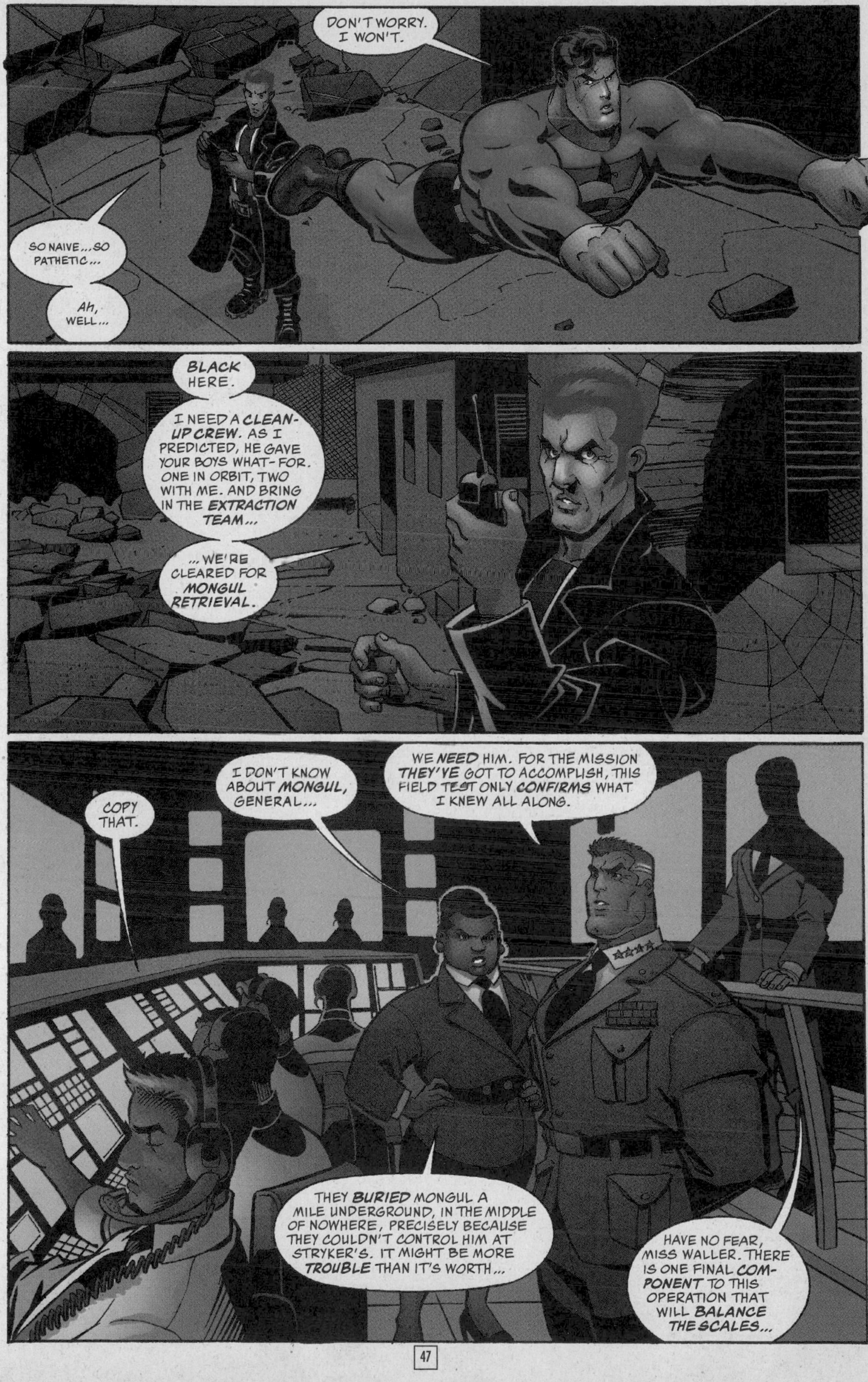
DON'T WORRY. I WON'T.
SO NAIVE... SO PATHETIC...
Ah, WELL...
BLACK HERE.
I NEED A CLEAN-UP CREW. AS I PREDICTED, HE GAVE YOUR BOYS WHAT-FOR. ONE IN ORBIT, TWO WITH ME. AND BRING IN THE EXTRACTION TEAM...
...WE'RE CLEARED FOR MONGUL RETRIEVAL.
COPY THAT.
I DON'T KNOW ABOUT MONGUL, GENERAL...
WE NEED HIM. FOR THE MISSION THEY'VE GOT TO ACCOMPLISH, THIS FIELD TEST ONLY CONFIRMS WHAT I KNEW ALL ALONG.
THEY BURIED MONGUL A MILE UNDERGROUND, IN THE MIDDLE OF NOWHERE, PRECISELY BECAUSE THEY COULDN'T CONTROL HIM AT STRYKER'S. IT MIGHT BE MORE TROUBLE THAN IT'S WORTH...
HAVE NO FEAR, MISS WALLER. THERE IS ONE FINAL COMPONENT TO THIS OPERATION THAT WILL BALANCE THE SCALES...

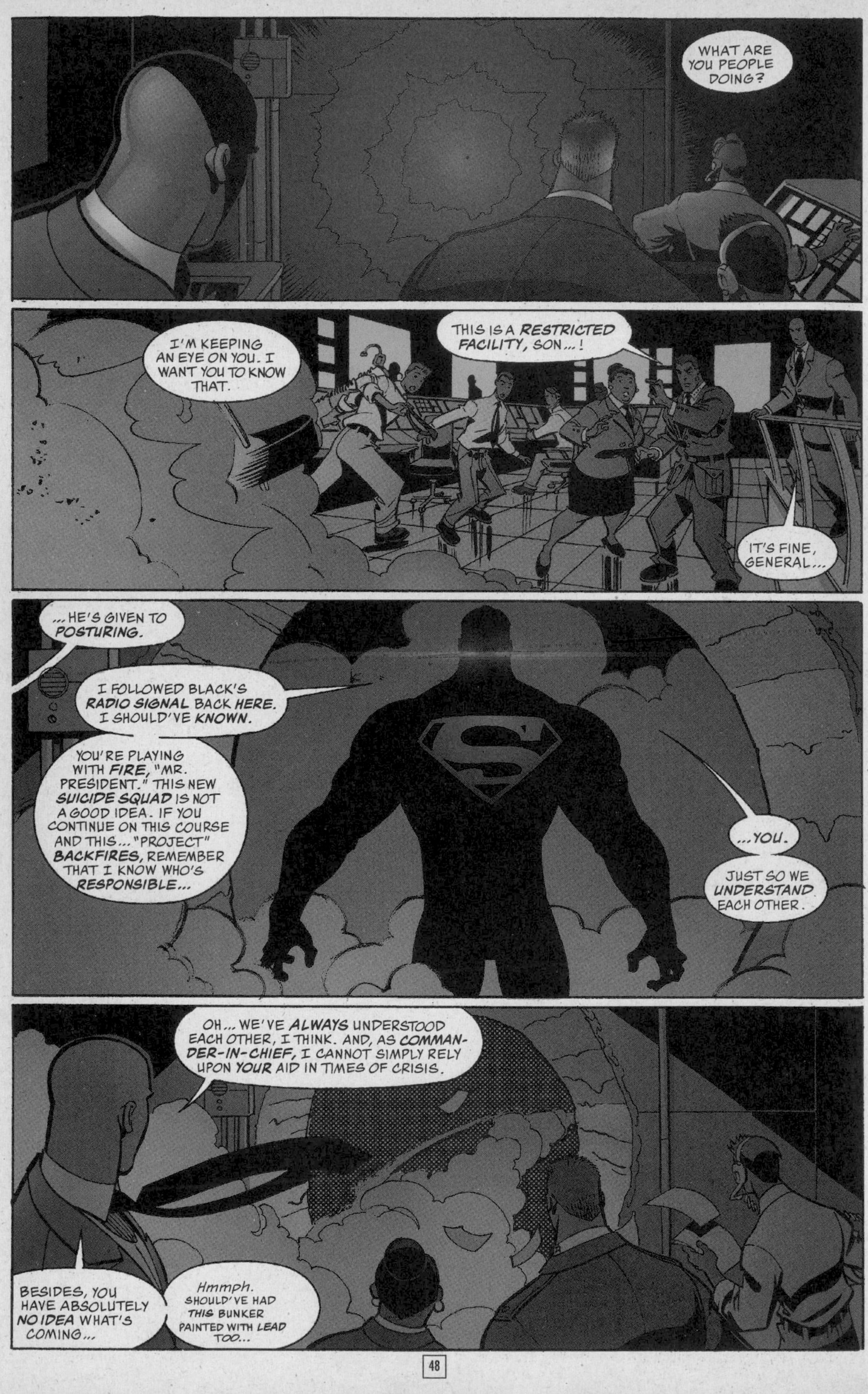

WHAT ARE YOU PEOPLE DOING?
I'M KEEPING AN EYE ON YOU. I WANT YOU TO KNOW THAT.
THIS IS A RESTRICTED FACILITY, SON...!
IT'S FINE, GENERAL...
...HE'S GIVEN TO POSTURING.
I FOLLOWED BLACK'S RADIO SIGNAL BACK HERE. I SHOULD'VE KNOWN.
YOU'RE PLAYING WITH FIRE, "MR. PRESIDENT." THIS NEW SUICIDE SQUAD IS NOT A GOOD IDEA. IF YOU CONTINUE ON THIS COURSE AND THIS... "PROJECT" BACKFIRES, REMEMBER THAT I KNOW WHO'S RESPONSIBLE...
...YOU.
JUST SO WE UNDERSTAND EACH OTHER.
OH... WE'VE ALWAYS UNDERSTOOD EACH OTHER, I THINK. AND, AS COMMANDER-IN-CHIEF, I CANNOT SIMPLY RELY UPON YOUR AID IN TIMES OF CRISIS.
BESIDES, YOU HAVE ABSOLUTELY NO IDEA WHAT'S COMING...
Hmmph. SHOULD'VE HAD THIS BUNKER PAINTED WITH LEAD TOO...

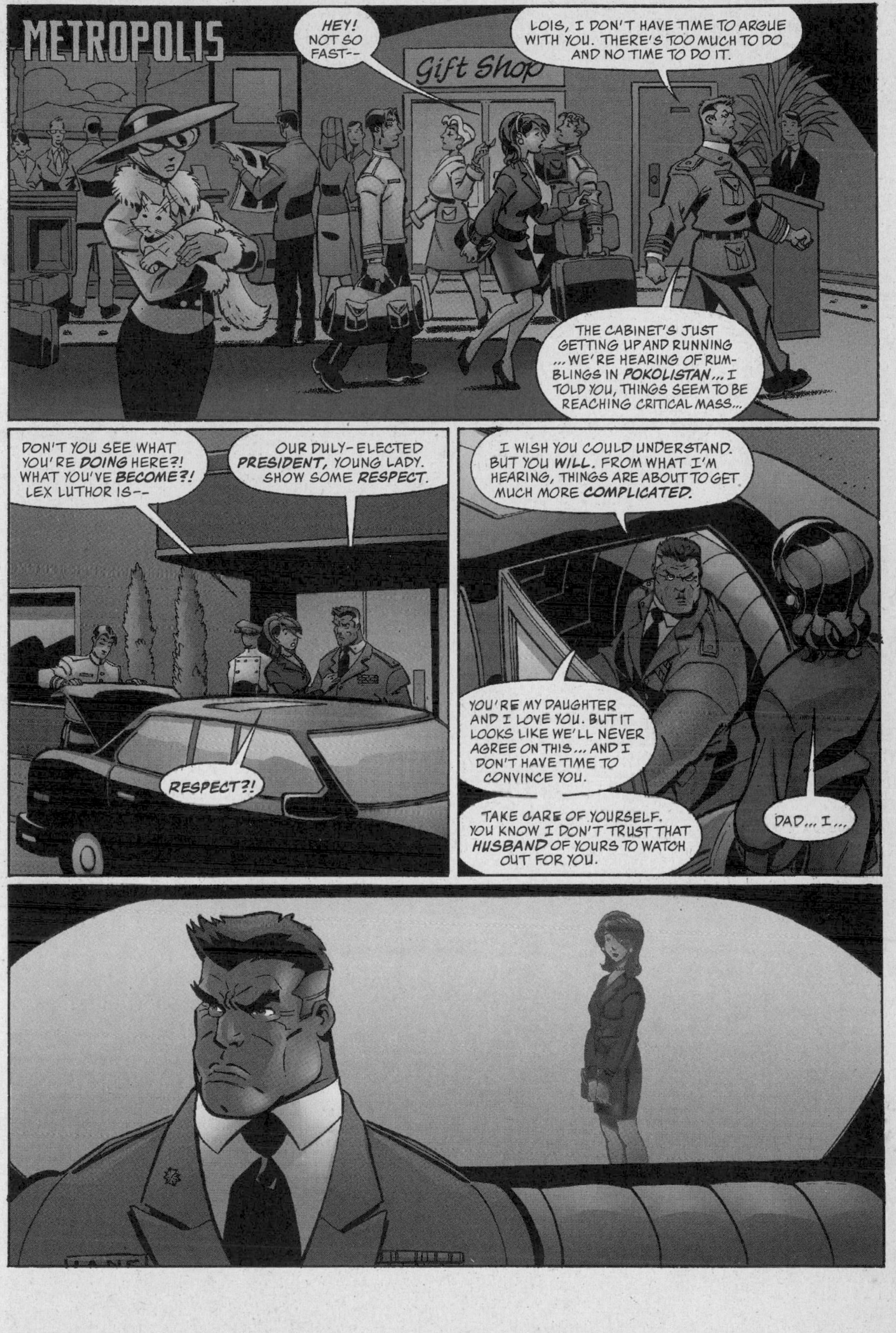
METROPOLIS
HEY! NOT SO FAST--
LOIS, I DON'T HAVE TIME TO ARGUE WITH YOU. THERE'S TOO MUCH TO DO AND NO TIME TO DO IT.
Gift Shop
THE CABINET'S JUST GETTING UP AND RUNNING ... WE'RE HEARING OF RUMBLINGS IN POKOLISTAN... I TOLD YOU, THINGS SEEM TO BE REACHING CRITICAL MASS...
DON'T YOU SEE WHAT YOU'RE DOING HERE?! WHAT YOU'VE BECOME?! LEX LUTHOR IS--
OUR DULY-ELECTED PRESIDENT, YOUNG LADY. SHOW SOME RESPECT.
RESPECT?!
I WISH YOU COULD UNDERSTAND. BUT YOU WILL. FROM WHAT I'M HEARING, THINGS ARE ABOUT TO GET MUCH MORE COMPLICATED.
YOU'RE MY DAUGHTER AND I LOVE YOU. BUT IT LOOKS LIKE WE'LL NEVER AGREE ON THIS... AND I DON'T HAVE TIME TO CONVINCE YOU.
TAKE CARE OF YOURSELF. YOU KNOW I DON'T TRUST THAT HUSBAND OF YOURS TO WATCH OUT FOR YOU.
DAD... I...

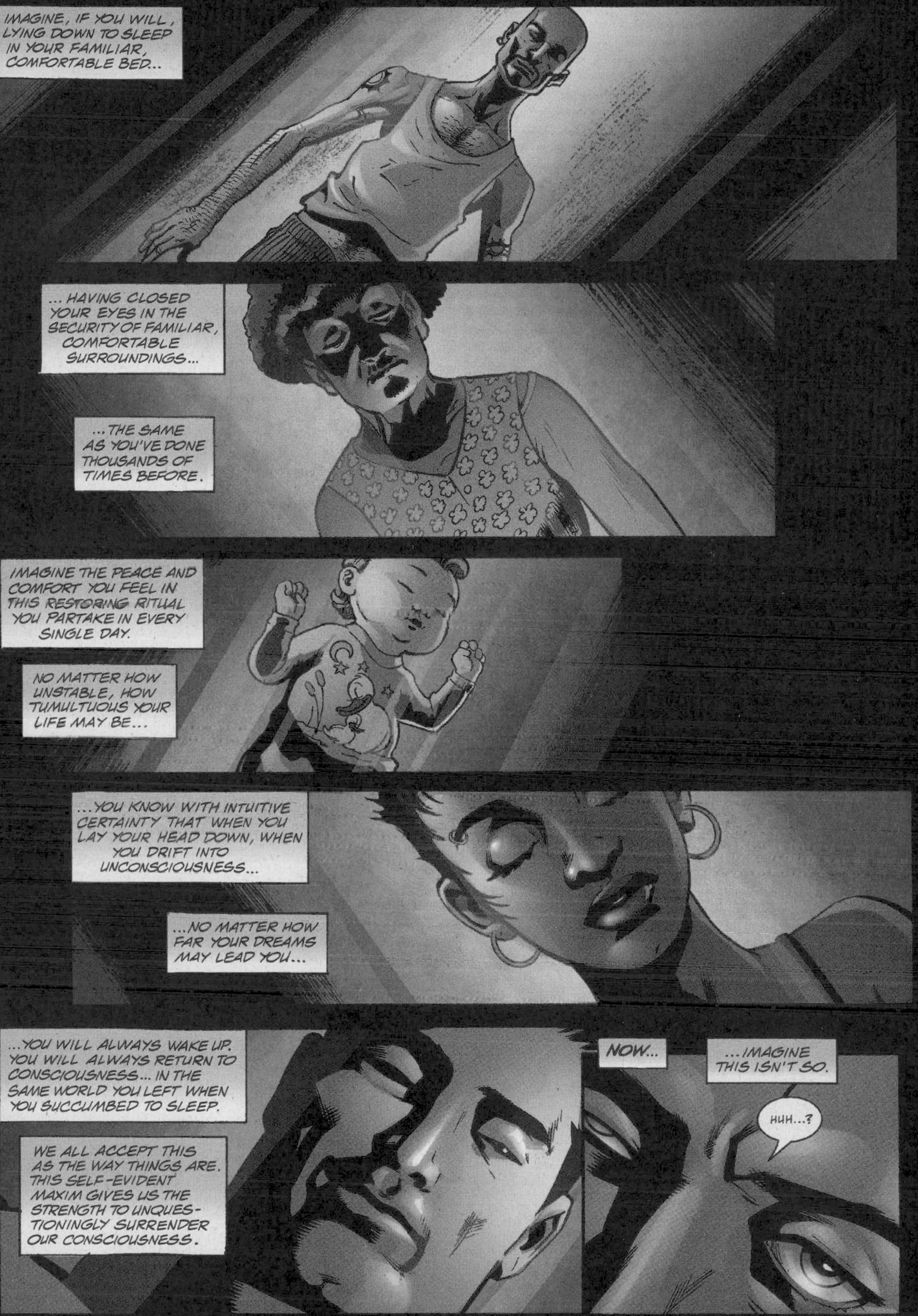
IMAGINE, IF YOU WILL, LYING DOWN TO SLEEP IN YOUR FAMILIAR, COMFORTABLE BED...
... HAVING CLOSED YOUR EYES IN THE SECURITY OF FAMILIAR, COMFORTABLE SURROUNDINGS...
...THE SAME AS YOU'VE DONE THOUSANDS OF TIMES BEFORE.
IMAGINE THE PEACE AND COMFORT YOU FEEL IN THIS RESTORING RITUAL YOU PARTAKE IN EVERY SINGLE DAY.
NO MATTER HOW UNSTABLE, HOW TUMULTUOUS YOUR LIFE MAY BE...
...YOU KNOW WITH INTUITIVE CERTAINTY THAT WHEN YOU LAY YOUR HEAD DOWN, WHEN YOU DRIFT INTO UNCONSCIOUSNESS...
...NO MATTER HOW FAR YOUR DREAMS MAY LEAD YOU...
...YOU WILL ALWAYS WAKE UP. YOU WILL ALWAYS RETURN TO CONSCIOUSNESS... IN THE SAME WORLD YOU LEFT WHEN YOU SUCCUMBED TO SLEEP.
WE ALL ACCEPT THIS AS THE WAY THINGS ARE. THIS SELF-EVIDENT MAXIM GIVES US THE STRENGTH TO UNQUESTIONINGLY SURRENDER OUR CONSCIOUSNESS.
NOW...
...IMAGINE THIS ISN'T SO.
HUH...?

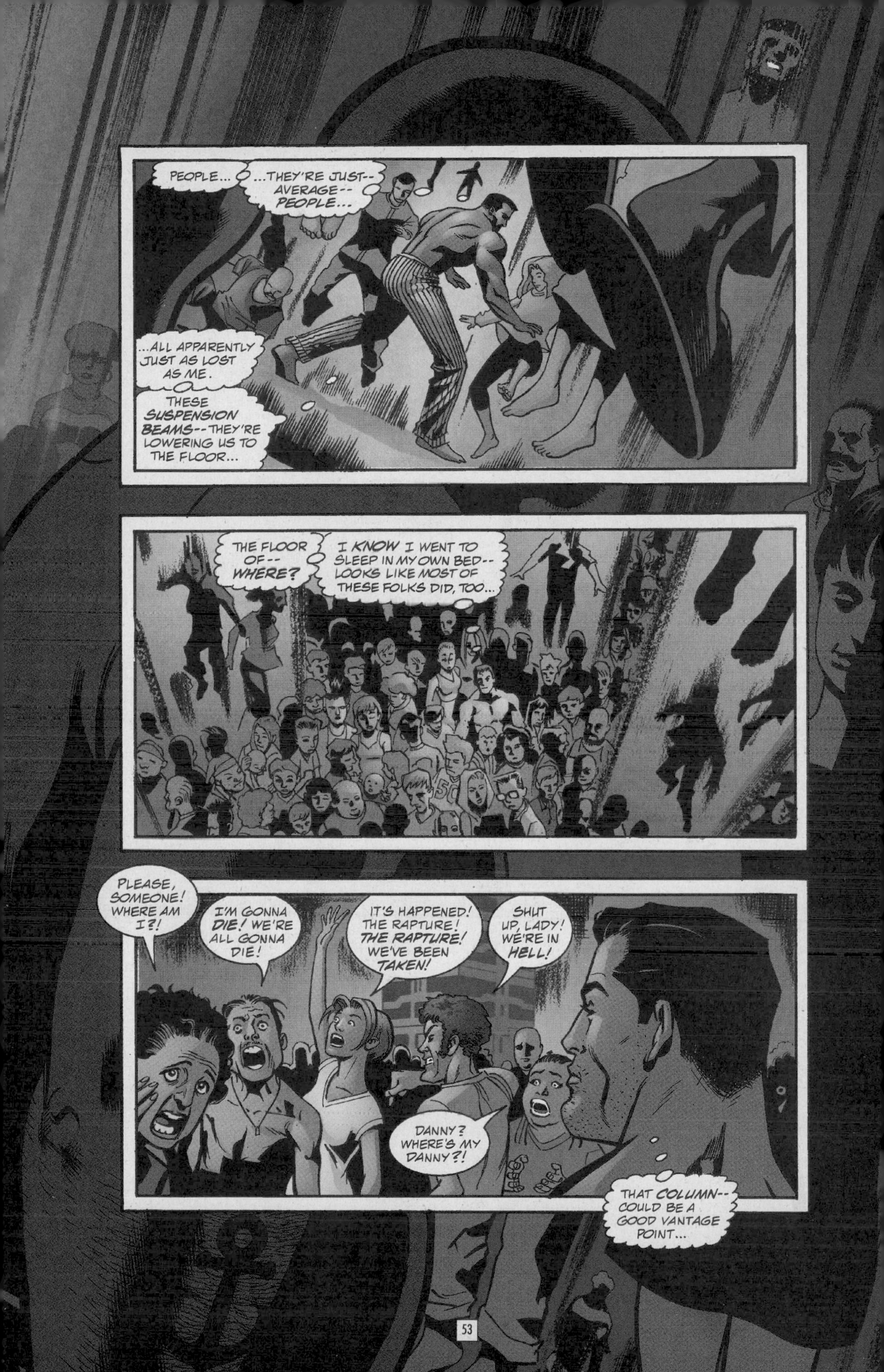
PEOPLE...
...THEY'RE JUST--AVERAGE--PEOPLE...
...ALL APPARENTLY JUST AS LOST AS ME.
THESE SUSPENSION BEAMS--THEY'RE LOWERING US TO THE FLOOR...
THE FLOOR OF--WHERE?
I KNOW I WENT TO SLEEP IN MY OWN BED--LOOKS LIKE MOST OF THESE FOLKS DID, TOO...
PLEASE, SOMEONE! WHERE AM I?!
I'M GONNA DIE! WE'RE ALL GONNA DIE!
IT'S HAPPENED! THE RAPTURE! THE RAPTURE! WE'VE BEEN TAKEN!
SHUT UP, LADY! WE'RE IN HELL!
DANNY? WHERE'S MY DANNY?!
THAT COLUMN--COULD BE A GOOD VANTAGE POINT...

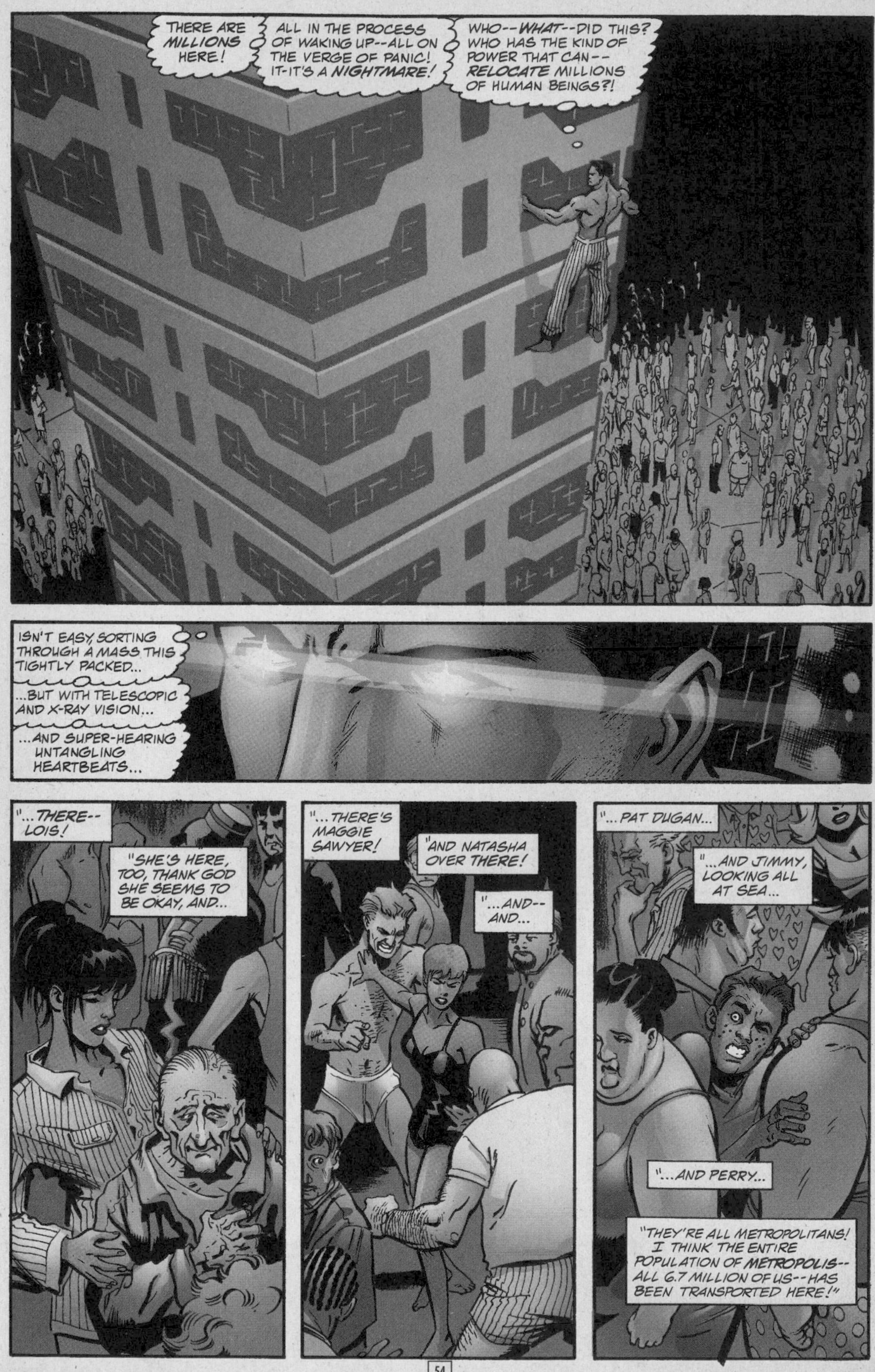

THERE ARE MILLIONS HERE!
ALL IN THE PROCESS OF WAKING UP--ALL ON THE VERGE OF PANIC! IT-IT'S A NIGHTMARE!
WHO--WHAT--DID THIS? WHO HAS THE KIND OF POWER THAT CAN--RELOCATE MILLIONS OF HUMAN BEINGS?!
ISN'T EASY, SORTING THROUGH A MASS THIS TIGHTLY PACKED...
...BUT WITH TELESCOPIC AND X-RAY VISION...
...AND SUPER-HEARING UNTANGLING HEARTBEATS...
"...THERE--LOIS!
"SHE'S HERE, TOO, THANK GOD SHE SEEMS TO BE OKAY, AND...
"...THERE'S MAGGIE SAWYER!
"AND NATASHA OVER THERE!
"...AND--AND...
"...PAT DUGAN...
"...AND JIMMY, LOOKING ALL AT SEA...
"...AND PERRY...
"THEY'RE ALL METROPOLITANS! I THINK THE ENTIRE POPULATION OF METROPOLIS--ALL 6.7 MILLION OF US--HAS BEEN TRANSPORTED HERE!"

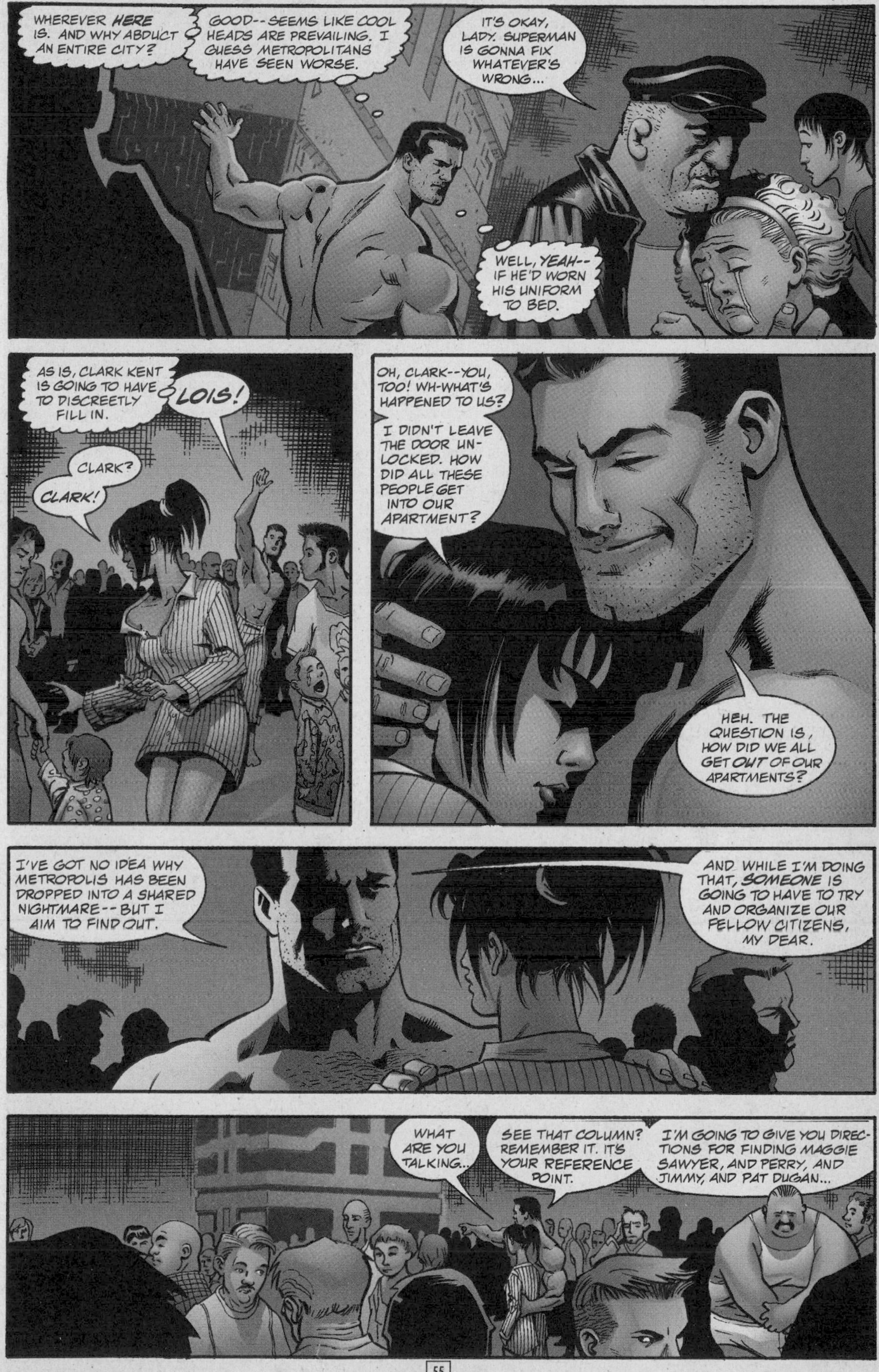
WHEREVER HERE IS. AND WHY ABDUCT AN ENTIRE CITY?
GOOD--SEEMS LIKE COOL HEADS ARE PREVAILING. I GUESS METROPOLITANS HAVE SEEN WORSE.
IT'S OKAY, LADY. SUPERMAN IS GONNA FIX WHATEVER'S WRONG...
WELL, YEAH--IF HE'D WORN HIS UNIFORM TO BED.
AS IS, CLARK KENT IS GOING TO HAVE TO DISCREETLY FILL IN.
LOIS!
CLARK?
CLARK!
OH, CLARK--YOU, TOO! WH-WHAT'S HAPPENED TO US?
I DIDN'T LEAVE THE DOOR UNLOCKED. HOW DID ALL THESE PEOPLE GET INTO OUR APARTMENT?
HEH. THE QUESTION IS, HOW DID WE ALL GET OUT OF OUR APARTMENTS?
I'VE GOT NO IDEA WHY METROPOLIS HAS BEEN DROPPED INTO A SHARED NIGHTMARE--BUT I AIM TO FIND OUT.
AND WHILE I'M DOING THAT, SOMEONE IS GOING TO HAVE TO TRY AND ORGANIZE OUR FELLOW CITIZENS, MY DEAR.
WHAT ARE YOU TALKING...
SEE THAT COLUMN? REMEMBER IT. IT'S YOUR REFERENCE POINT.
I'M GOING TO GIVE YOU DIRECTIONS FOR FINDING MAGGIE SAWYER, AND PERRY, AND JIMMY, AND PAT DUGAN...

I WANT YOU TO *LINK UP* WITH THEM AND...

CLARK! *LOOK!*

ATTENTION, PEOPLE OF METROPOLIS!

YOU ARE NOT IN *DANGER!* YOU WILL *NOT* BE HARMED! PLEASE REMAIN *CALM* AND *ORDERLY!*

ALL CITY OFFICIALS AND METAHUMANS WILL NOW PRESENT THEMSELVES!

THAT DOESN'T SOUND GOOD FOR *YOU.* WHO...?

I DON'T KNOW. BUT I'M BEGINNING TO THINK THIS IS A *PRISON CAMP.*

LOIS, I'M GOING TO GET TO THE *BOTTOM* OF THIS AND GET US ALL BACK *HOME,* BUT WHILE I'M DOING *THAT* I WANT *YOU* TO NEGOTIATE FOR *OUR* PEOPLE.

Y-YOU WANT *ME* TO...?

÷SIGH÷ CAN'T FIND THEM.

WHAT ABOUT *JOHN HENRY?* A-AND *PROFESSOR HAMILTON...?*

YOU'LL DO *FINE,* LOIS. YOU'RE *GOOD* AT WHIPPING THINGS INTO SHAPE.

LOOK, I DON'T KNOW HOW LONG THIS WILL TAKE--WHEN WE'LL *SEE* EACH OTHER AGAIN--BUT...

I *WILL.*

SMALLVILLE-- BE CAREFUL...

YOU JUST FIND THE *OTHERS,* AND DO YOUR BEST TO TAKE CARE OF OUR PEOPLE--THERE'S GOING TO BE *ANGELS* AND *PREDATORS* AMONG THEM. JUST--JUST...

"...REMEMBER-- I LOVE YOU..."

LOIS, I KNOW I'M ASKING AN *AWFUL* LOT--MAYBE THE *IMPOSSIBLE...*

...BUT IF THERE EVER WAS A *NATURAL-BORN* LEADER WAITING TO *HAPPEN...*

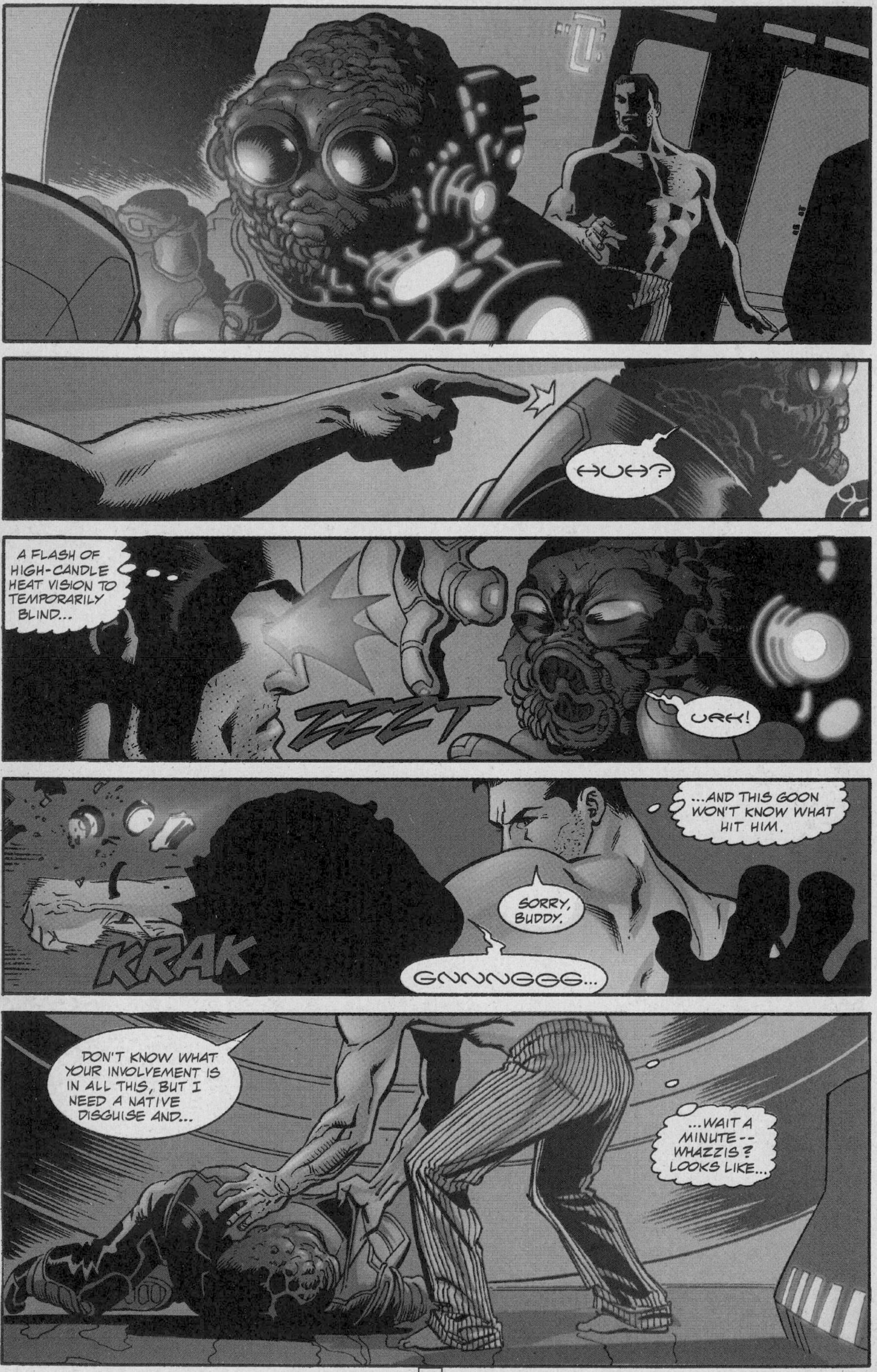
HUH?
A FLASH OF HIGH-CANDLE HEAT VISION TO TEMPORARILY BLIND...
ZZZT
URK!
...AND THIS GOON WON'T KNOW WHAT HIT HIM.
SORRY, BUDDY.
KRAK
GNNNGGG...
DON'T KNOW WHAT YOUR INVOLVEMENT IS IN ALL THIS, BUT I NEED A NATIVE DISGUISE AND...
...WAIT A MINUTE-- WHAZZIS? LOOKS LIKE...

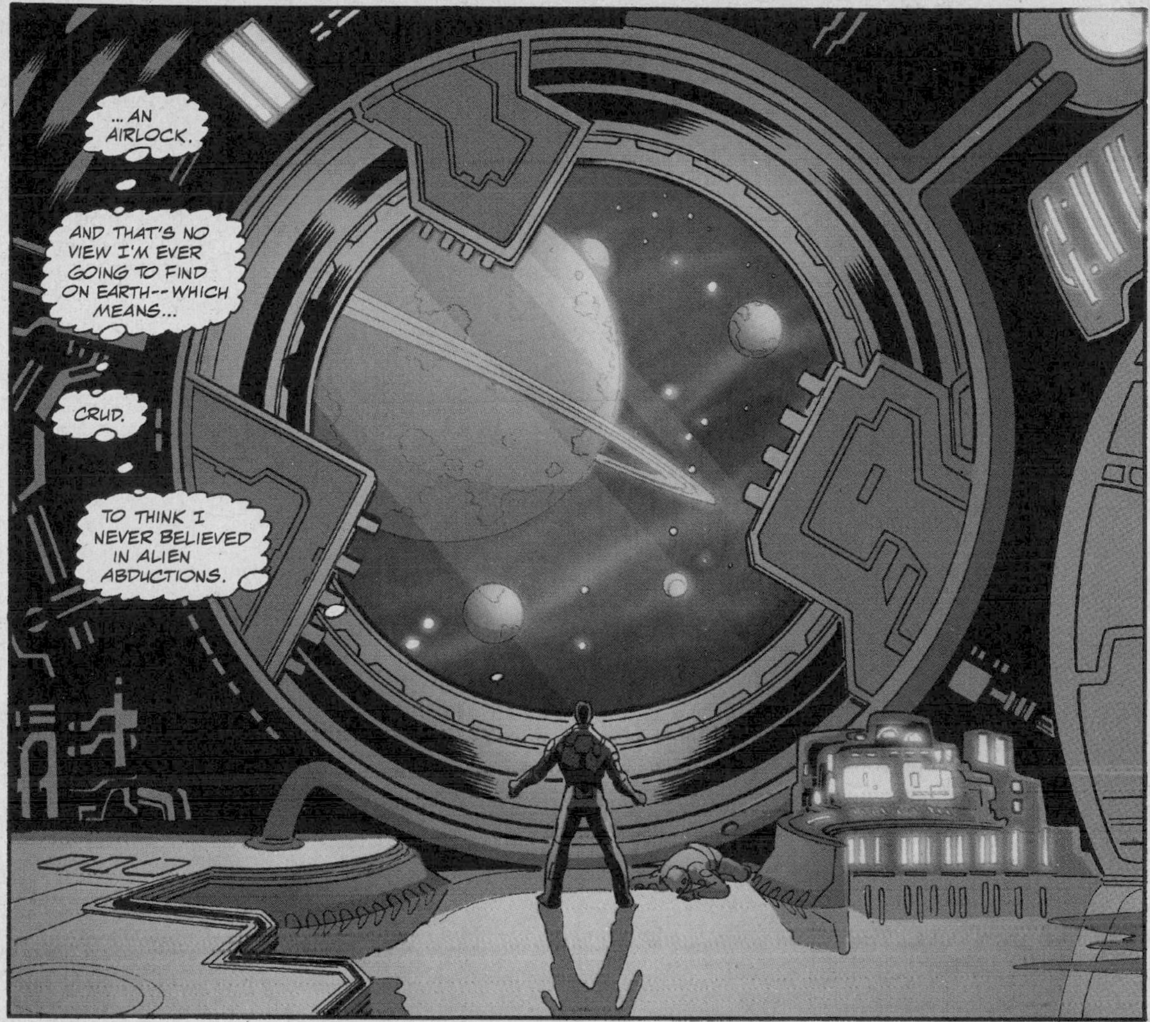
...AN AIRLOCK.
AND THAT'S NO VIEW I'M EVER GOING TO FIND ON EARTH--WHICH MEANS...
CRUD.
TO THINK I NEVER BELIEVED IN ALIEN ABDUCTIONS.

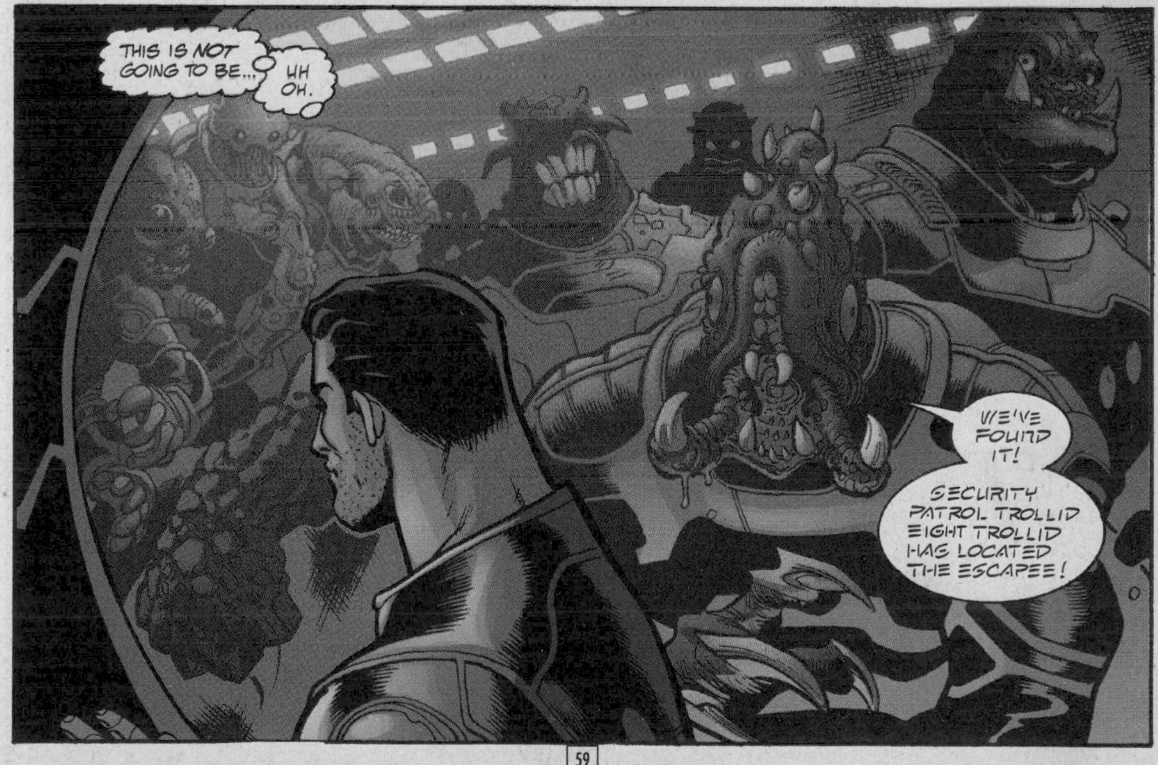
THIS IS NOT GOING TO BE...
UH OH.
WE'VE FOUND IT!
SECURITY PATROL TROLLID EIGHT TROLLID HAS LOCATED THE ESCAPEE!

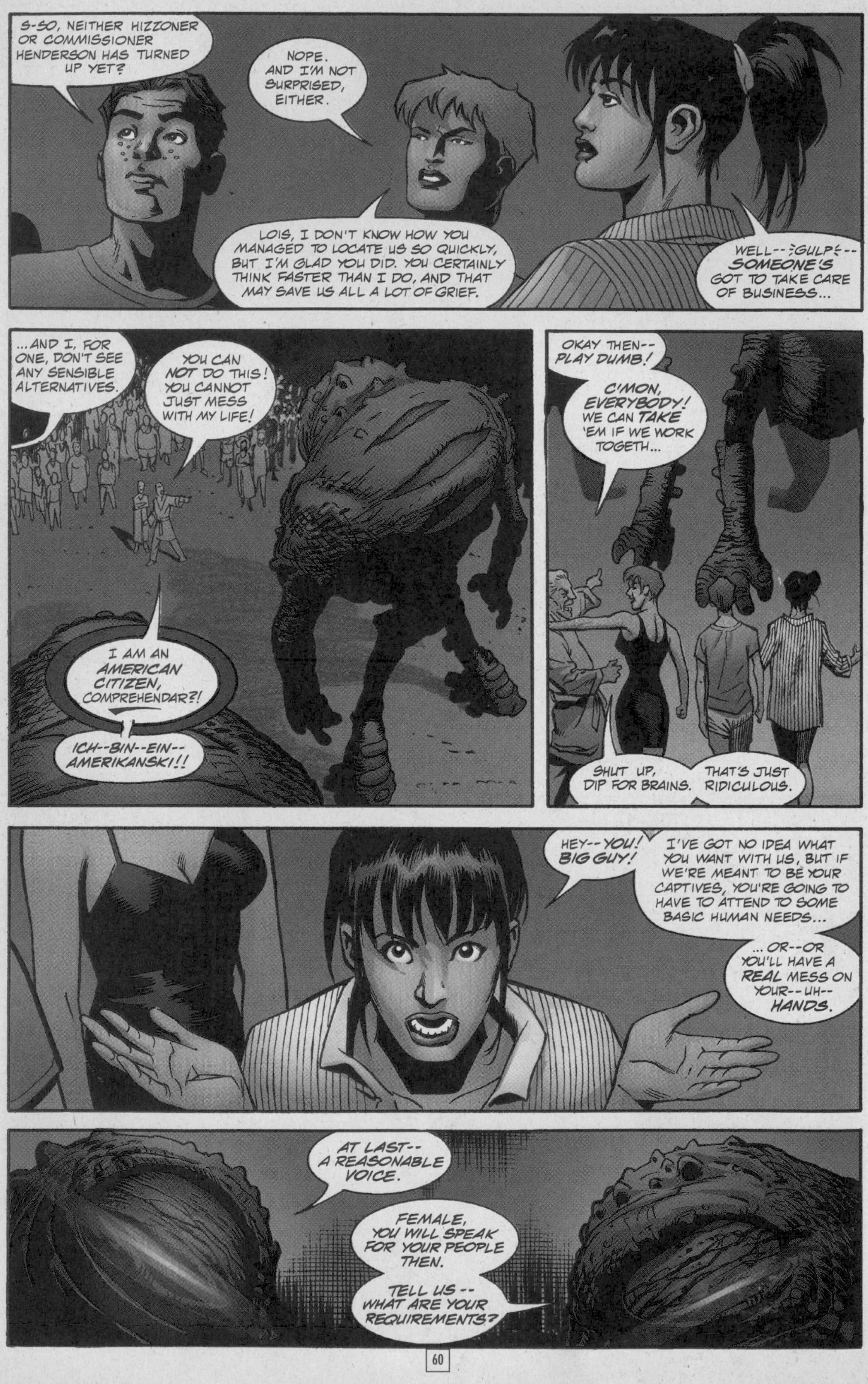
S-SO, NEITHER HIZZONER OR COMMISSIONER HENDERSON HAS TURNED UP YET?
NOPE. AND I'M NOT SURPRISED, EITHER.
LOIS, I DON'T KNOW HOW YOU MANAGED TO LOCATE US SO QUICKLY, BUT I'M GLAD YOU DID. YOU CERTAINLY THINK FASTER THAN I DO, AND THAT MAY SAVE US ALL A LOT OF GRIEF.
WELL-- GULP --SOMEONE'S GOT TO TAKE CARE OF BUSINESS...
...AND I, FOR ONE, DON'T SEE ANY SENSIBLE ALTERNATIVES.
YOU CAN NOT DO THIS! YOU CANNOT JUST MESS WITH MY LIFE!
I AM AN AMERICAN CITIZEN, COMPREHENDAR?!
ICH--BIN--EIN--AMERIKANSKI!!
OKAY THEN-- PLAY DUMB!
C'MON, EVERYBODY! WE CAN TAKE 'EM IF WE WORK TOGETH...
SHUT UP, DIP FOR BRAINS.
THAT'S JUST RIDICULOUS.
HEY-- YOU! BIG GUY!
I'VE GOT NO IDEA WHAT YOU WANT WITH US, BUT IF WE'RE MEANT TO BE YOUR CAPTIVES, YOU'RE GOING TO HAVE TO ATTEND TO SOME BASIC HUMAN NEEDS...
...OR--OR YOU'LL HAVE A REAL MESS ON YOUR--UH-- HANDS.
AT LAST-- A REASONABLE VOICE.
FEMALE, YOU WILL SPEAK FOR YOUR PEOPLE THEN.
TELL US -- WHAT ARE YOUR REQUIREMENTS?

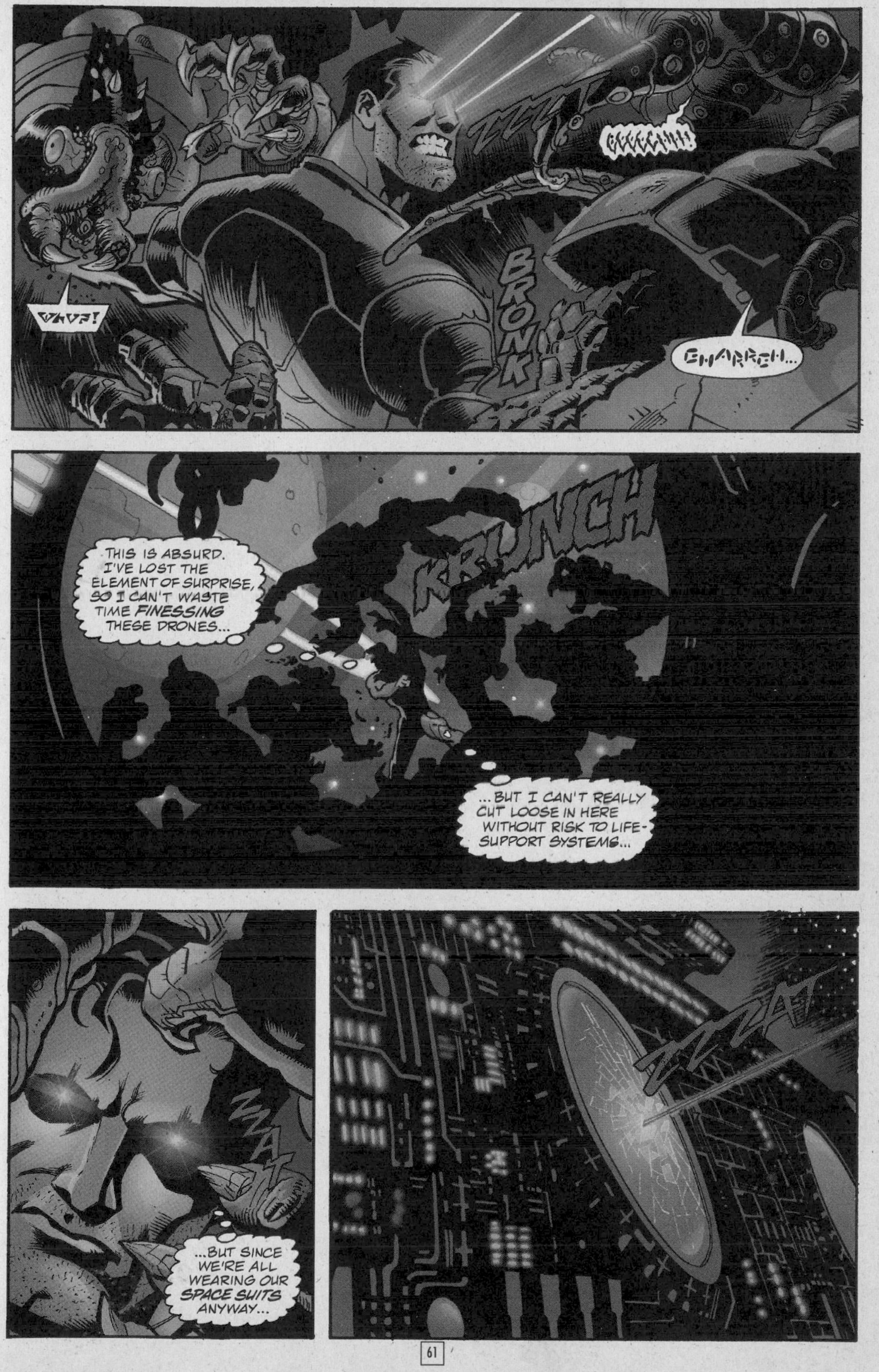
BRONK
KRUNCH
THIS IS ABSURD. I'VE LOST THE ELEMENT OF SURPRISE, SO I CAN'T WASTE TIME *FINESSING* THESE DRONES...
... BUT I CAN'T REALLY CUT LOOSE IN HERE WITHOUT RISK TO LIFE-SUPPORT SYSTEMS...
...BUT SINCE WE'RE ALL WEARING OUR *SPACE SUITS* ANYWAY...

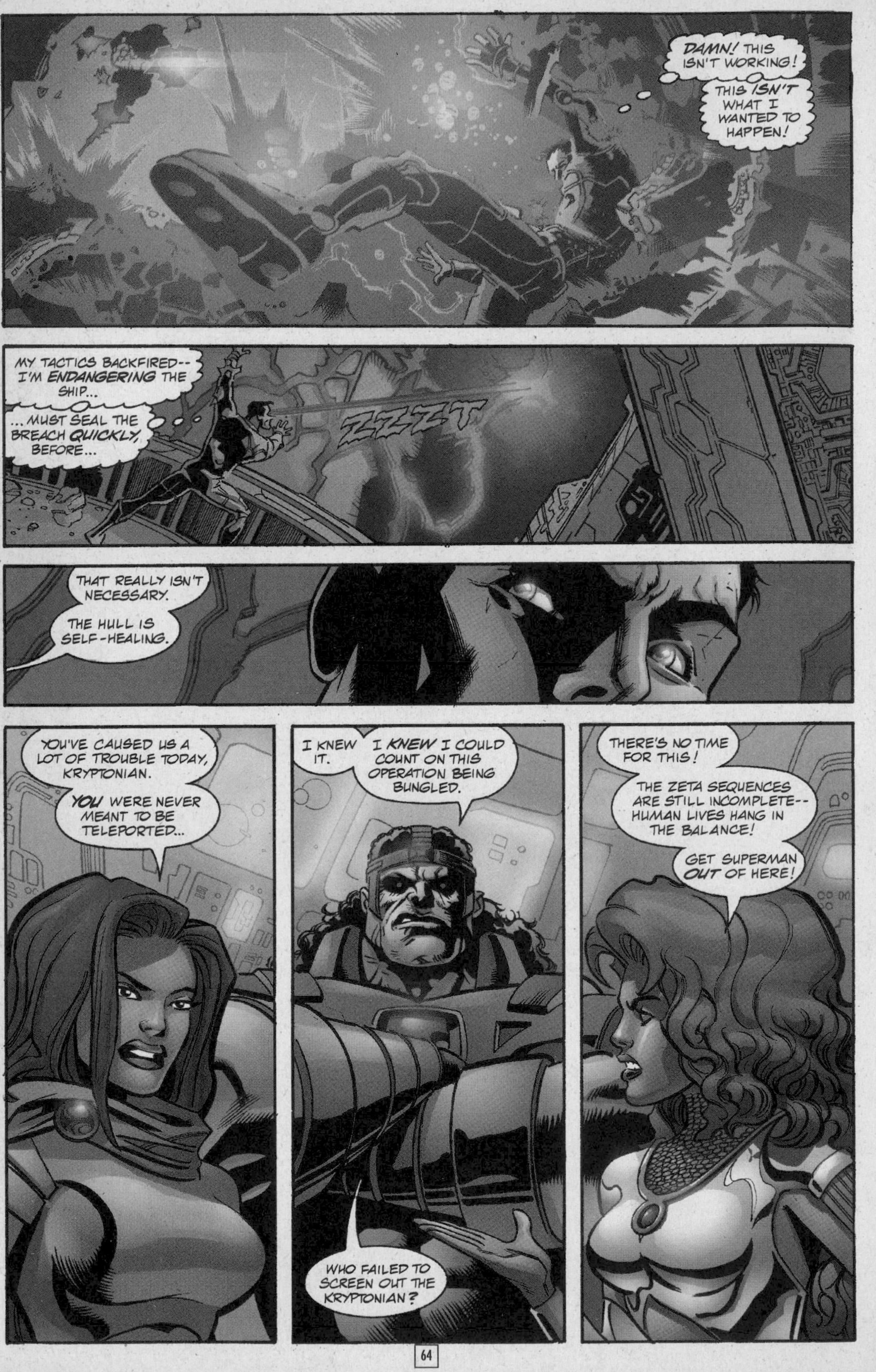
DAMN! THIS ISN'T WORKING!
THIS ISN'T WHAT I WANTED TO HAPPEN!
MY TACTICS BACKFIRED-- I'M ENDANGERING THE SHIP...
...MUST SEAL THE BREACH QUICKLY, BEFORE...
ZZZZT
THAT REALLY ISN'T NECESSARY.
THE HULL IS SELF-HEALING.
YOU'VE CAUSED US A LOT OF TROUBLE TODAY, KRYPTONIAN.
YOU WERE NEVER MEANT TO BE TELEPORTED...
I KNEW IT.
I KNEW I COULD COUNT ON THIS OPERATION BEING BUNGLED.
WHO FAILED TO SCREEN OUT THE KRYPTONIAN?
THERE'S NO TIME FOR THIS!
THE ZETA SEQUENCES ARE STILL INCOMPLETE-- HUMAN LIVES HANG IN THE BALANCE!
GET SUPERMAN OUT OF HERE!

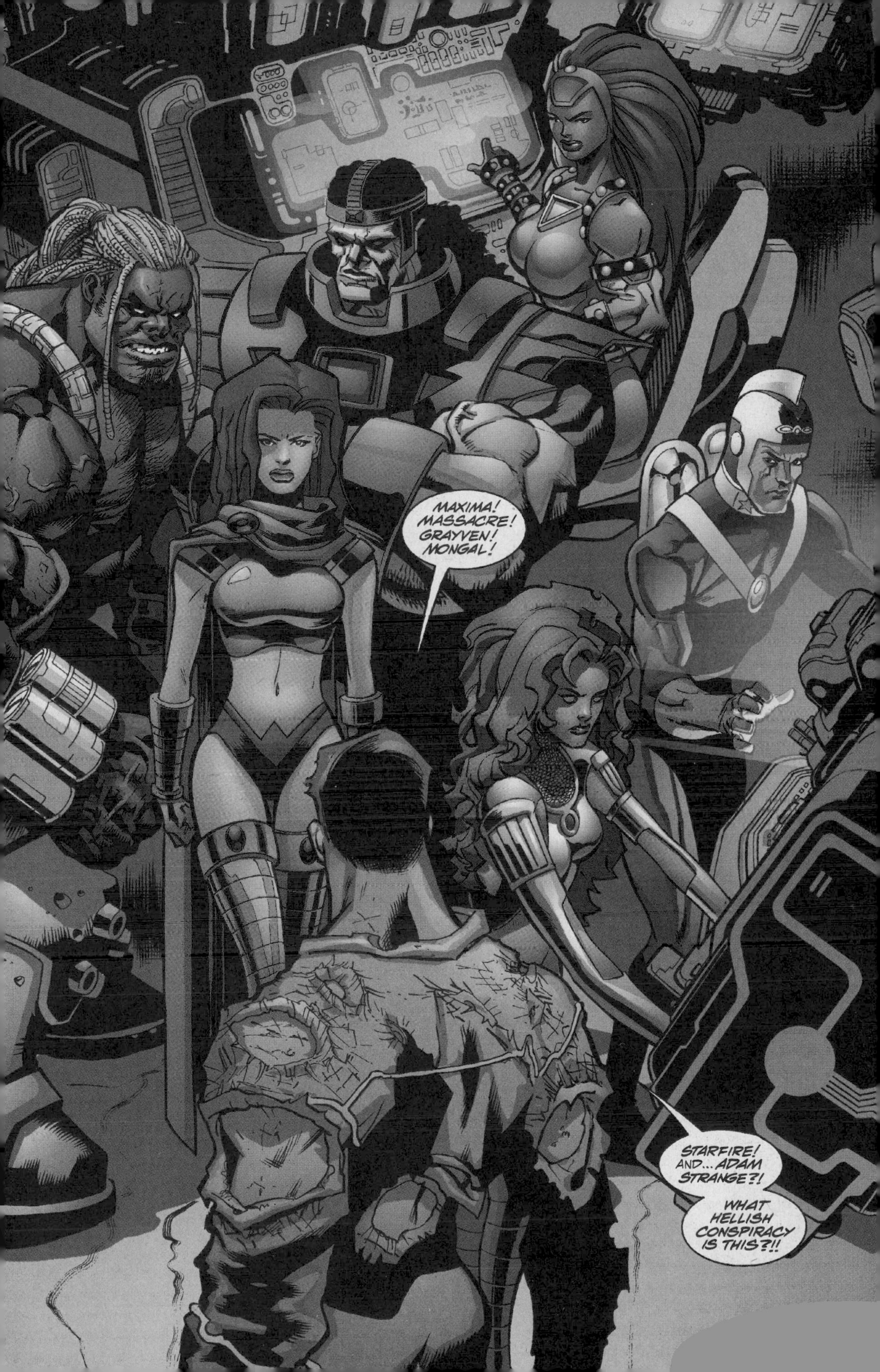
MAXIMA! MASSACRE! GRAYVEN! MONGAL!
STARFIRE! AND... ADAM STRANGE?!
WHAT HELLISH CONSPIRACY IS THIS?!!

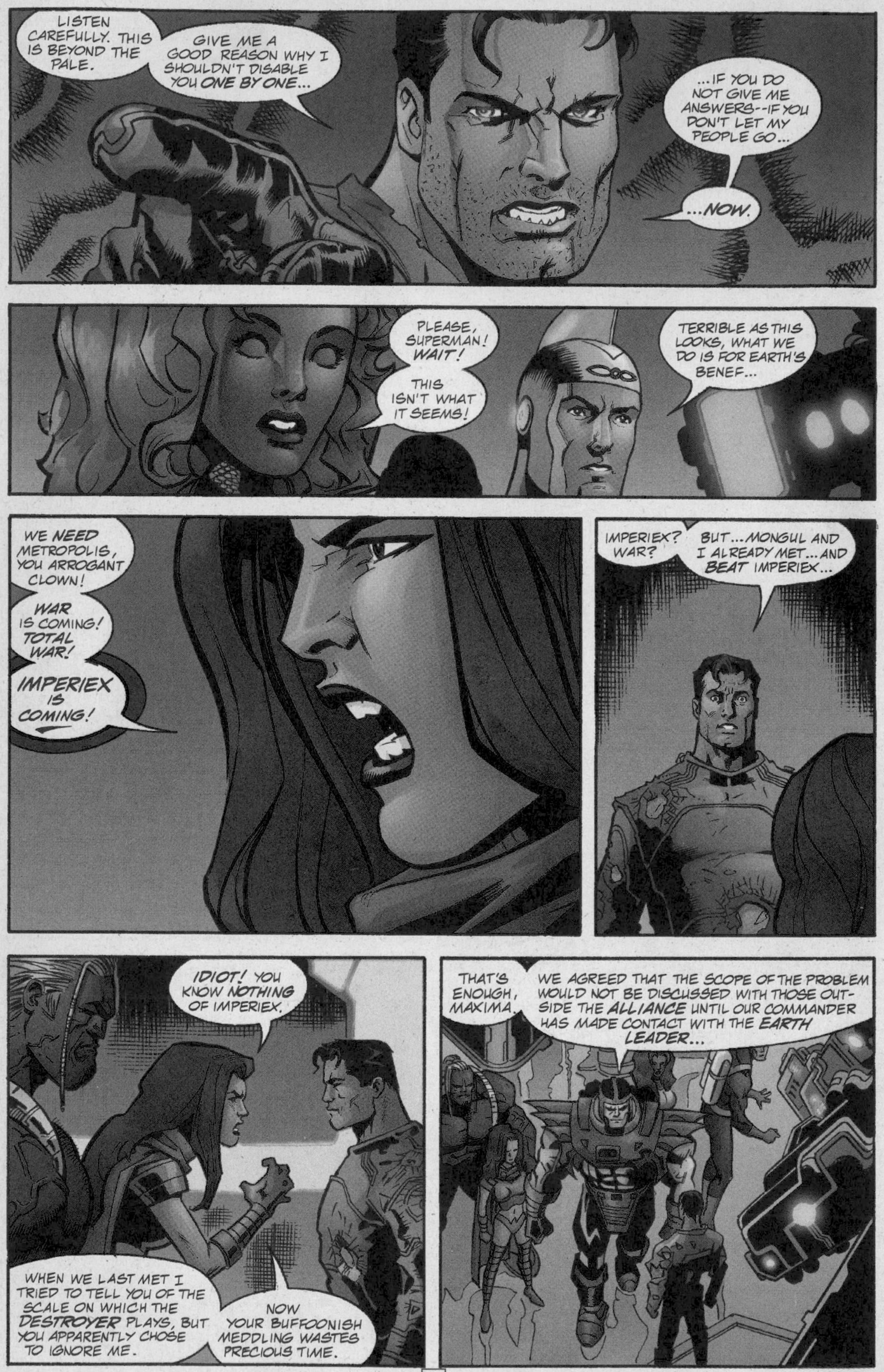

LISTEN CAREFULLY. THIS IS BEYOND THE PALE.
GIVE ME A GOOD REASON WHY I SHOULDN'T DISABLE YOU ONE BY ONE...
...IF YOU DO NOT GIVE ME ANSWERS--IF YOU DON'T LET MY PEOPLE GO...
...NOW.
PLEASE, SUPERMAN! WAIT!
THIS ISN'T WHAT IT SEEMS!
TERRIBLE AS THIS LOOKS, WHAT WE DO IS FOR EARTH'S BENEF...
WE NEED METROPOLIS, YOU ARROGANT CLOWN!
WAR IS COMING! TOTAL WAR!
IMPERIEX IS COMING!
IMPERIEX? WAR?
BUT...MONGUL AND I ALREADY MET...AND BEAT IMPERIEX...
IDIOT! YOU KNOW NOTHING OF IMPERIEX.
WHEN WE LAST MET I TRIED TO TELL YOU OF THE SCALE ON WHICH THE DESTROYER PLAYS, BUT YOU APPARENTLY CHOSE TO IGNORE ME.
NOW YOUR BUFFOONISH MEDDLING WASTES PRECIOUS TIME.
THAT'S ENOUGH, MAXIMA.
WE AGREED THAT THE SCOPE OF THE PROBLEM WOULD NOT BE DISCUSSED WITH THOSE OUTSIDE THE ALLIANCE UNTIL OUR COMMANDER HAS MADE CONTACT WITH THE EARTH LEADER...

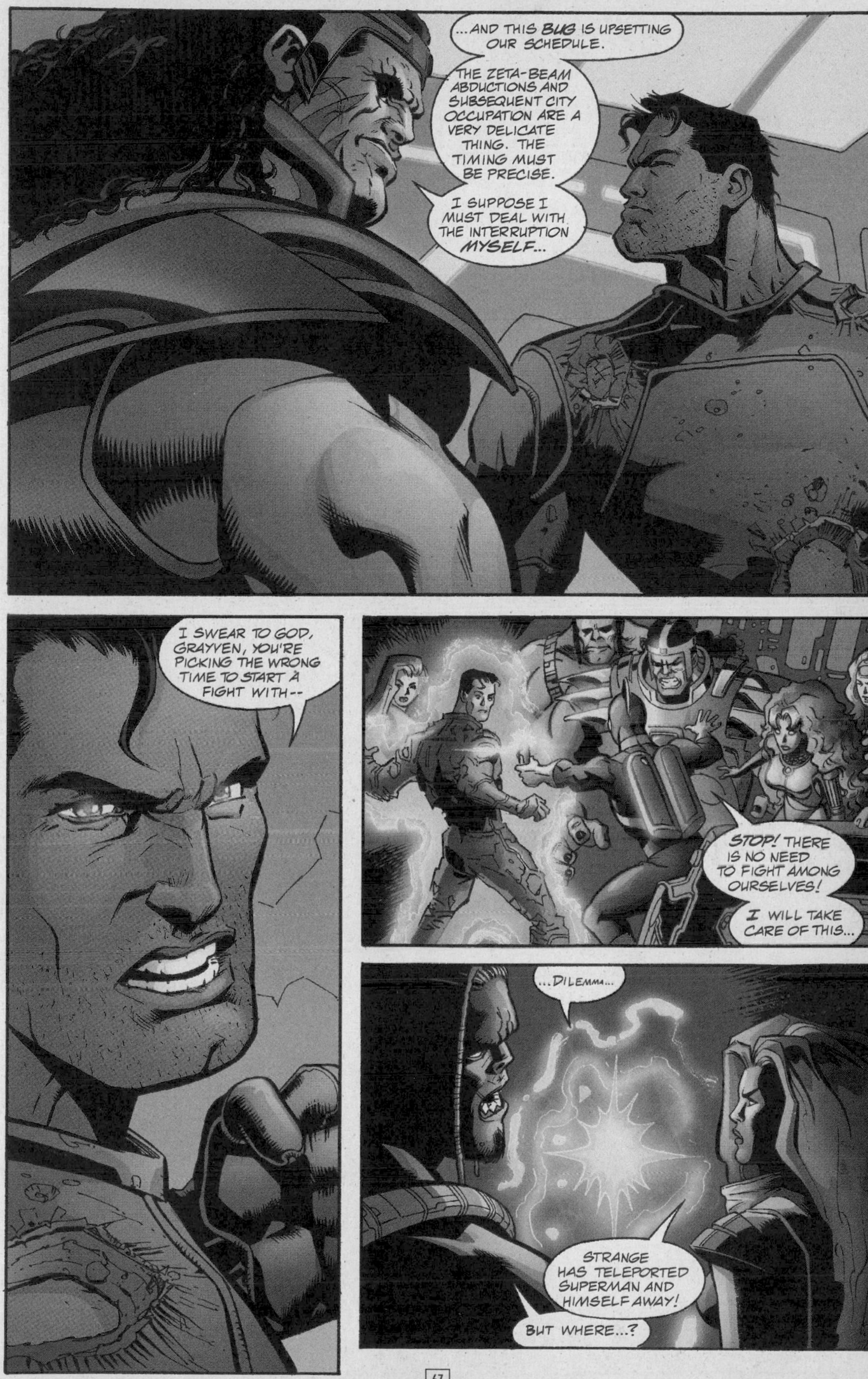
...AND THIS BUG IS UPSETTING OUR SCHEDULE.
THE ZETA-BEAM ABDUCTIONS AND SUBSEQUENT CITY OCCUPATION ARE A VERY DELICATE THING. THE TIMING MUST BE PRECISE.
I SUPPOSE I MUST DEAL WITH THE INTERRUPTION MYSELF...
I SWEAR TO GOD, GRAYVEN, YOU'RE PICKING THE WRONG TIME TO START A FIGHT WITH--
STOP! THERE IS NO NEED TO FIGHT AMONG OURSELVES!
I WILL TAKE CARE OF THIS...
...DILEMMA...
STRANGE HAS TELEPORTED SUPERMAN AND HIMSELF AWAY!
BUT WHERE...?

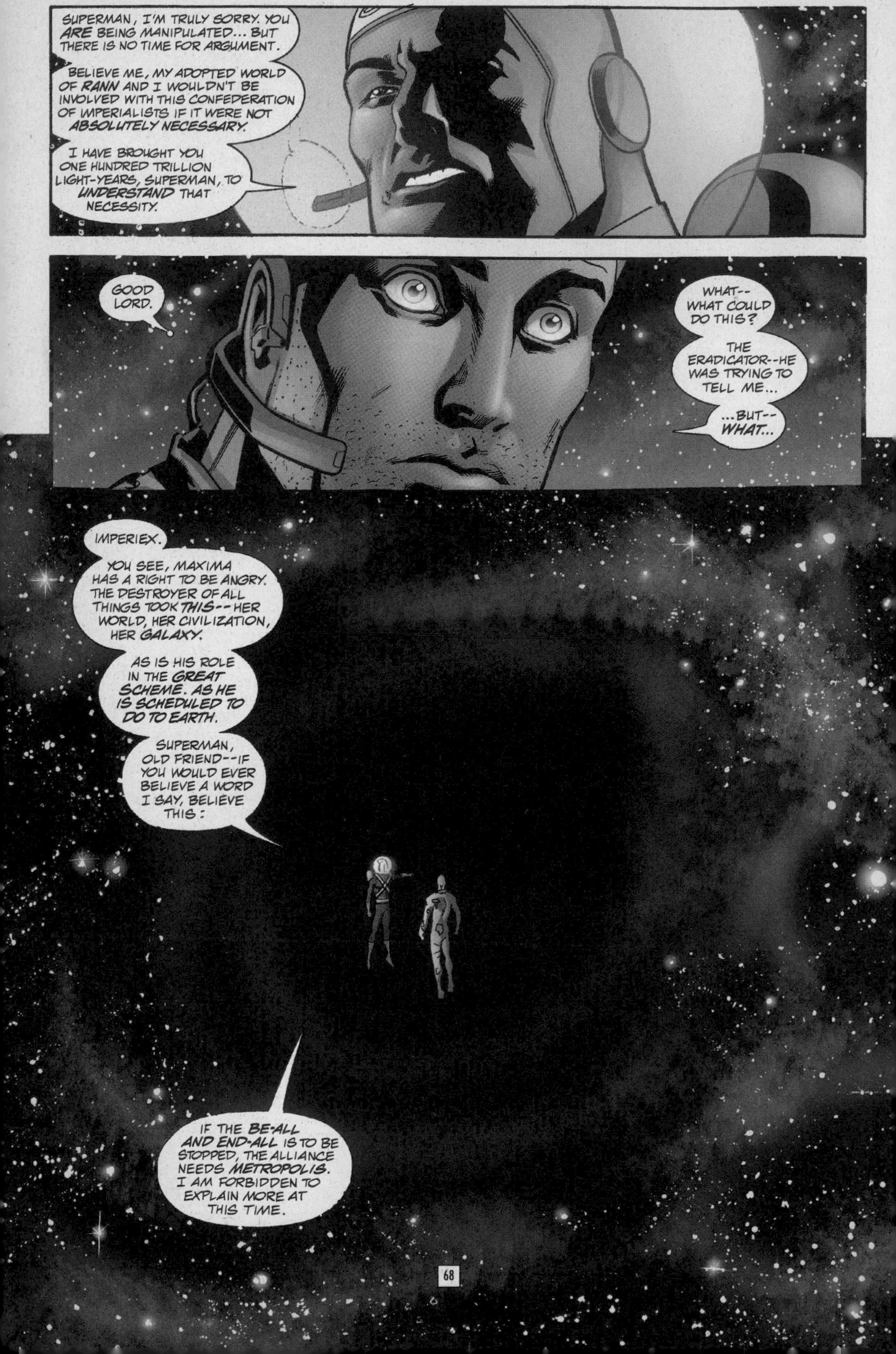
SUPERMAN, I'M TRULY SORRY. YOU ARE BEING MANIPULATED... BUT THERE IS NO TIME FOR ARGUMENT.
BELIEVE ME, MY ADOPTED WORLD OF RANN AND I WOULDN'T BE INVOLVED WITH THIS CONFEDERATION OF IMPERIALISTS IF IT WERE NOT ABSOLUTELY NECESSARY.
I HAVE BROUGHT YOU ONE HUNDRED TRILLION LIGHT-YEARS, SUPERMAN, TO UNDERSTAND THAT NECESSITY.
GOOD LORD.
WHAT-- WHAT COULD DO THIS?
THE ERADICATOR--HE WAS TRYING TO TELL ME...
...BUT-- WHAT...
IMPERIEX.
YOU SEE, MAXIMA HAS A RIGHT TO BE ANGRY. THE DESTROYER OF ALL THINGS TOOK THIS--HER WORLD, HER CIVILIZATION, HER GALAXY.
AS IS HIS ROLE IN THE GREAT SCHEME. AS HE IS SCHEDULED TO DO TO EARTH.
SUPERMAN, OLD FRIEND--IF YOU WOULD EVER BELIEVE A WORD I SAY, BELIEVE THIS:
IF THE BE-ALL AND END-ALL IS TO BE STOPPED, THE ALLIANCE NEEDS METROPOLIS. I AM FORBIDDEN TO EXPLAIN MORE AT THIS TIME.

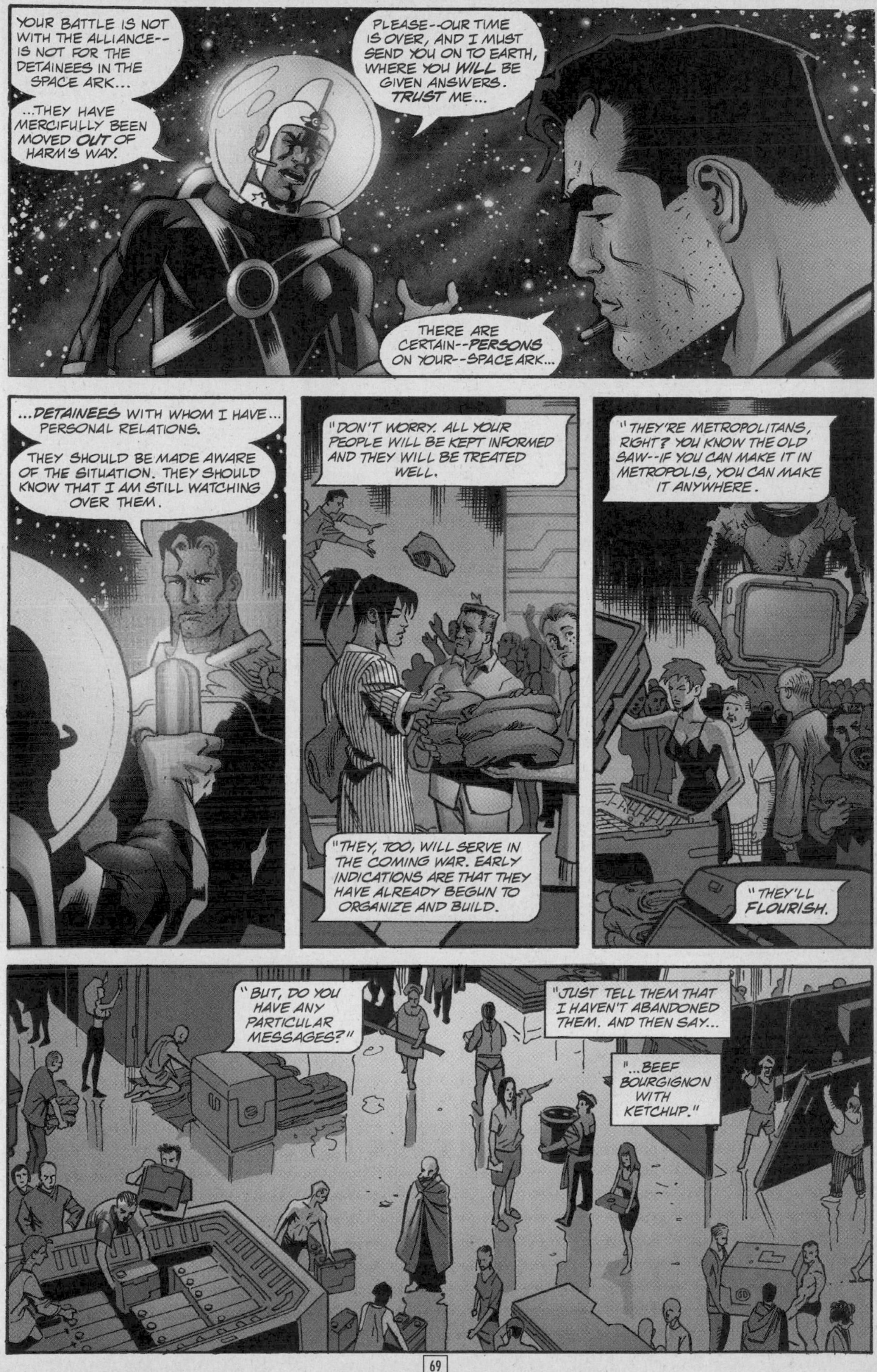
YOUR BATTLE IS NOT WITH THE ALLIANCE-- IS NOT FOR THE DETAINEES IN THE SPACE ARK...
...THEY HAVE MERCIFULLY BEEN MOVED OUT OF HARM'S WAY.
PLEASE--OUR TIME IS OVER, AND I MUST SEND YOU ON TO EARTH, WHERE YOU WILL BE GIVEN ANSWERS. TRUST ME...
THERE ARE CERTAIN--PERSONS ON YOUR--SPACE ARK...
...DETAINEES WITH WHOM I HAVE... PERSONAL RELATIONS.
THEY SHOULD BE MADE AWARE OF THE SITUATION. THEY SHOULD KNOW THAT I AM STILL WATCHING OVER THEM.
"DON'T WORRY. ALL YOUR PEOPLE WILL BE KEPT INFORMED AND THEY WILL BE TREATED WELL.
"THEY, TOO, WILL SERVE IN THE COMING WAR. EARLY INDICATIONS ARE THAT THEY HAVE ALREADY BEGUN TO ORGANIZE AND BUILD.
"THEY'RE METROPOLITANS, RIGHT? YOU KNOW THE OLD SAW--IF YOU CAN MAKE IT IN METROPOLIS, YOU CAN MAKE IT ANYWHERE.
"THEY'LL FLOURISH.
"BUT, DO YOU HAVE ANY PARTICULAR MESSAGES?"
"JUST TELL THEM THAT I HAVEN'T ABANDONED THEM. AND THEN SAY...
"...BEEF BOURGIGNON WITH KETCHUP."

"THE APPROPRIATE PARTY WILL KNOW WHAT I MEAN.

"I'M TRUSTING YOU, ADAM..."

METROPOLIS! MODIFIED ZETA-BEAM TECHNOLOGY-- INSTANTANEOUS TRAVEL ACROSS HALF THE UNIVERSE...

THAT'S HOW THE ALLIANCE EFFECTED THE EVACUATION OF METROPOLIS...

...AND--MY GOD! THE OCCUPATION OF THE CITY!

METROPOLIS UNDER ALIEN CONTROL!

MY PEOPLE IN CAPTIVITY!

I'VE BEEN A REASONABLE MAN, BUT NOW I WANT ANSWERS.

I NEED...

BOOM

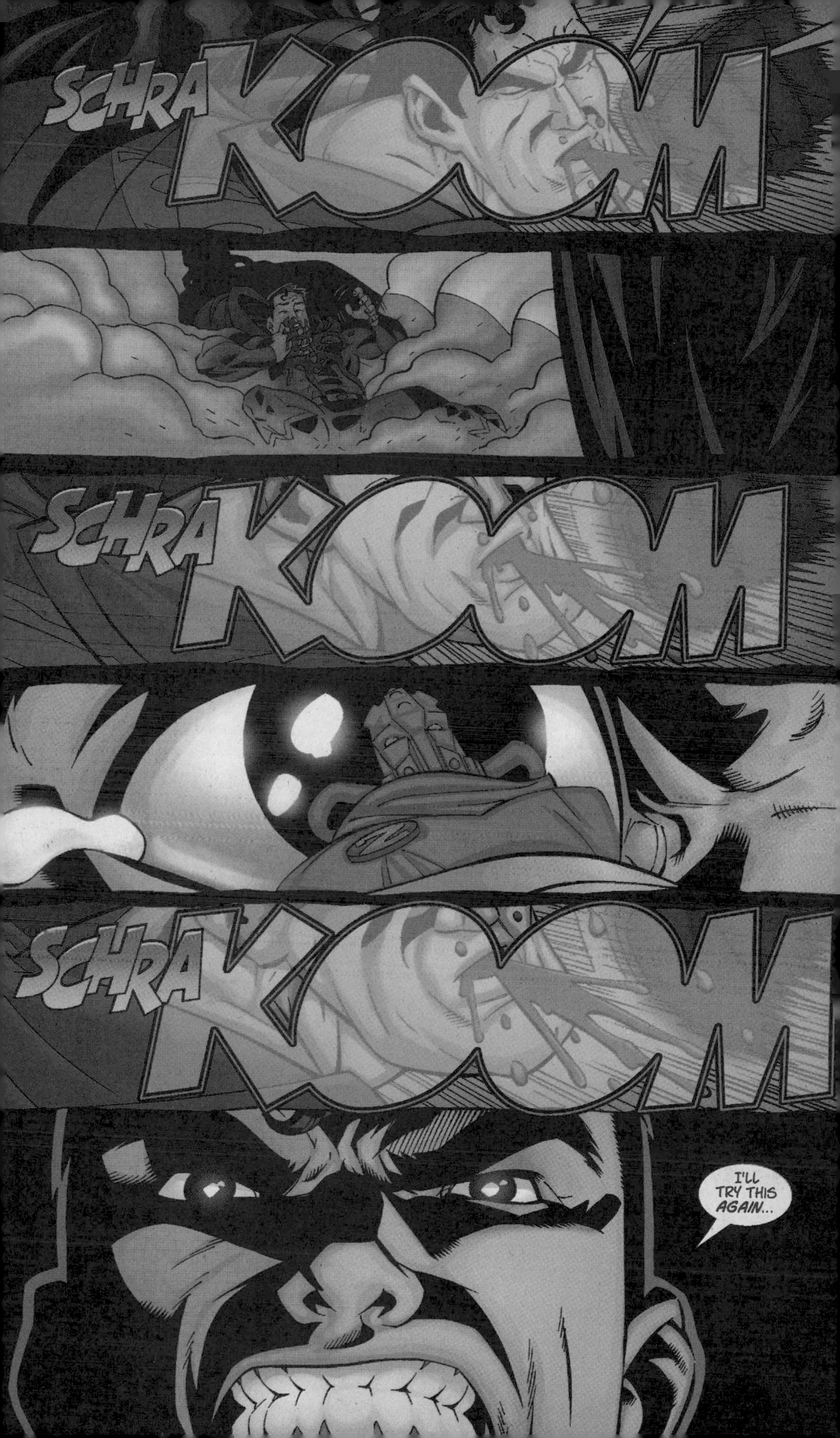
SCHRAKOOM
SCHRAKOOM
SCHRAKOOM
I'LL TRY THIS AGAIN...

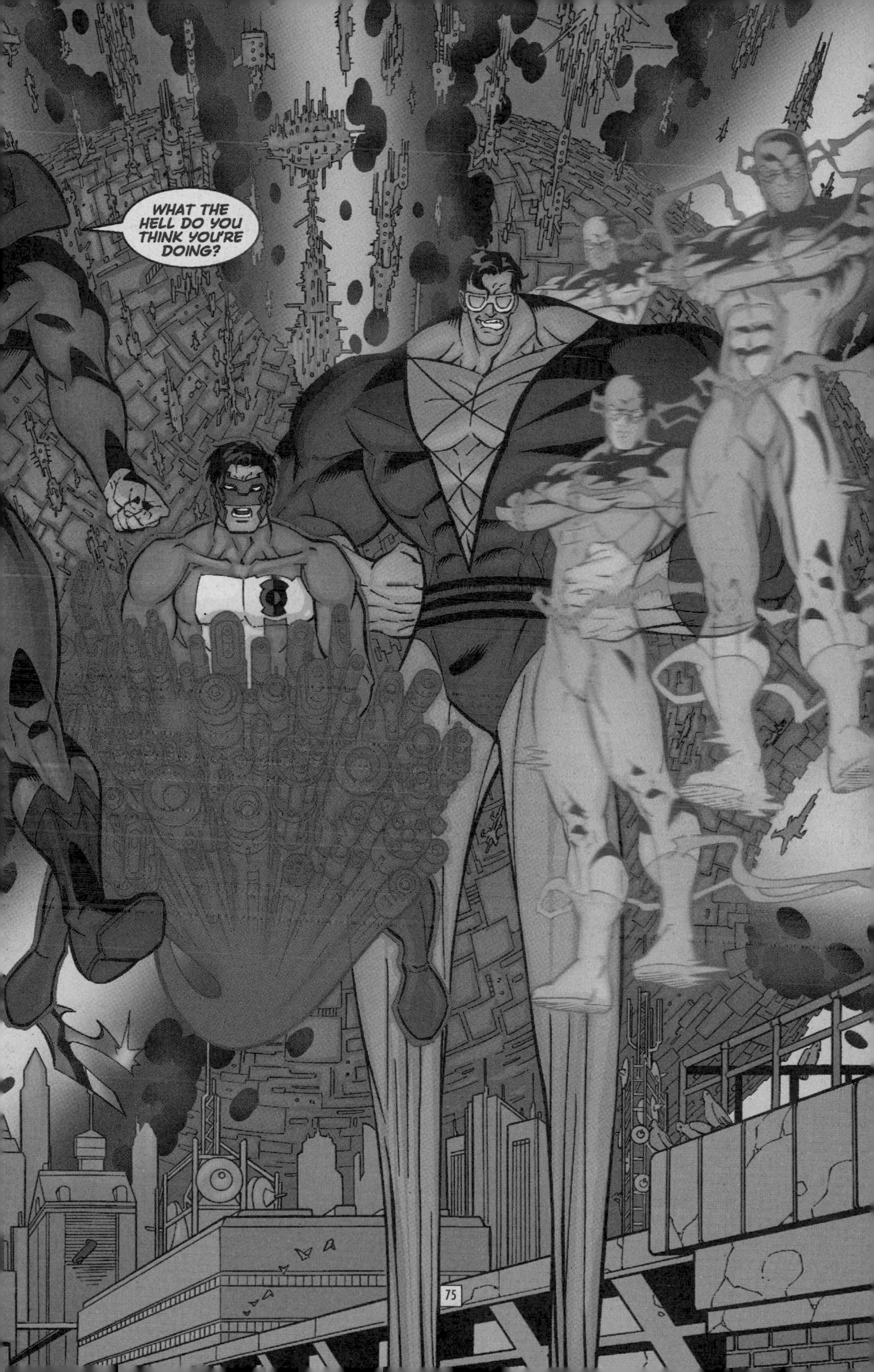
WHAT THE HELL DO YOU THINK YOU'RE DOING?

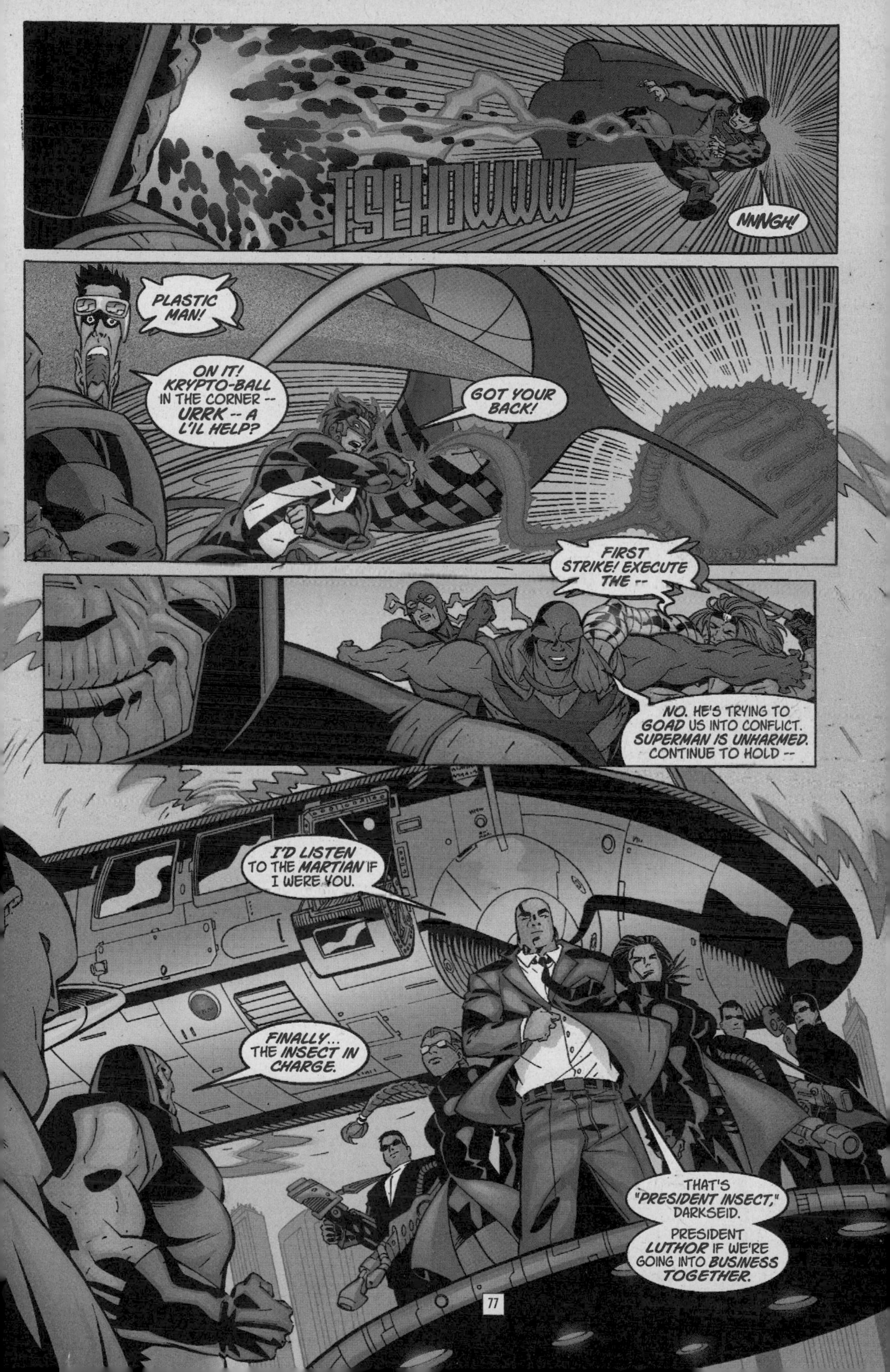
TSCHOWWW
NNNGH!
PLASTIC MAN!
ON IT! KRYPTO-BALL IN THE CORNER -- URRK -- A L'IL HELP?
GOT YOUR BACK!
FIRST STRIKE! EXECUTE THE --
NO. HE'S TRYING TO GOAD US INTO CONFLICT. SUPERMAN IS UNHARMED. CONTINUE TO HOLD --
I'D LISTEN TO THE MARTIAN IF I WERE YOU.
FINALLY... THE INSECT IN CHARGE.
THAT'S "PRESIDENT INSECT," DARKSEID.
PRESIDENT LUTHOR IF WE'RE GOING INTO BUSINESS TOGETHER.

YOU KNEW?!

SERIOUSLY, IT WAS A *PLEASURE*... NO NEED TO *THANK* ME --

-- COULD SOMEONE USE THEIR *GREAT POWER* TO HELP ME FIND MY *PANCREAS?*

I'M THE *PRESIDENT OF THE UNITED STATES,* SUPERMAN. OF COURSE *"I KNEW."*

I TRUST ALL IS ACCORDING TO *SPECIFICATIONS?*

YOUR *TIDES* ARE ON *SCHEDULE.* YOUR *MOON* HAS NOT SPIRALED INTO THE *SUN.*

YOU HAVE A GIFT FOR UNDERSTATEMENT. HOW MUCH TIME DO WE HAVE?

DAYS, AT LEAST --

LUTHOR, WHAT'S GOING ON? WHY WEREN'T WE *NOTIFIED* --?

YOU WOULD HAVE BEEN, HAD YOU NOT BEEN SO *GUNG HO* TO ATTACK AN *ALLY.*

COME, LEAGUERS, THERE IS MUCH TO DISCUSS. *PREPARATIONS* TO BE MADE...

...*EXCEPT* FOR YOU, SUPERMAN.

LEX, I'VE HAD *ENOUGH* OF THE *RUN-AROUND.* PRESIDENT OR NO, YOU'RE *NOT* CUTTING ME OUT OF --

SUPERMAN... I *PROMISE,* YOU WILL BE INVOLVED IN THIS OPERATION, BUT THERE IS A MATTER *MORE PRESSING.*

PEOPLE... PEOPLE ARE *DYING.* A *MADMAN* HAS UNLEASHED MILITARY FORCES IN *BERLIN.* I BELIEVE YOU'VE *MET...*

...THE *"GENERAL."*

FROM *POKOLISTAN.*

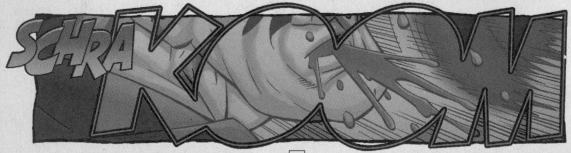

SCHRA KKOOM

78

I'M *NOT LEAVING.*

SUPERMAN, I *APPRECIATE* YOUR CONCERN FOR BOTH THE CITIZENS OF *METROPOLIS* -- AND YOUR -- AHEM -- *BELOVED PRESIDENT.*

BUT EVERY SECOND YOU STAND HERE *POUTING* BECAUSE YOUR LEADER IS DOING THE WORK OF *LEADING* -- PEOPLE ARE *DYING* IN *BERLIN.*

THIS IS THE SORT OF CONFLICT THAT STARTS *WARS,* SUPERMAN...

... AND I'M TO ASKING YOU TO HELP ME *SNUFF OUT* THE *MATCH* BEFORE IT BECOMES A *FOREST FIRE.*

YOU *WILL BE INTEGRAL* TO SOLVING THIS *"DARKSEID CRISIS,"* BUT... *YOU* CAN GET TO *BERLIN FIRST.* YOU CAN KEEP *AMERICA OUT* OF CONFLICT FOR A LITTLE WHILE LONGER.

PLEASE.

IF IT MAKES THE DECISION EASIER... I'VE LOCKED THE WATCHTOWER TELEPORTER ON HIS OMEGA BEAM ENERGY SIGNATURE.

HE SO MUCH AS ADJUSTS A CONTACT LENS, AND HE'LL BE ON *NEPTUNE* IN FIVE HUNDREDTHS OF A NANOSECOND.

"THERE IS A *LOGICAL STEP* MISSING WHEN ONE *ANALYZES* THE MOVE FROM A *STRATEGIC* POINT OF VIEW."

"MY PEOPLE AT THE *PENTAGON* ARE BETTING BERLIN IS MORE FOR A *PSYCHOLOGICAL EFFECT* THAN ANYTHING ELSE."

"WHICH MAKES HIM EITHER *INSANE, DELUDED,* OR UTTERLY *BRILLIANT.*"

HE BROKE MY *JAW.*

"HE SNUCK UP THROUGH THE *CZECH REPUBLIC.* APPARENTLY, *SATELLITES* AREN'T AN ISSUE. NEITHER IS *MANPOWER.*"

HE BROKE MY *JAW.*

"THE UNITED STATES *WILL* GET INVOLVED, I ALREADY HAVE *TROOPS* MOBILIZING, BUT AFTER *YOUR* INCIDENT IN POKOLISTAN..."

"...I THOUGHT YOU MIGHT WANT *FIRST CRACK.* WHAT IS IT BETWEEN YOU *TWO?*"

HE BROKE MY *JAW.*

"I DON'T KNOW, *LEX...* I DON'T KNOW."

80

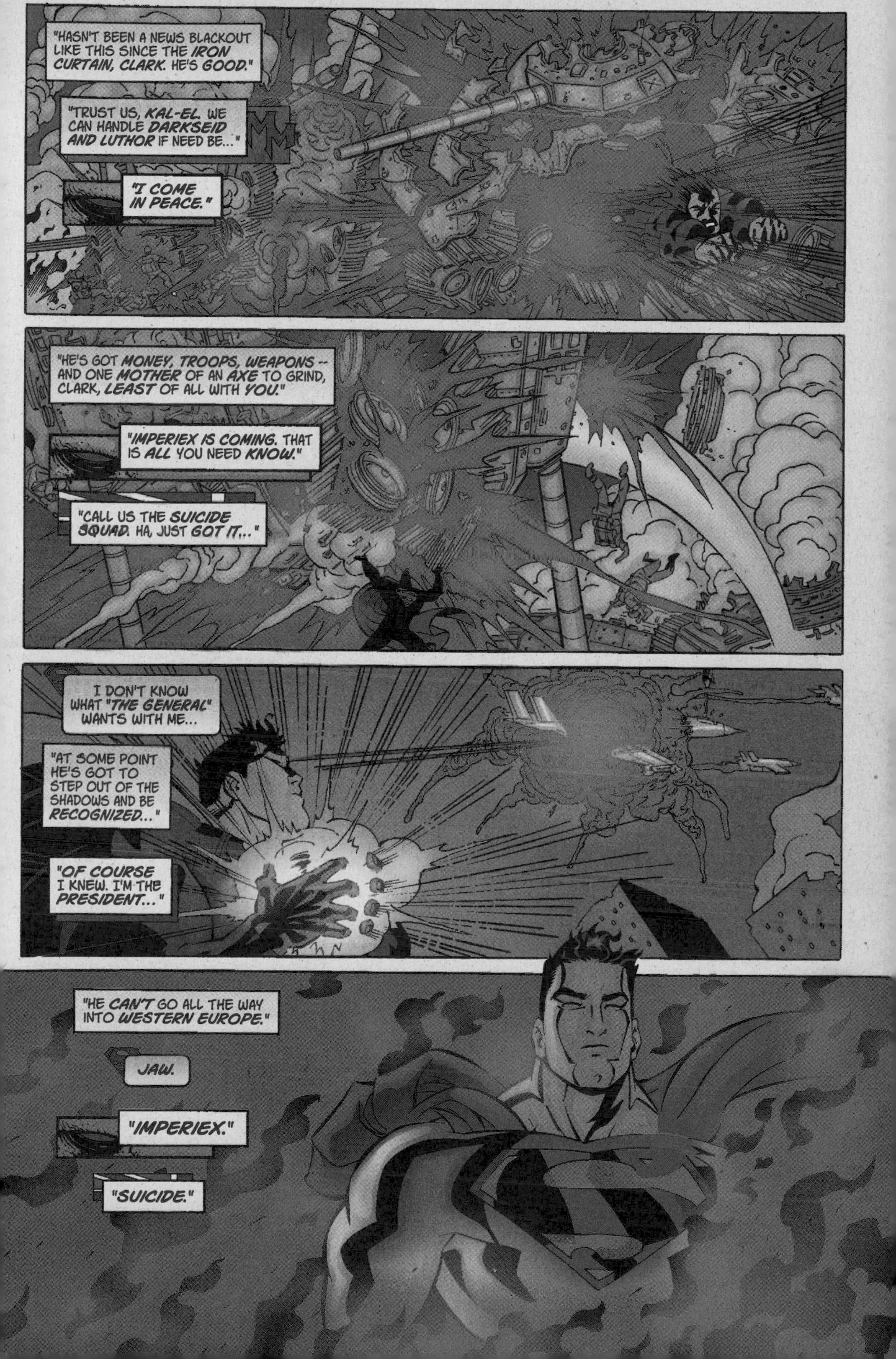
"HASN'T BEEN A NEWS BLACKOUT LIKE THIS SINCE THE IRON CURTAIN, CLARK. HE'S GOOD."
"TRUST US, KAL-EL. WE CAN HANDLE DARKSEID AND LUTHOR IF NEED BE..."
"I COME IN PEACE."
"HE'S GOT MONEY, TROOPS, WEAPONS -- AND ONE MOTHER OF AN AXE TO GRIND, CLARK, LEAST OF ALL WITH YOU."
"IMPERIEX IS COMING. THAT IS ALL YOU NEED KNOW."
"CALL US THE SUICIDE SQUAD. HA, JUST GOT IT..."
I DON'T KNOW WHAT "THE GENERAL" WANTS WITH ME...
"AT SOME POINT HE'S GOT TO STEP OUT OF THE SHADOWS AND BE RECOGNIZED..."
"OF COURSE I KNEW. I'M THE PRESIDENT..."
"HE CAN'T GO ALL THE WAY INTO WESTERN EUROPE."
JAW.
"IMPERIEX."
"SUICIDE."

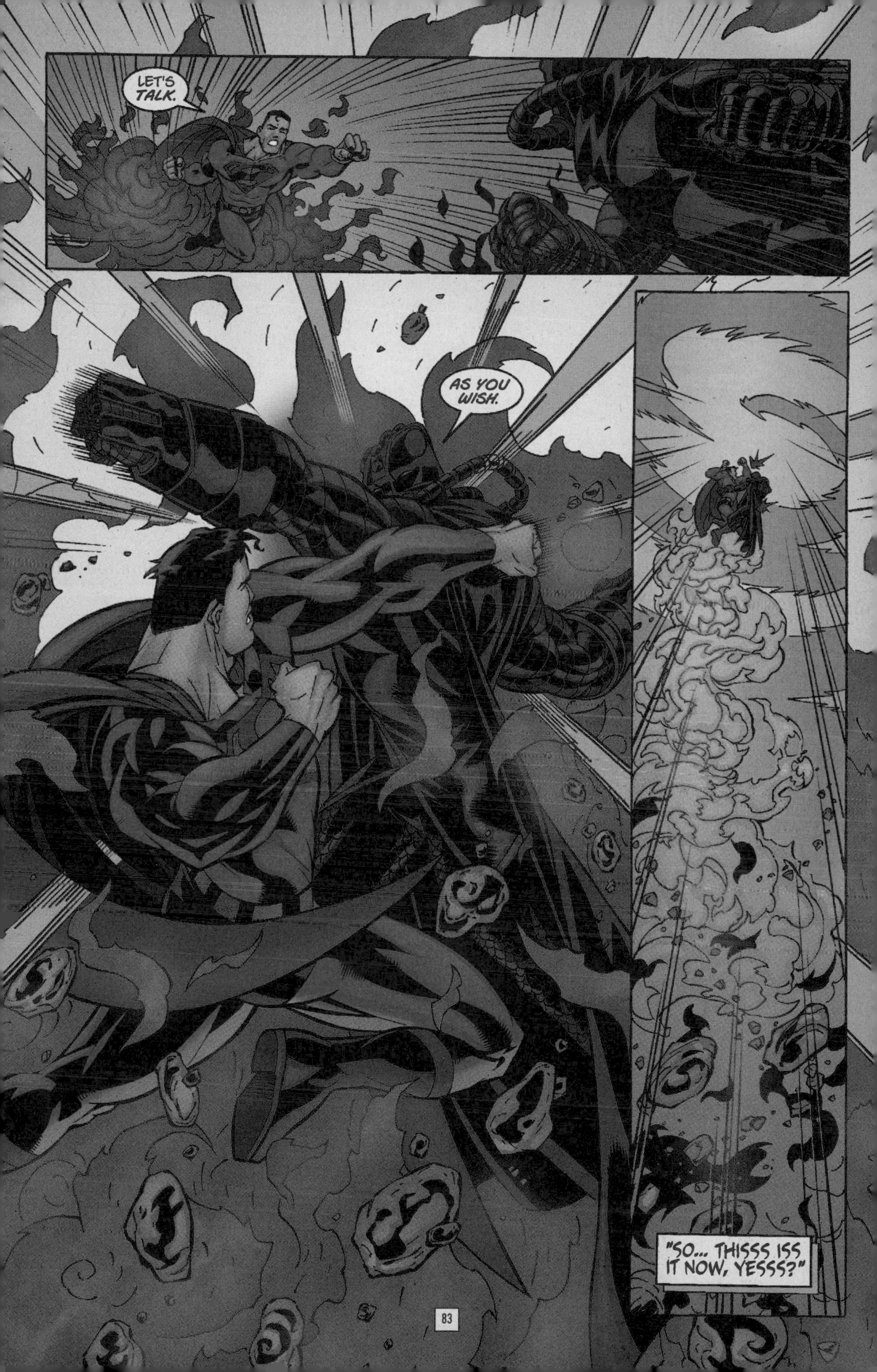
LET'S TALK.
AS YOU WISH.
"SO... THISSS ISS IT NOW, YESSS?"

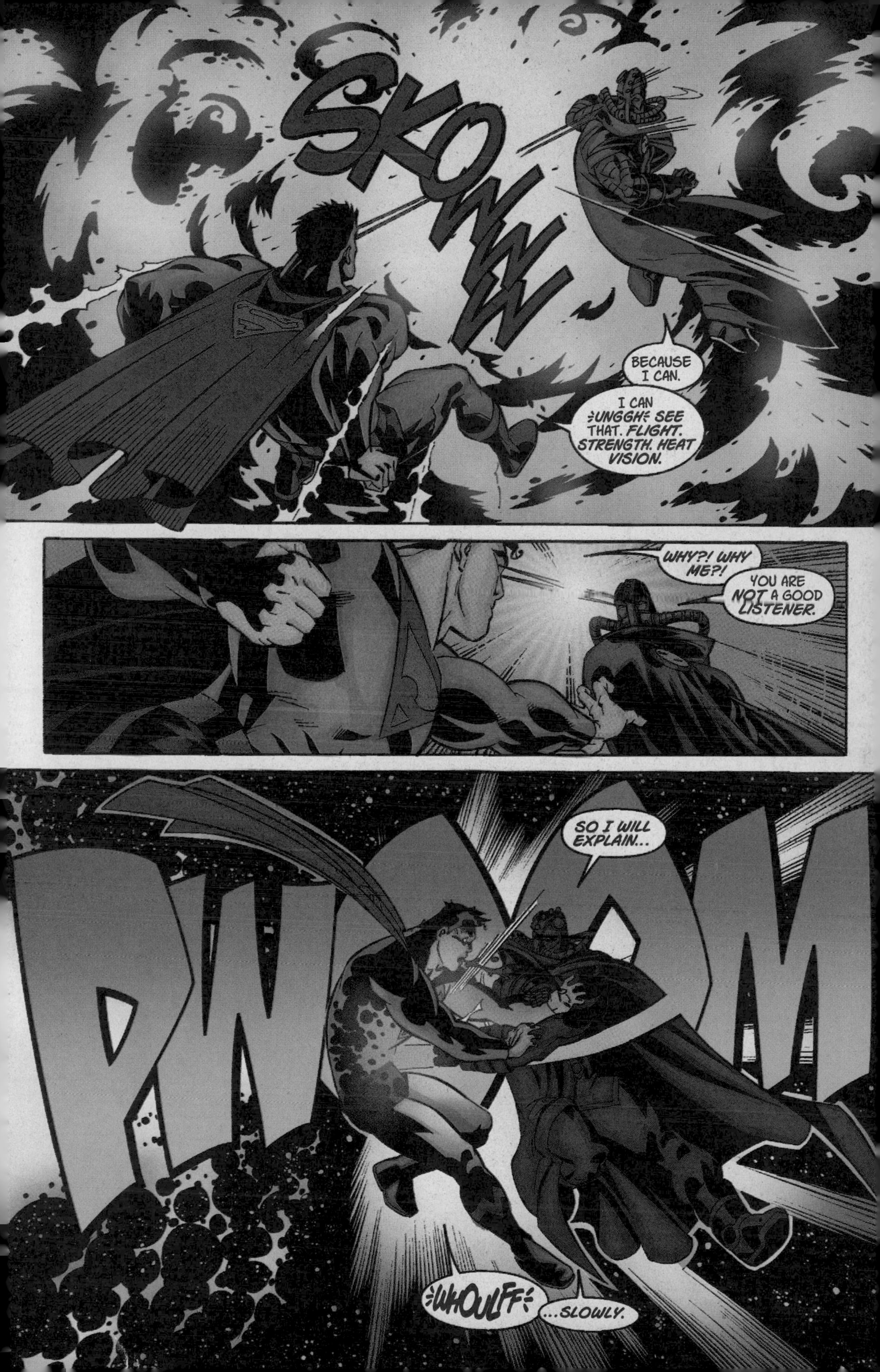
SKOWWW
BECAUSE I CAN.
I CAN ~UNGGH~ SEE THAT. FLIGHT. STRENGTH. HEAT VISION.
WHY?! WHY ME?!
YOU ARE NOT A GOOD LISTENER.
SO I WILL EXPLAIN...
PWOOM
~WHOULFF~
...SLOWLY.

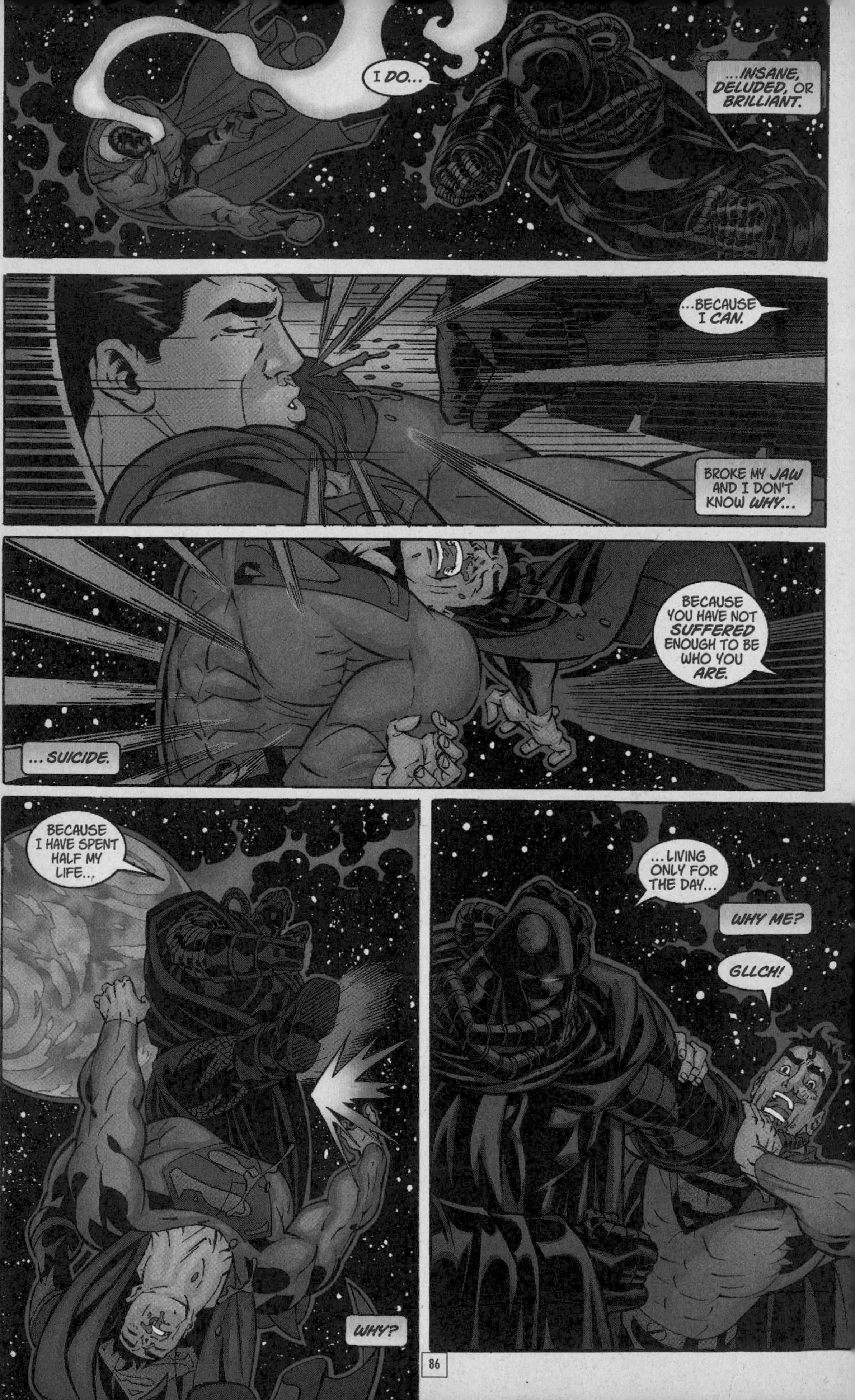
I DO...
...INSANE, DELUDED, OR BRILLIANT.
...BECAUSE I CAN.
BROKE MY JAW AND I DON'T KNOW WHY...
BECAUSE YOU HAVE NOT SUFFERED ENOUGH TO BE WHO YOU ARE.
...SUICIDE.
BECAUSE I HAVE SPENT HALF MY LIFE...
WHY?
...LIVING ONLY FOR THE DAY...
WHY ME?
GLLCH!

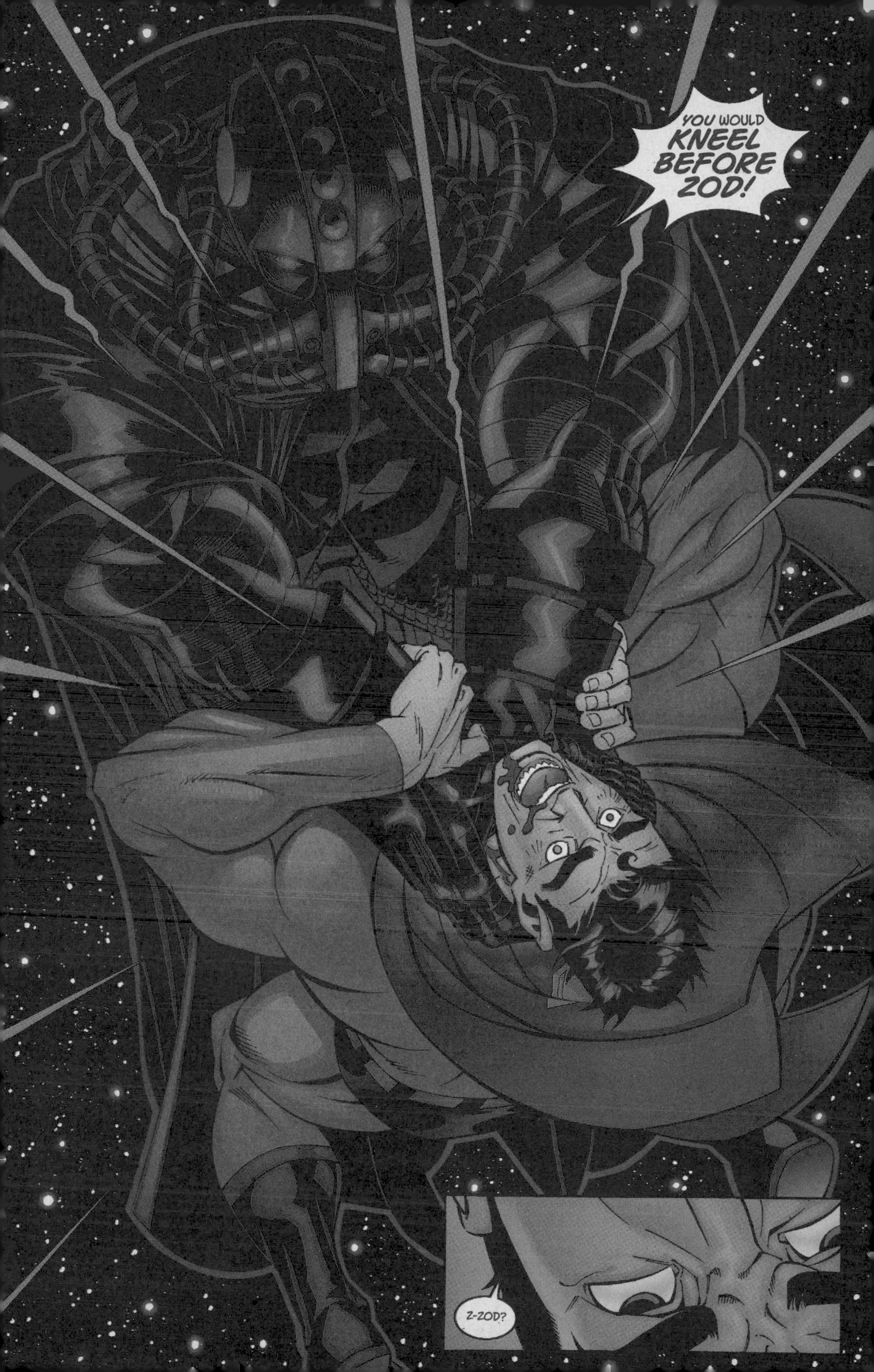
YOU WOULD KNEEL BEFORE ZOD!
Z-ZOD?

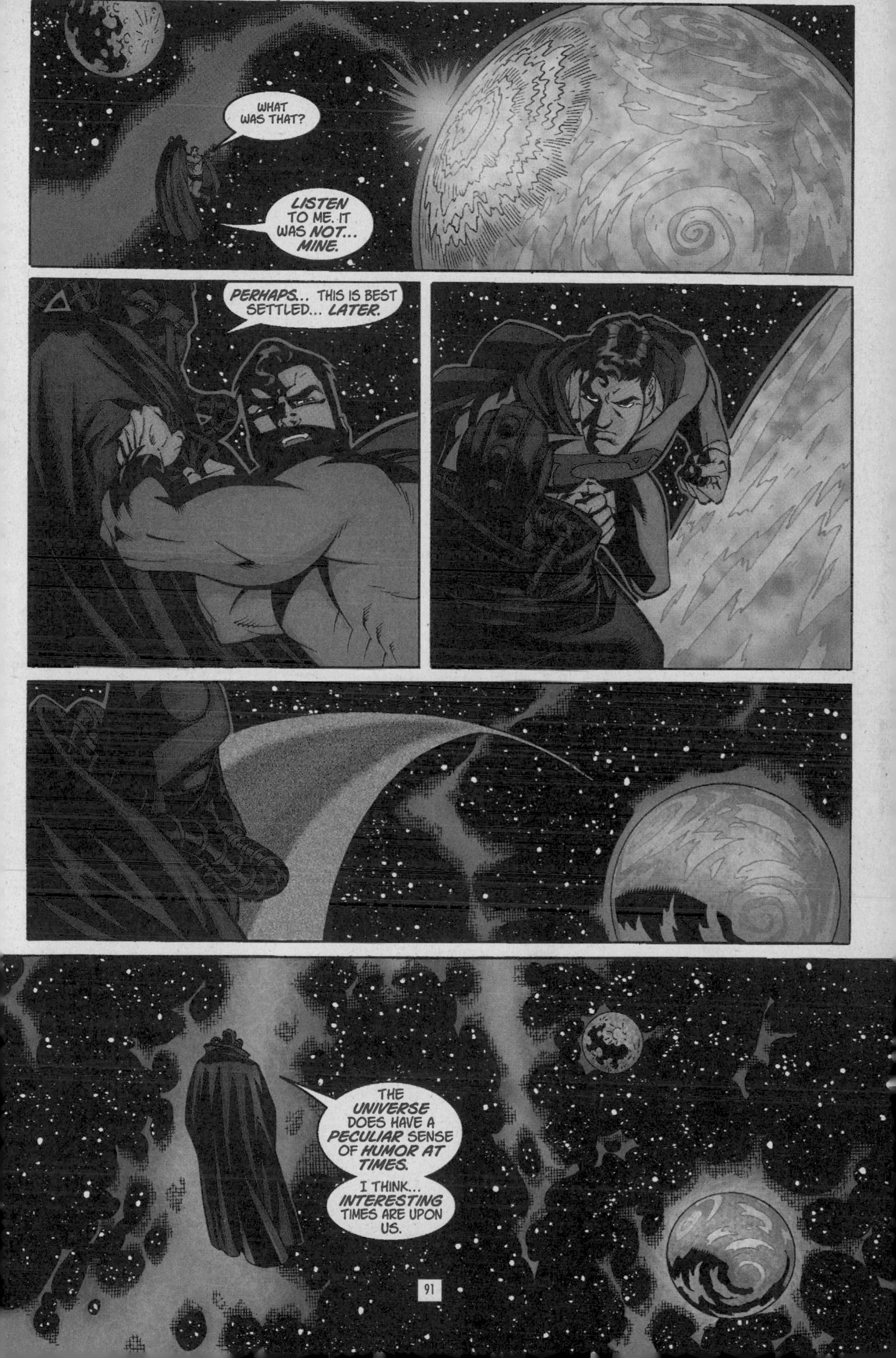
WHAT WAS THAT?
LISTEN TO ME. IT WAS NOT... MINE.
PERHAPS... THIS IS BEST SETTLED... LATER.
THE UNIVERSE DOES HAVE A PECULIAR SENSE OF HUMOR AT TIMES.
I THINK... INTERESTING TIMES ARE UPON US.

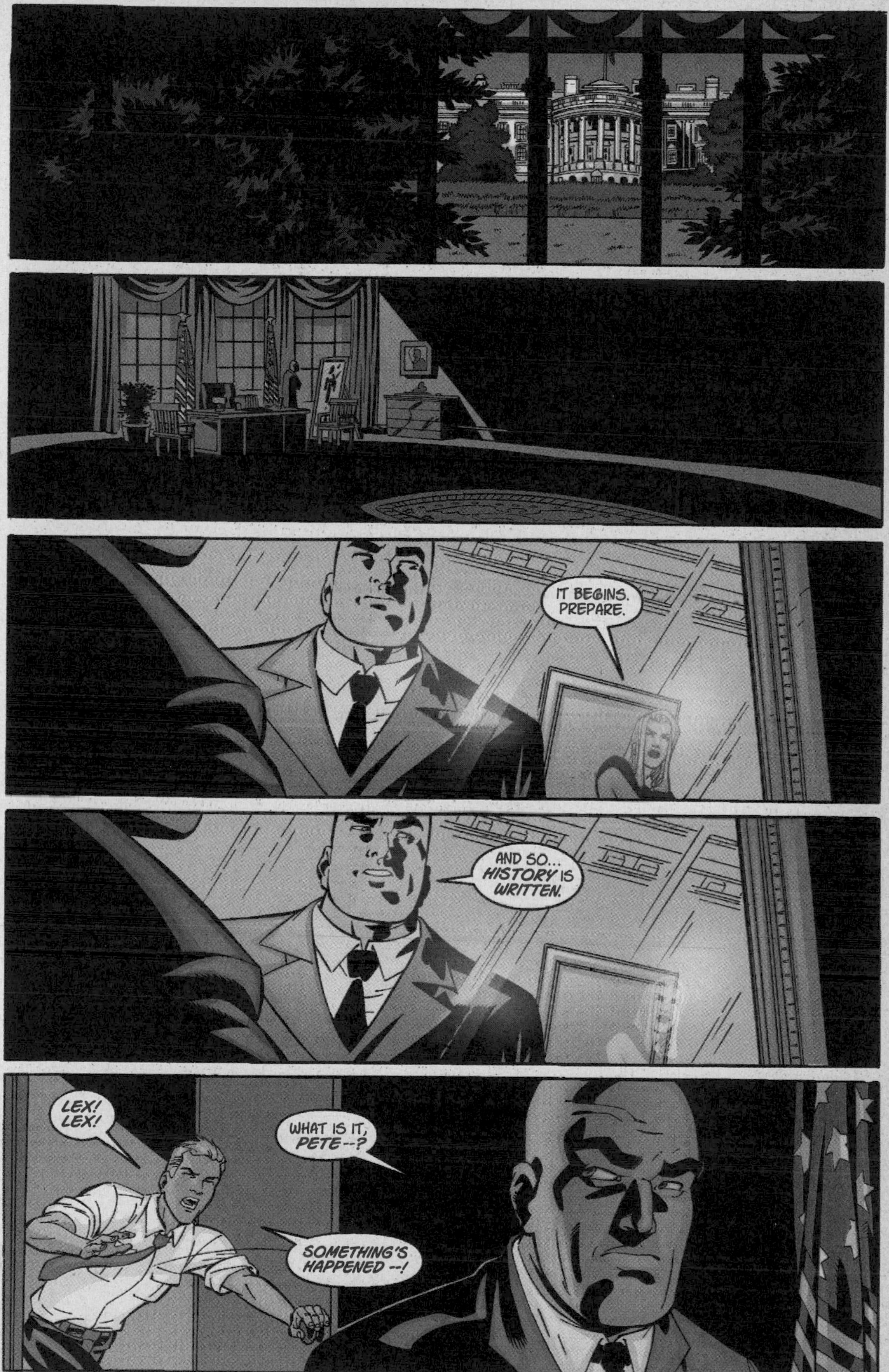
IT BEGINS. PREPARE.
AND SO... HISTORY IS WRITTEN.
LEX! LEX!
WHAT IS IT, PETE--?
SOMETHING'S HAPPENED --!

"-- SOMETHING HAPPENED TO *KANSAS.*" "SOMETHING *CATASTROPHIC.*"

JOE KELLY   KANO   MARLO ALQUIZA
WRITER   PENCILLER   INKER

THE END OF

"There are times we sleepwalk through our days, oblivious to the signs around us, until we suddenly wake up and realize that we're not walking at all. We're sliding. Down a greased hill. Towards a boiling pit of... life."
Clark Kent, Daily Planet, June 2001.

THE BEGINNING

ROB SCHWAGER
COLORS

COMICRAFT
LETTERS

TOM PALMER JR.
ASSISTANT EDITOR

EDDIE BERGANZA
EDITOR

Superman Created by
JERRY SIEGEL and JOE SHUSTER

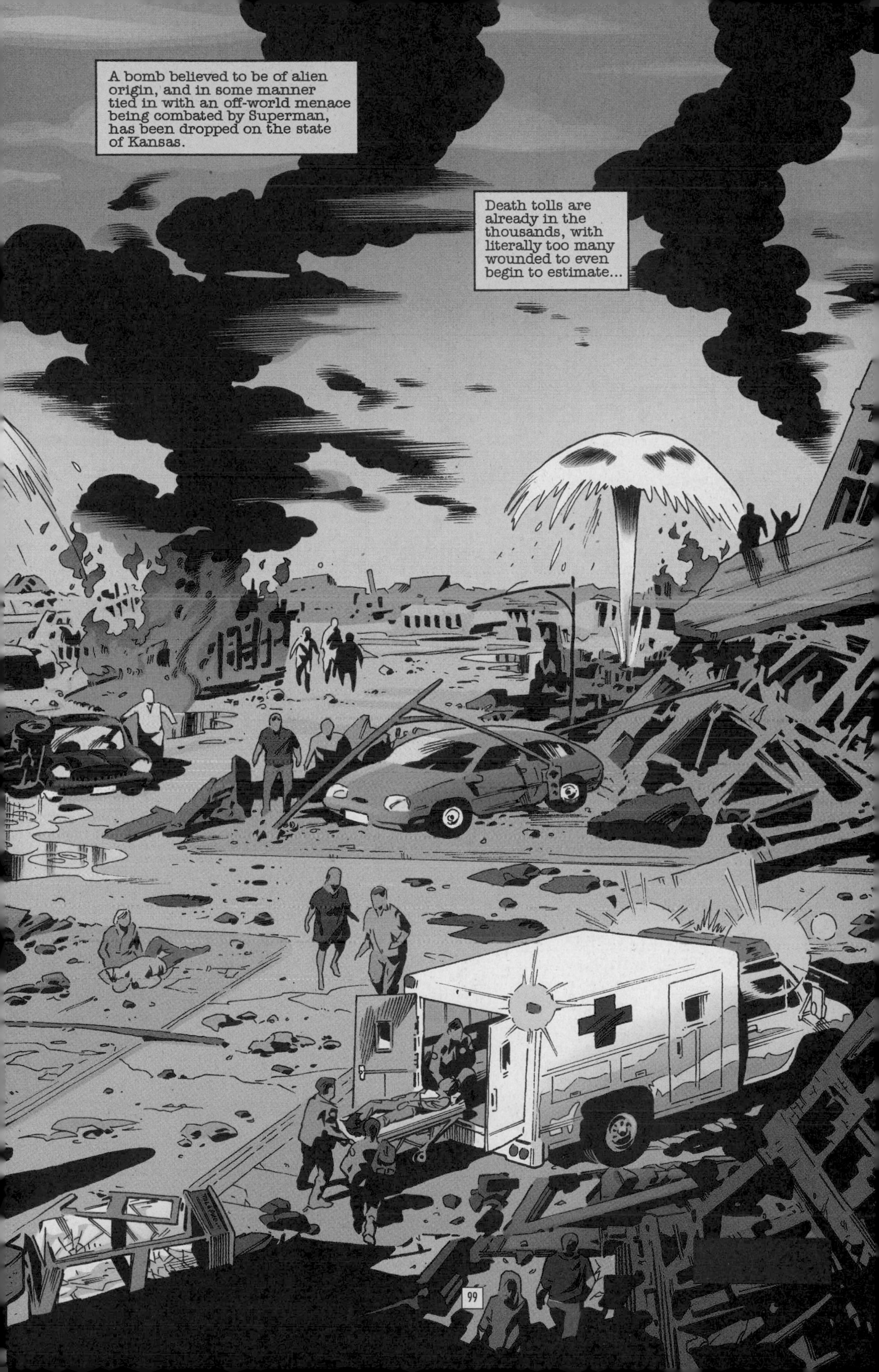
A bomb believed to be of alien origin, and in some manner tied in with an off-world menace being combated by Superman, has been dropped on the state of Kansas.
Death tolls are already in the thousands, with literally too many wounded to even begin to estimate...

We were passing through *Kansas*, Buzz and I, following the Chaos Stream, searching for Supergirl, the Fallen angel...

I was just in the process of calling Ma and Pa...

...and I figured it'd be a nice opportunity to get together with Ma and Pa Kent. But I wasn't about to bring *Buzz* to see them and risk his piecing together *Clark's* identity.

So I made up a story about a photo exhibit and some friends and dropped him at a pub. He seemed perfectly *happy* about it.

...and suddenly it was... it...

I don't know *what* it was...

YOU!

Huh?

AHHH! DON'T HURT ME!

DON'T BE RIDICULOUS. I'M **SUPERGIRL.** I'M NOT GOING TO HURT YOU.

THE EXPLOSION... WHAT **CAUSED** IT?

Nuh... NOBODY'S SURE. THERE'S REPORTS ABOUT... ABOUT **ALIENS.** THE NEWS SAID SOMETHING ABOUT SOMETHING CALLED... "IMPERICAL," I THINK IT WAS...

...AND THERE WAS FOOTAGE OF SOME ALIEN GUY LANDING IN METROPOLIS ...AND THE **JLA** WAS CALLED IN...

The **JLA?** If **they're** in the thick of it, then hopefully they'll help stop the situation from getting worse. Meantime, I've got to find out if Ma and Pa are okay...

DO YOU HAVE A CELL PHONE?

WHAT? SURE, BUT...

BUT **WHAT?**

PHONE SERVICE IS DOWN **EVERYWHERE.** I MEAN, MAYBE IF YOU'RE CALLING SOMEONE **ELSE** WITH A CELL...

LOOK... SUPERGIRL... IF THAT'S WHO YOU **ARE...**

YEAH?

Jeez, I don't know if Ma and Pa even **have** a cell phone. I don't think they do...

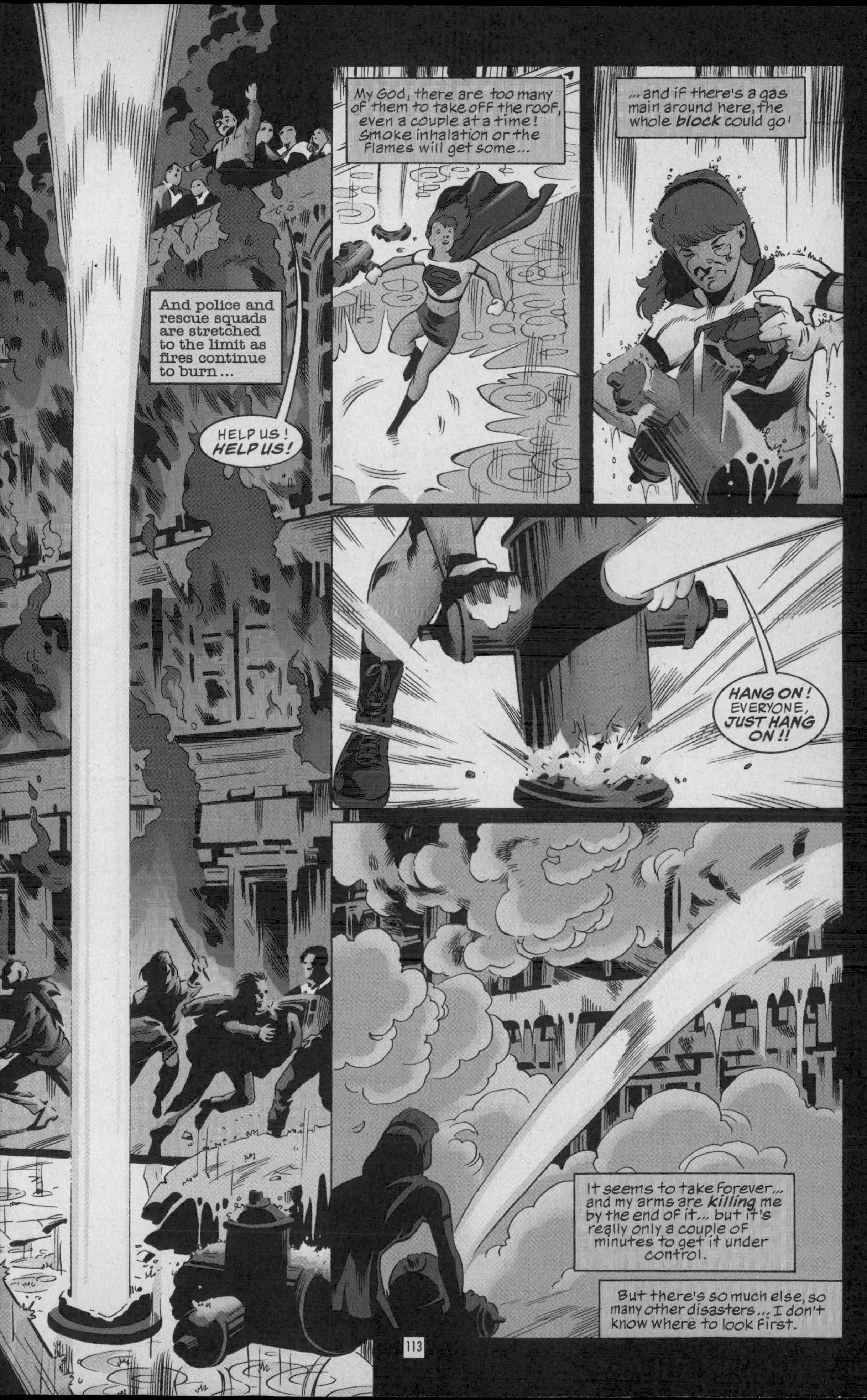

My God, there are too many of them to take off the roof, even a couple at a time! Smoke inhalation or the flames will get some...
...and if there's a gas main around here, the whole **block** could go!
And police and rescue squads are stretched to the limit as fires continue to burn...
HELP US! **HELP US!**
HANG ON! EVERYONE, **JUST HANG ON!!**
It seems to take forever... and my arms are *killing* me by the end of it... but it's really only a couple of minutes to get it under control.
But there's so much else, so many other disasters... I don't know where to look first.

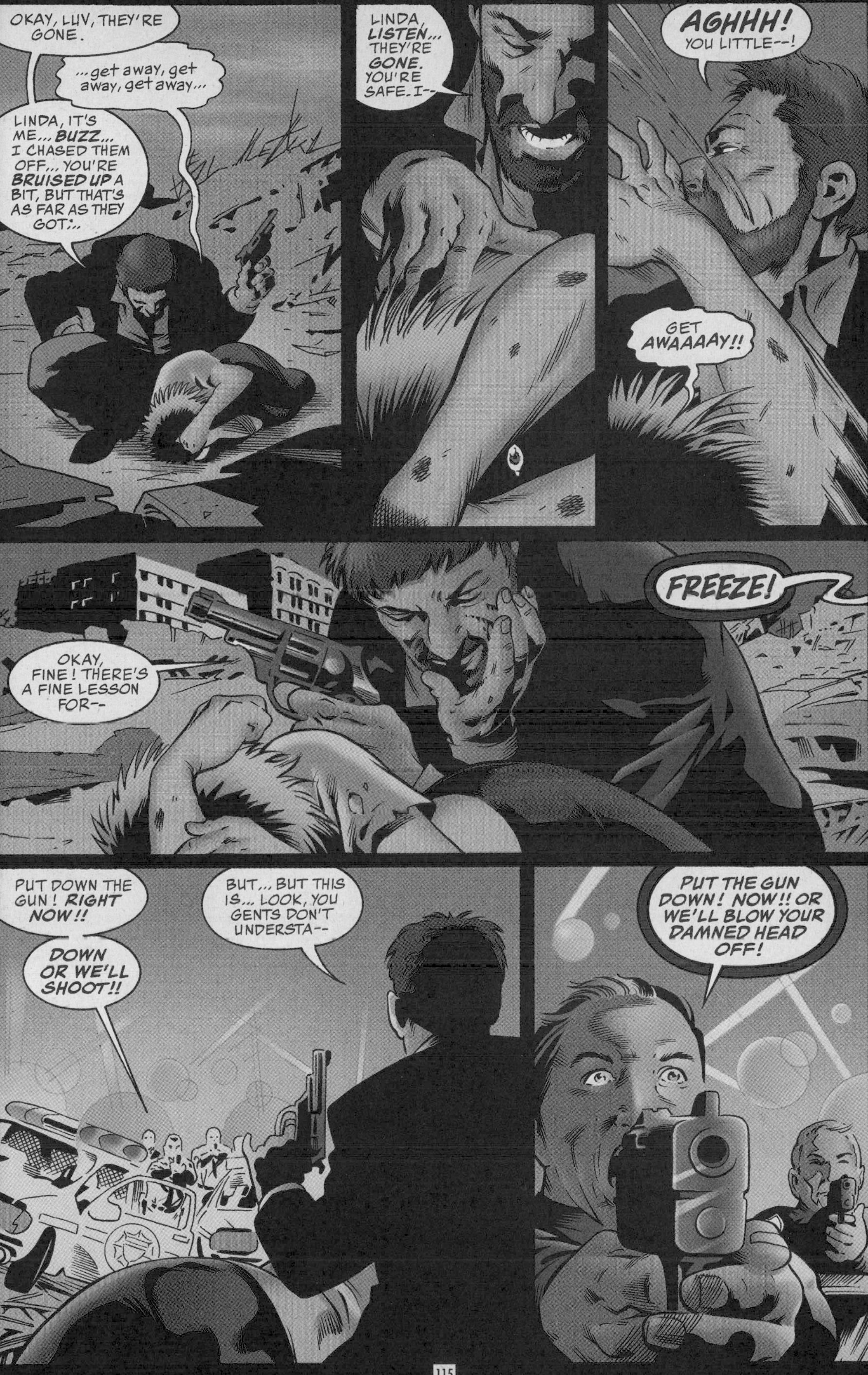
OKAY, LUV, THEY'RE GONE.
...get away, get away, get away...
LINDA, IT'S ME... BUZZ... I CHASED THEM OFF... YOU'RE BRUISED UP A BIT, BUT THAT'S AS FAR AS THEY GOT...
LINDA, LISTEN... THEY'RE GONE. YOU'RE SAFE. I--
AGHHH! YOU LITTLE--!
GET AWAAAAY!!
OKAY, FINE! THERE'S A FINE LESSON FOR--
FREEZE!
PUT DOWN THE GUN! RIGHT NOW!!
DOWN OR WE'LL SHOOT!!
BUT... BUT THIS IS... LOOK, YOU GENTS DON'T UNDERSTA--
PUT THE GUN DOWN! NOW!! OR WE'LL BLOW YOUR DAMNED HEAD OFF!

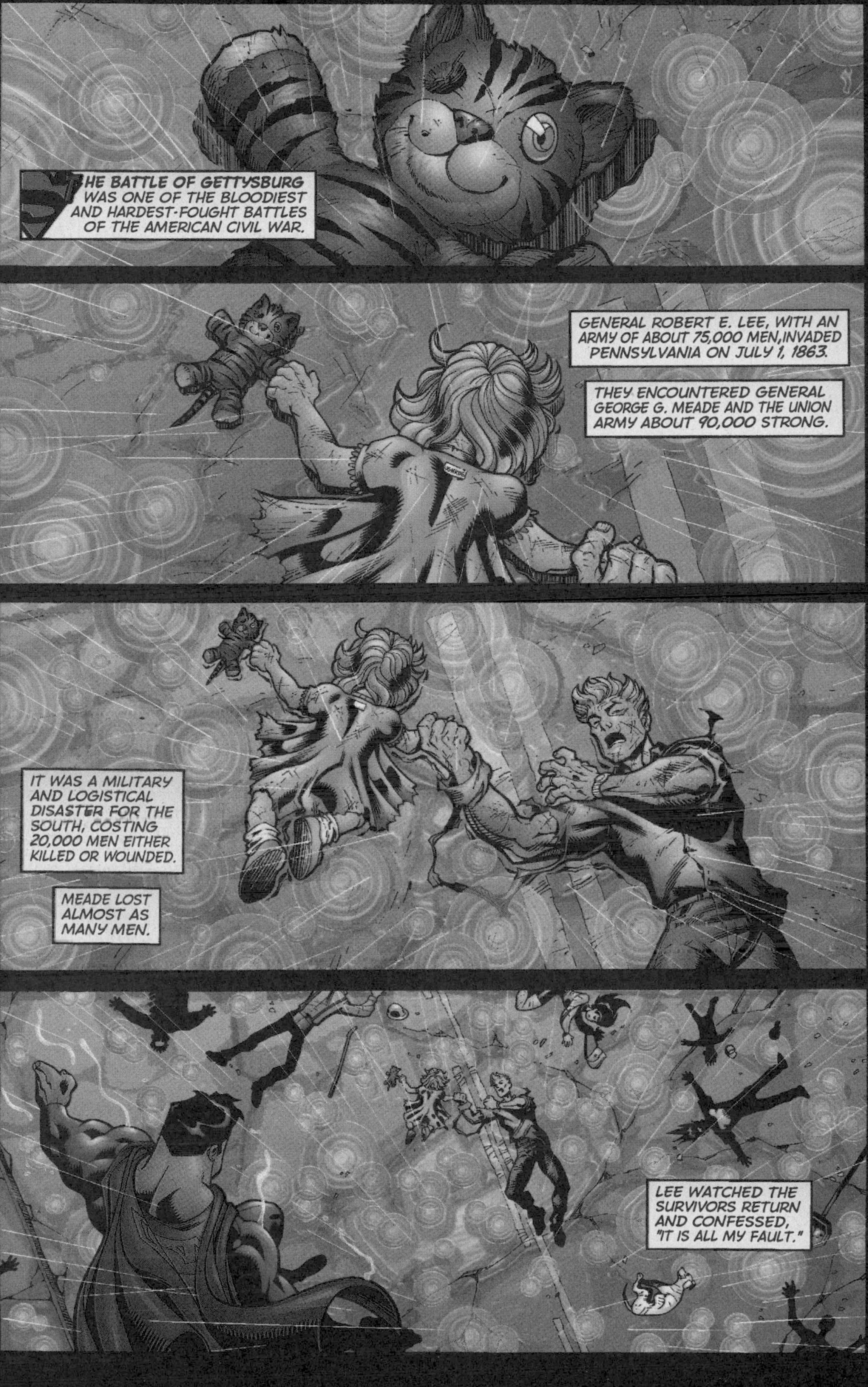
THE BATTLE OF GETTYSBURG WAS ONE OF THE BLOODIEST AND HARDEST-FOUGHT BATTLES OF THE AMERICAN CIVIL WAR.
GENERAL ROBERT E. LEE, WITH AN ARMY OF ABOUT 75,000 MEN, INVADED PENNSYLVANIA ON JULY 1, 1863.
THEY ENCOUNTERED GENERAL GEORGE G. MEADE AND THE UNION ARMY ABOUT 90,000 STRONG.
IT WAS A MILITARY AND LOGISTICAL DISASTER FOR THE SOUTH, COSTING 20,000 MEN EITHER KILLED OR WOUNDED.
MEADE LOST ALMOST AS MANY MEN.
LEE WATCHED THE SURVIVORS RETURN AND CONFESSED, "IT IS ALL MY FAULT."

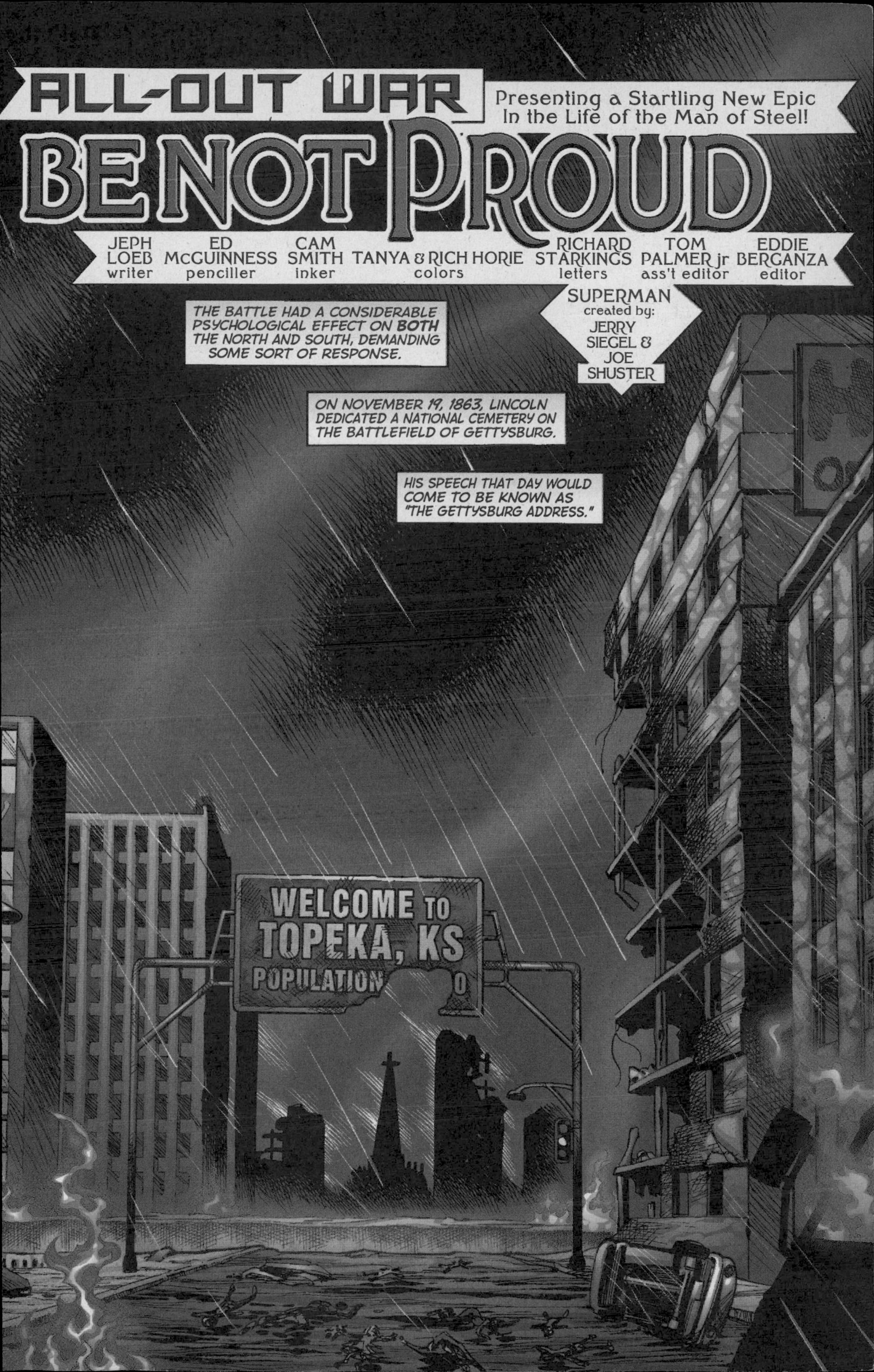
ALL-OUT WAR
Presenting a Startling New Epic In the Life of the Man of Steel!
BE NOT PROUD
JEPH LOEB writer
ED McGUINNESS penciller
CAM SMITH inker
TANYA & RICH HORIE colors
RICHARD STARKINGS letters
TOM PALMER jr ass't editor
EDDIE BERGANZA editor
SUPERMAN created by: JERRY SIEGEL & JOE SHUSTER
THE BATTLE HAD A CONSIDERABLE PSYCHOLOGICAL EFFECT ON BOTH THE NORTH AND SOUTH, DEMANDING SOME SORT OF RESPONSE.
ON NOVEMBER 19, 1863, LINCOLN DEDICATED A NATIONAL CEMETERY ON THE BATTLEFIELD OF GETTYSBURG.
HIS SPEECH THAT DAY WOULD COME TO BE KNOWN AS "THE GETTYSBURG ADDRESS."
WELCOME TO TOPEKA, KS
POPULATION 0

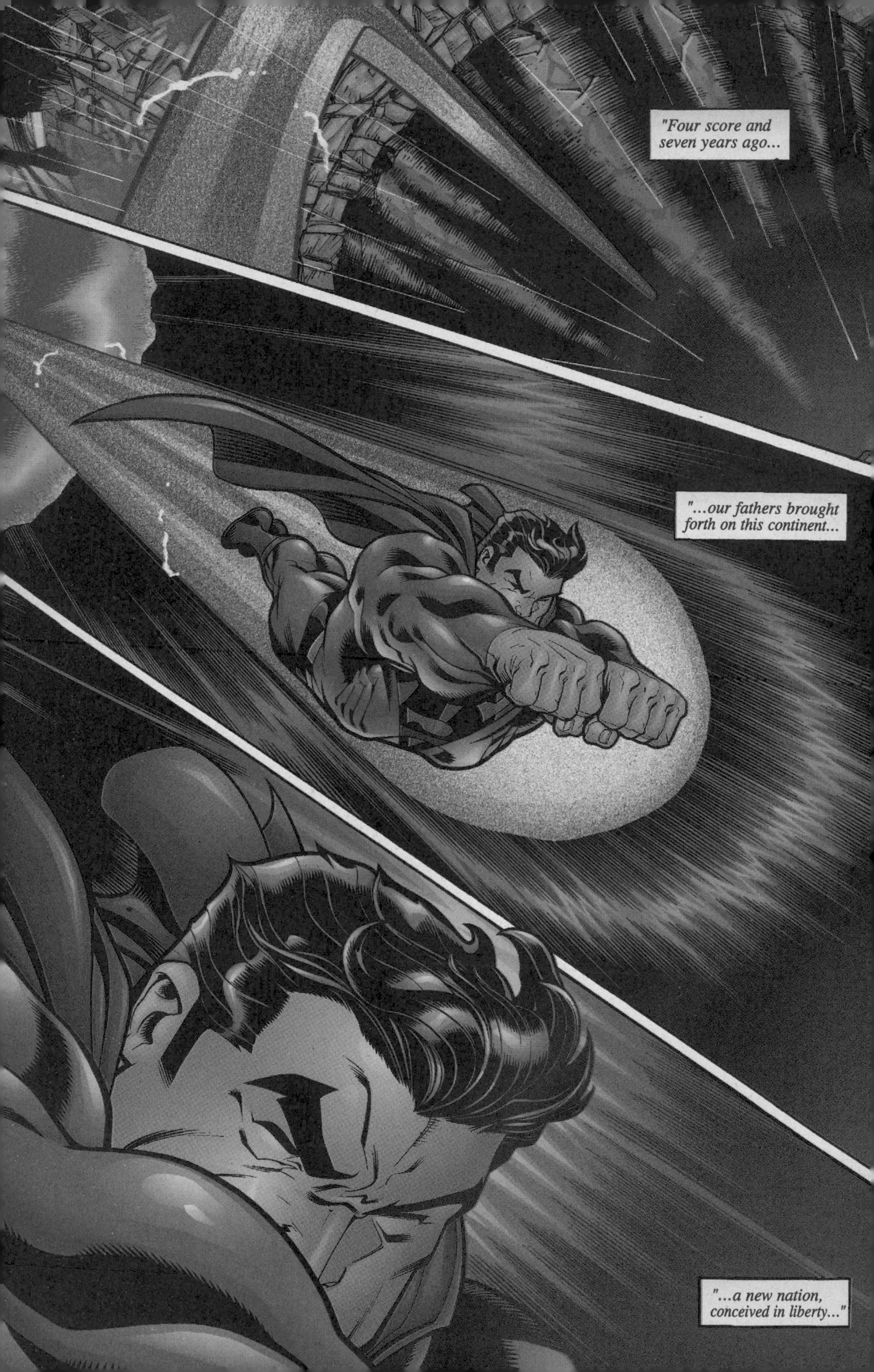
"Four score and seven years ago...
"...our fathers brought forth on this continent...
"...a new nation, conceived in liberty..."

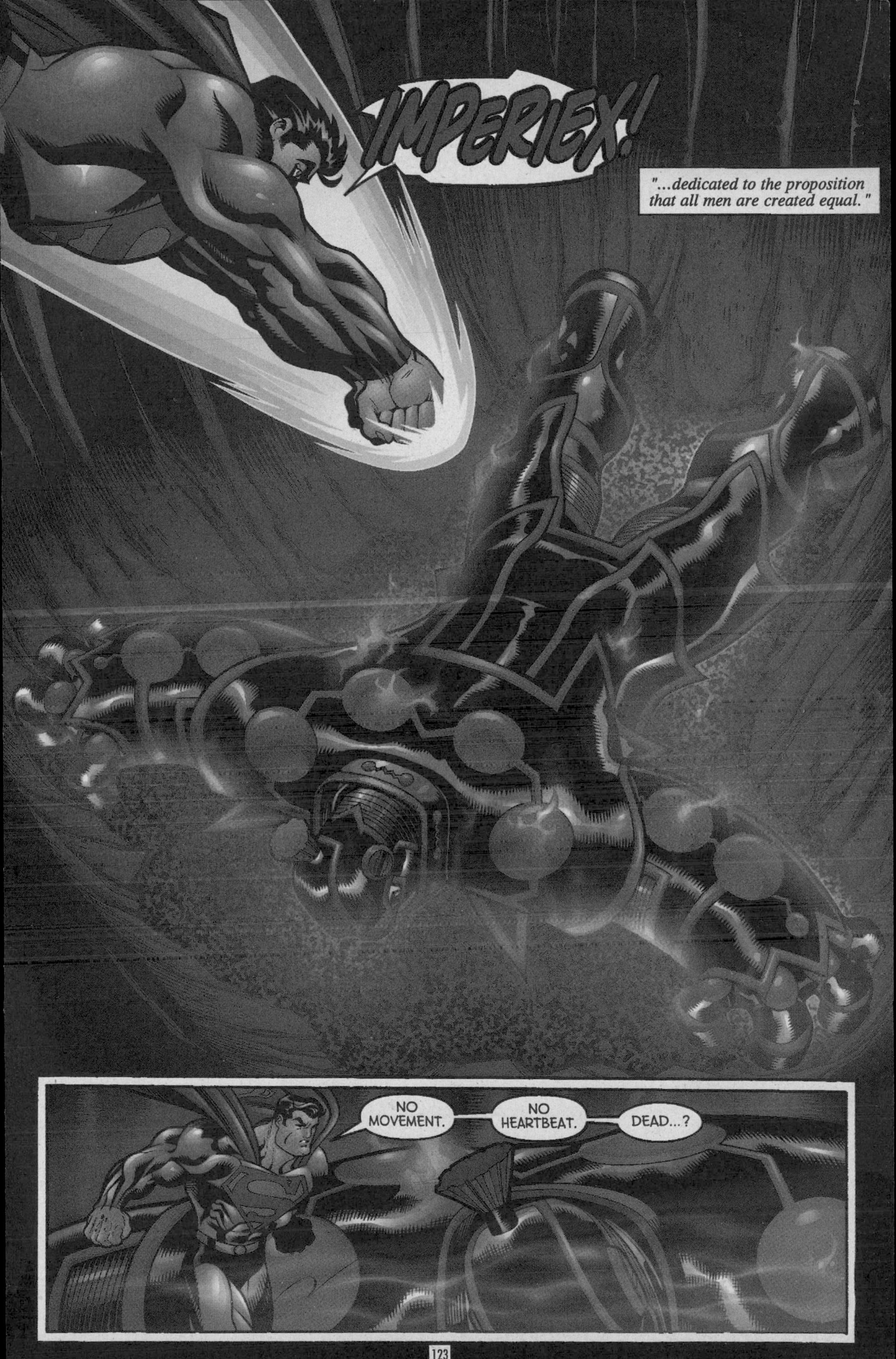
IMPERIEX!
"...dedicated to the proposition that all men are created equal."
NO MOVEMENT.
NO HEARTBEAT.
DEAD...?

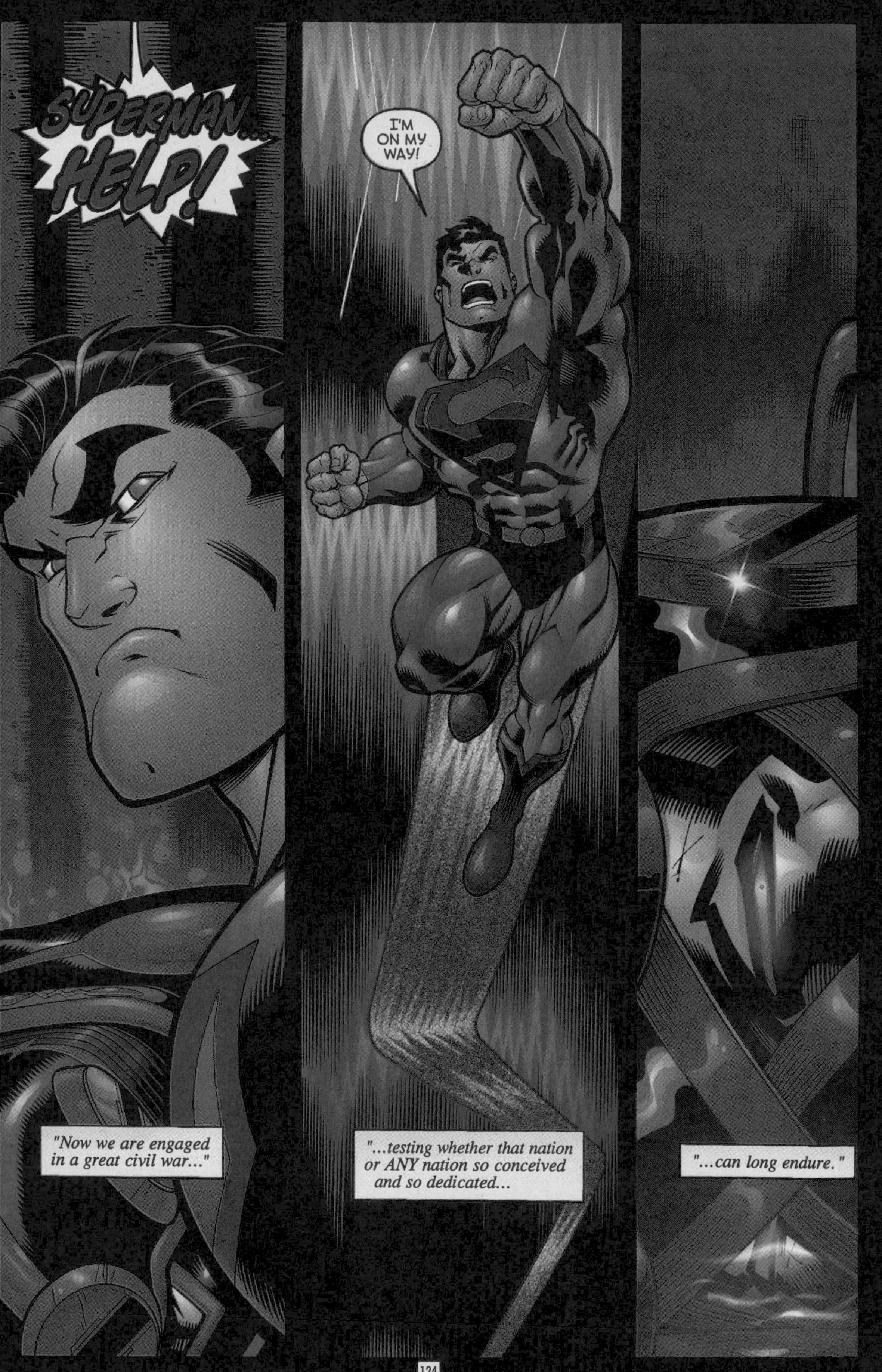
SUPERMAN... HELP!
"Now we are engaged in a great civil war..."
I'M ON MY WAY!
"...testing whether that nation or ANY nation so conceived and so dedicated...
"...can long endure."

"We are met on a great battlefield of that war."
EASY, NOW, SON. I'VE GOT YOU.
SUPERMAN -- I CAN'T FIND MY MOM OR DAD -- ANYBODY --
-- I'M SCARED!
I KNOW. I'M SCARED TOO.
NU-UHN. SUPERMAN'S NOT A'SCARED OF ANYTHING.
TELL YOU WHAT -- I'LL BE BRAVE, IF YOU'LL BE BRAVE.
I THINK I CAN DO THAT...
WHEOO-WHEOO-WHEOO-WHEOO-WHEOO-WHE

"...as a final resting place for those who here gave their lives that that nation might live."
FWOOSH
RUMMBLE
WAY TO GO, SUPERMAN!
HE -- HE SAVED US ALL!
NO.

"But, in a larger sense, we cannot dedicate --"
DID YOU LEARN NOTHING FROM OUR FIRST ENCOUNTER?
WHAM
I LEARNED YOU CAN BE BEATEN!
BASH
SEE SUPERMAN #153 -- ED.
" -- we cannot consecrate --"
A TEMPORARY SOLUTION, IF AT ALL.
KRAK
" -- we cannot hallow -- this ground."
THEN IT WILL BE PERMANENT THIS TIME!
VZZZ
THOOM
THOOM
THOOM

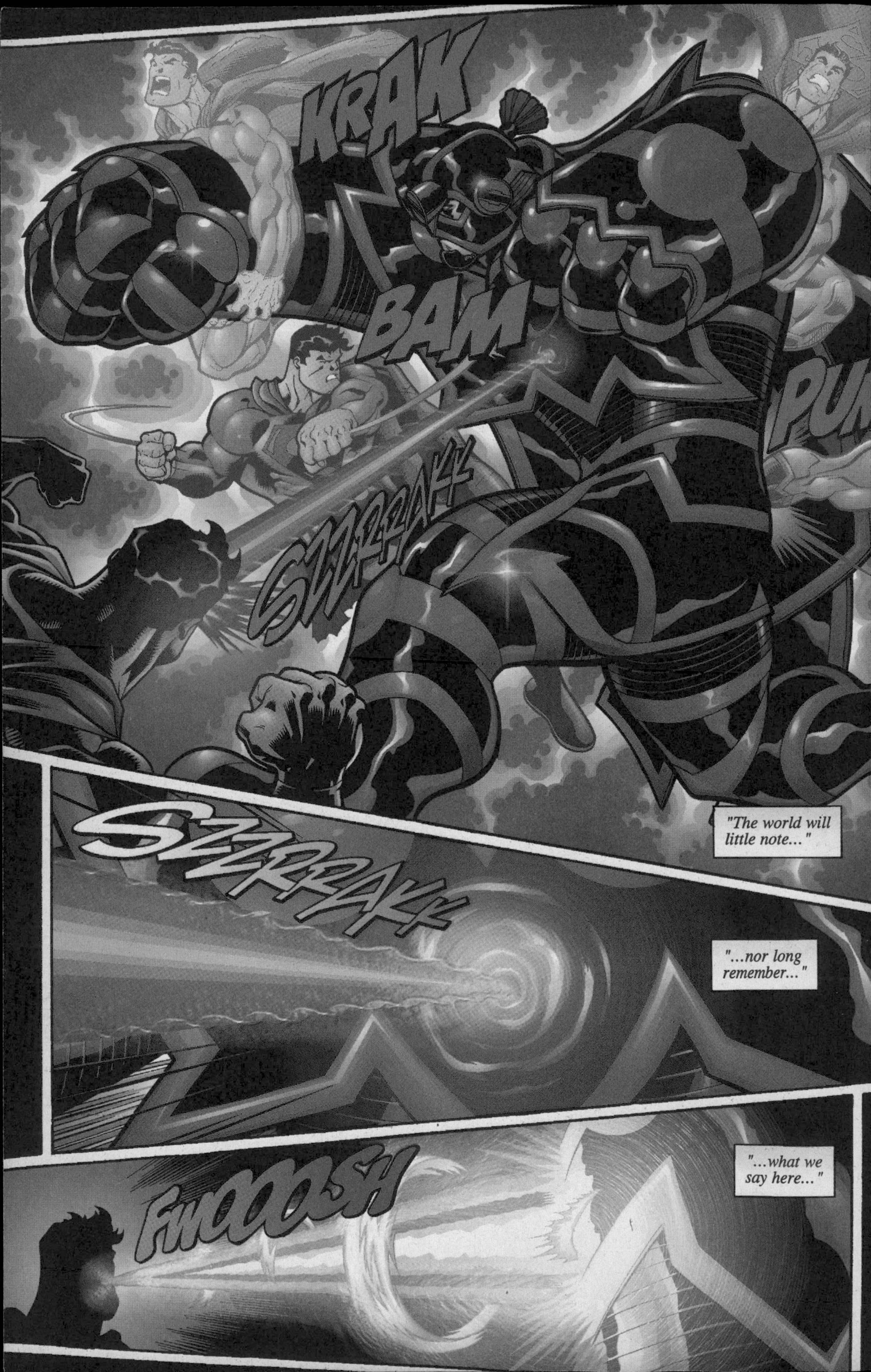
KRAK
BAM
PUM
SZZRRAKK
SZZRRAKK
"The world will little note..."
"...nor long remember..."
FWOOOSH
"...what we say here..."

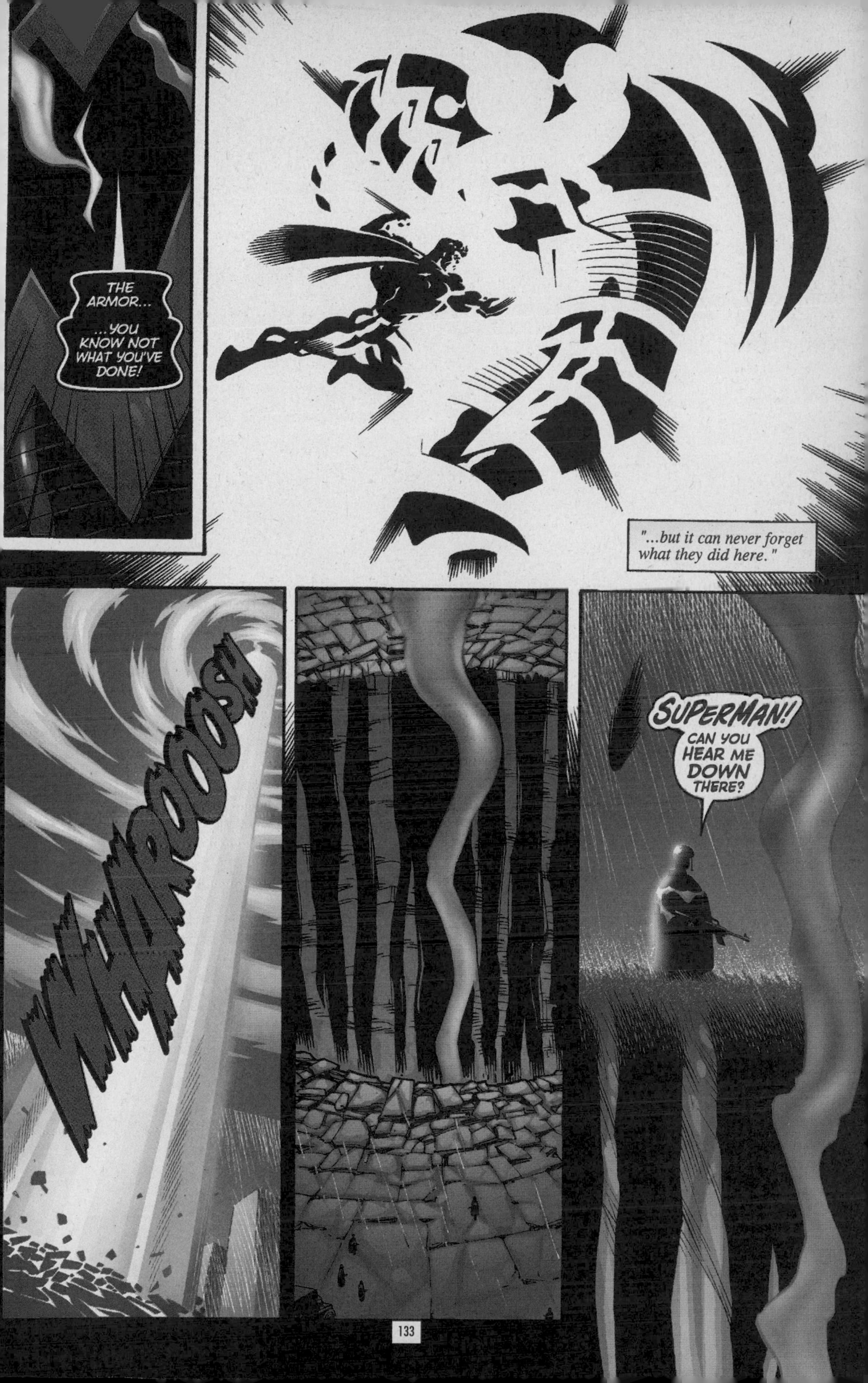
THE ARMOR...
...YOU KNOW NOT WHAT YOU'VE DONE!
"...but it can never forget what they did here."
WHAROOOSH
SUPERMAN! CAN YOU HEAR ME DOWN THERE?

WHAT'S HAPPENED HERE?

HUH...? WHERE'D YOU COME FROM?

WHAT'S HAPPENED HERE?

WHO ARE YOU SUPPOSED TO BE?

I'M NOT SUPPOSED TO BE ANYBODY.

IS... IS IT NIGHT ALREADY?

SUPERGIRL...?

I'M SUPERGIRL.

NO WAY. NOT ANY SUPERGIRL I'VE EVER --

THAT'S ME. HEY, YOU DON'T LOOK SO GOOD.

I NEED YOU TO HANDLE THINGS HERE WHILE I CHECK ON...

...SOME FOLKS NEARBY.

I UNDERSTAND.

HE, UH, DOESN'T STAY IN ONE PLACE TOO LONG, HUH?

NO. NO, HE DOESN'T.

"It is for us, the living, rather..."

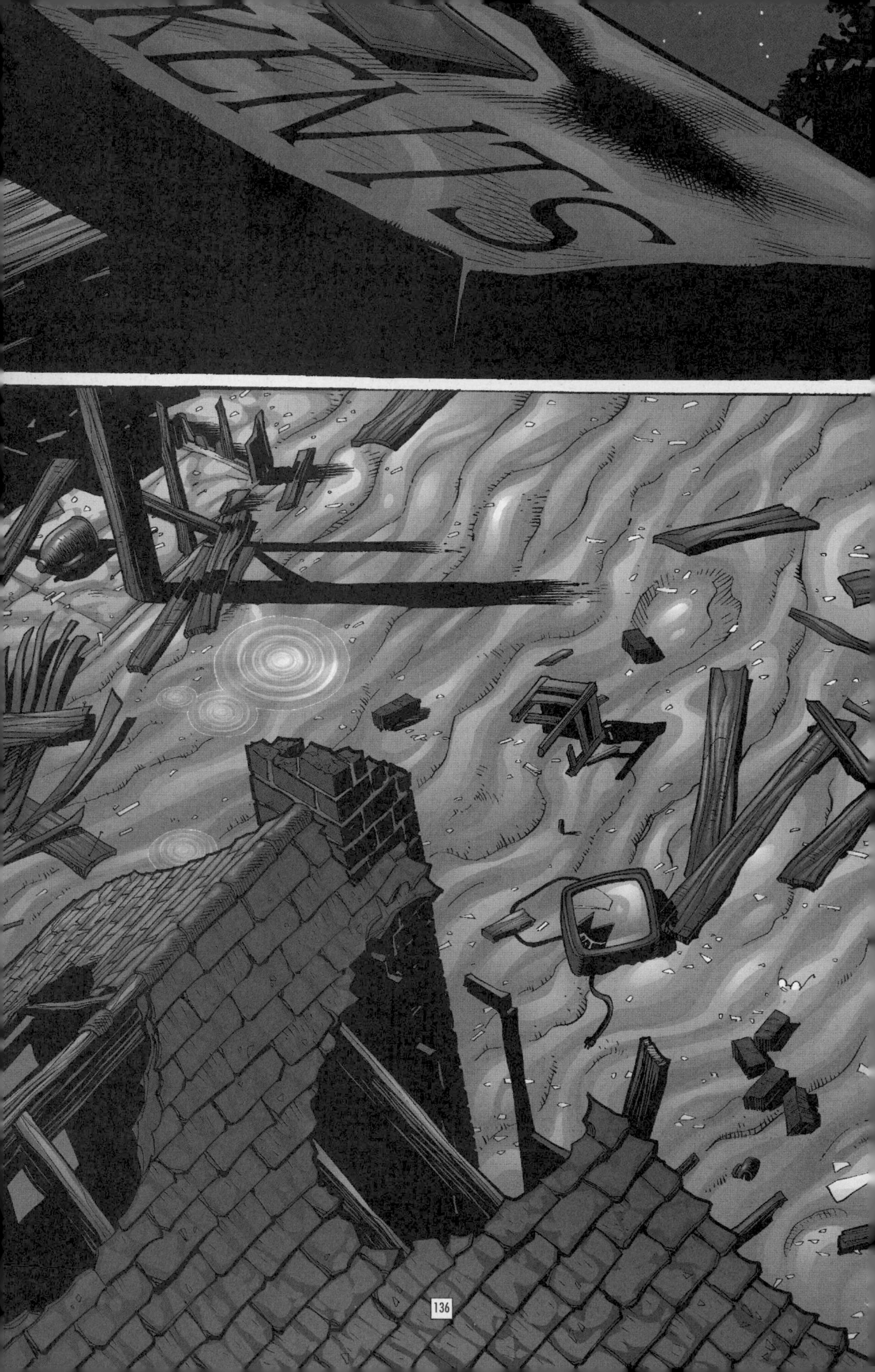
KENTS

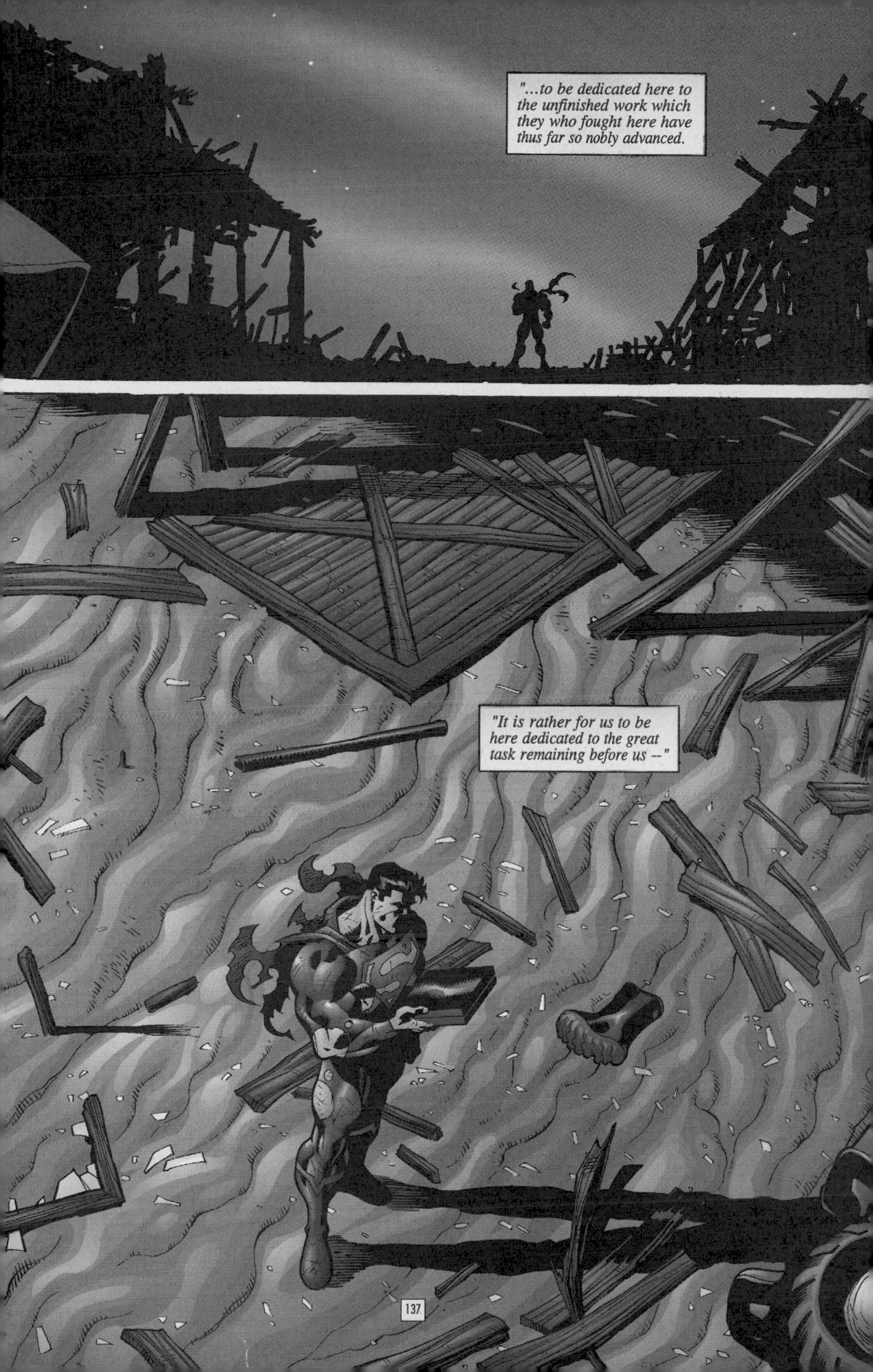
"...to be dedicated here to the unfinished work which they who fought here have thus far so nobly advanced.
"It is rather for us to be here dedicated to the great task remaining before us --"

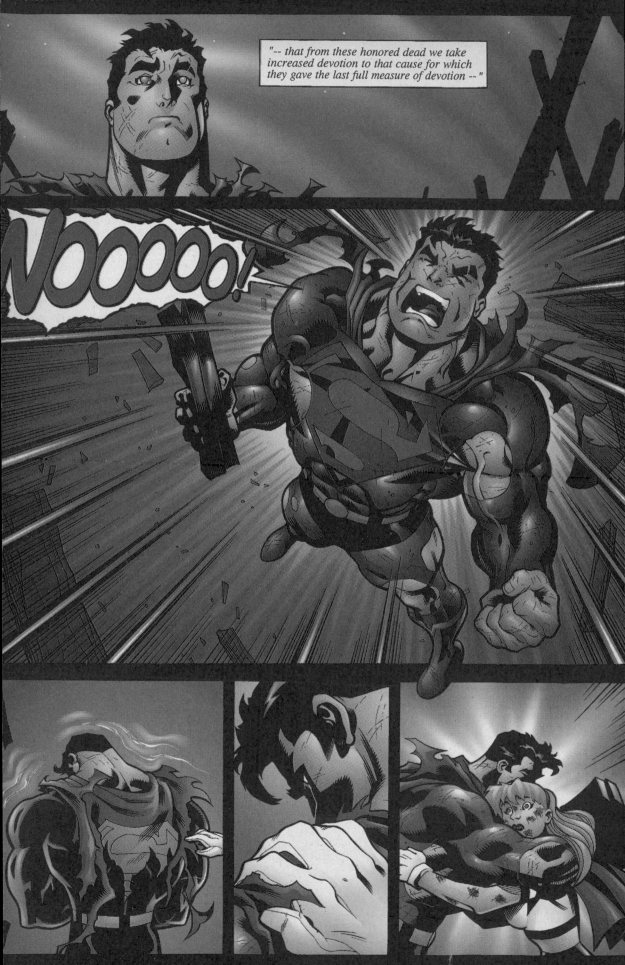

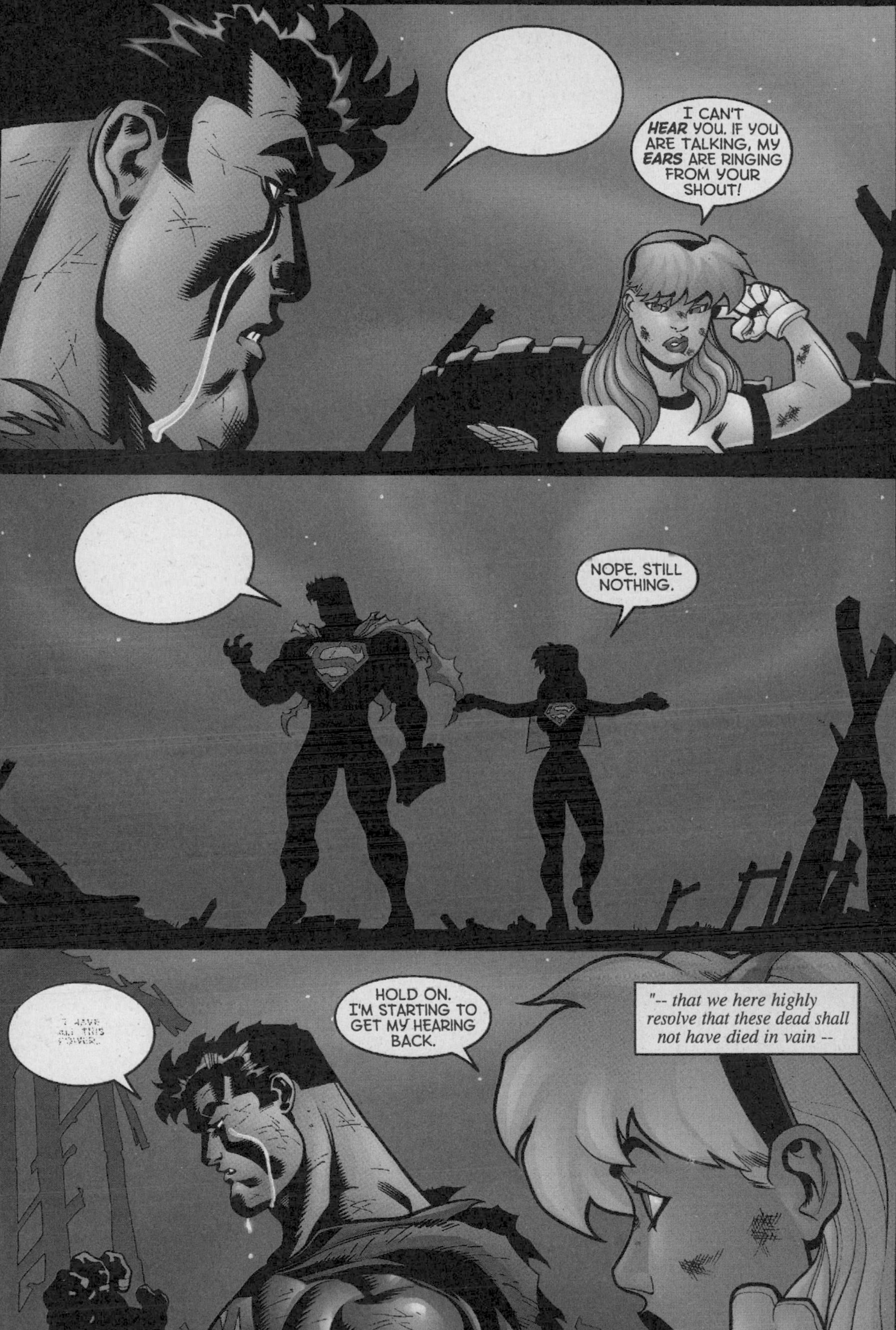
I CAN'T HEAR YOU. IF YOU ARE TALKING, MY EARS ARE RINGING FROM YOUR SHOUT!
NOPE. STILL NOTHING.
I HAVE ALL THIS POWER.
HOLD ON. I'M STARTING TO GET MY HEARING BACK.
"-- that we here highly resolve that these dead shall not have died in vain --

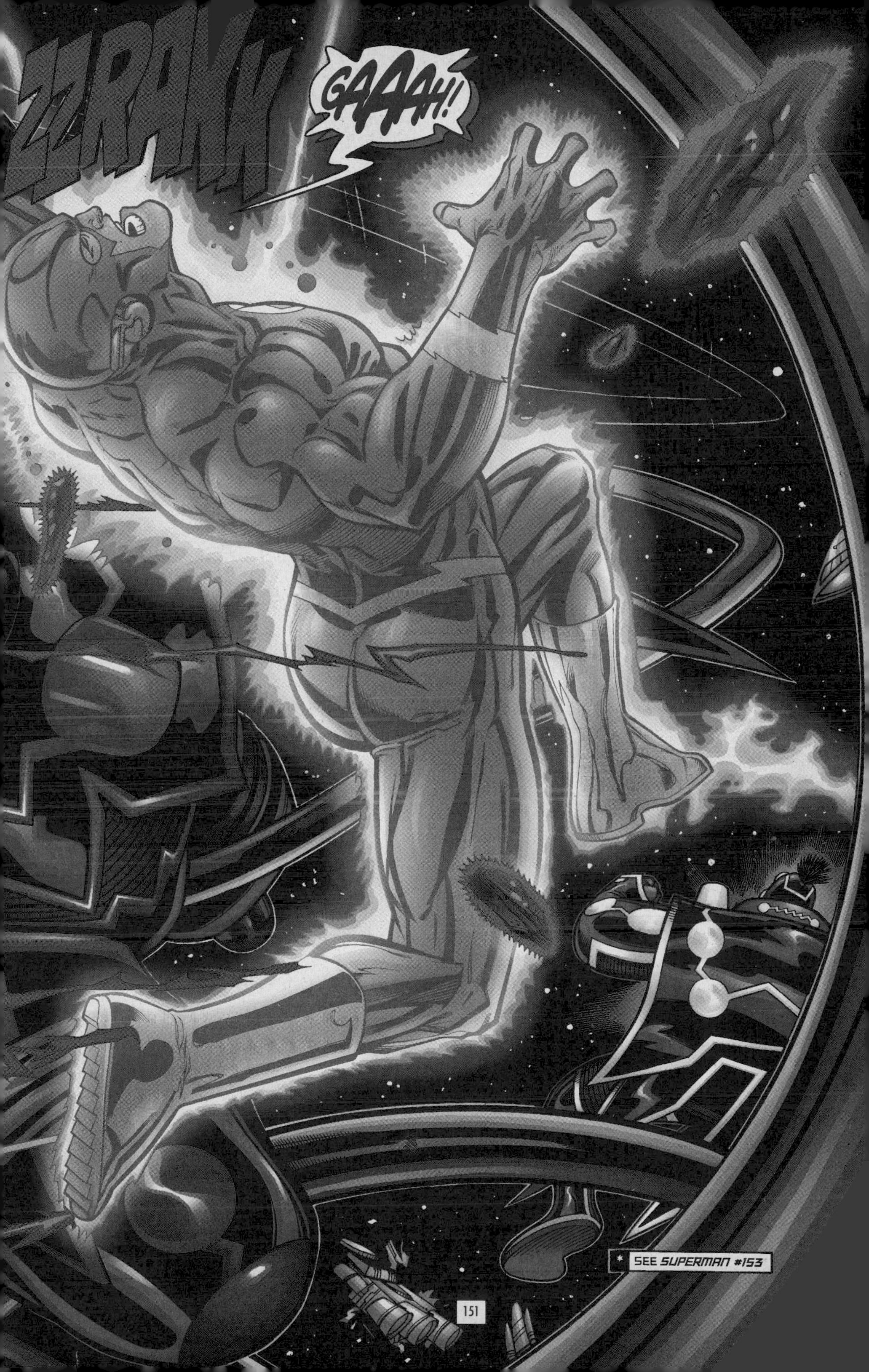

ZZRAKK
GAAAH!
* SEE SUPERMAN #153

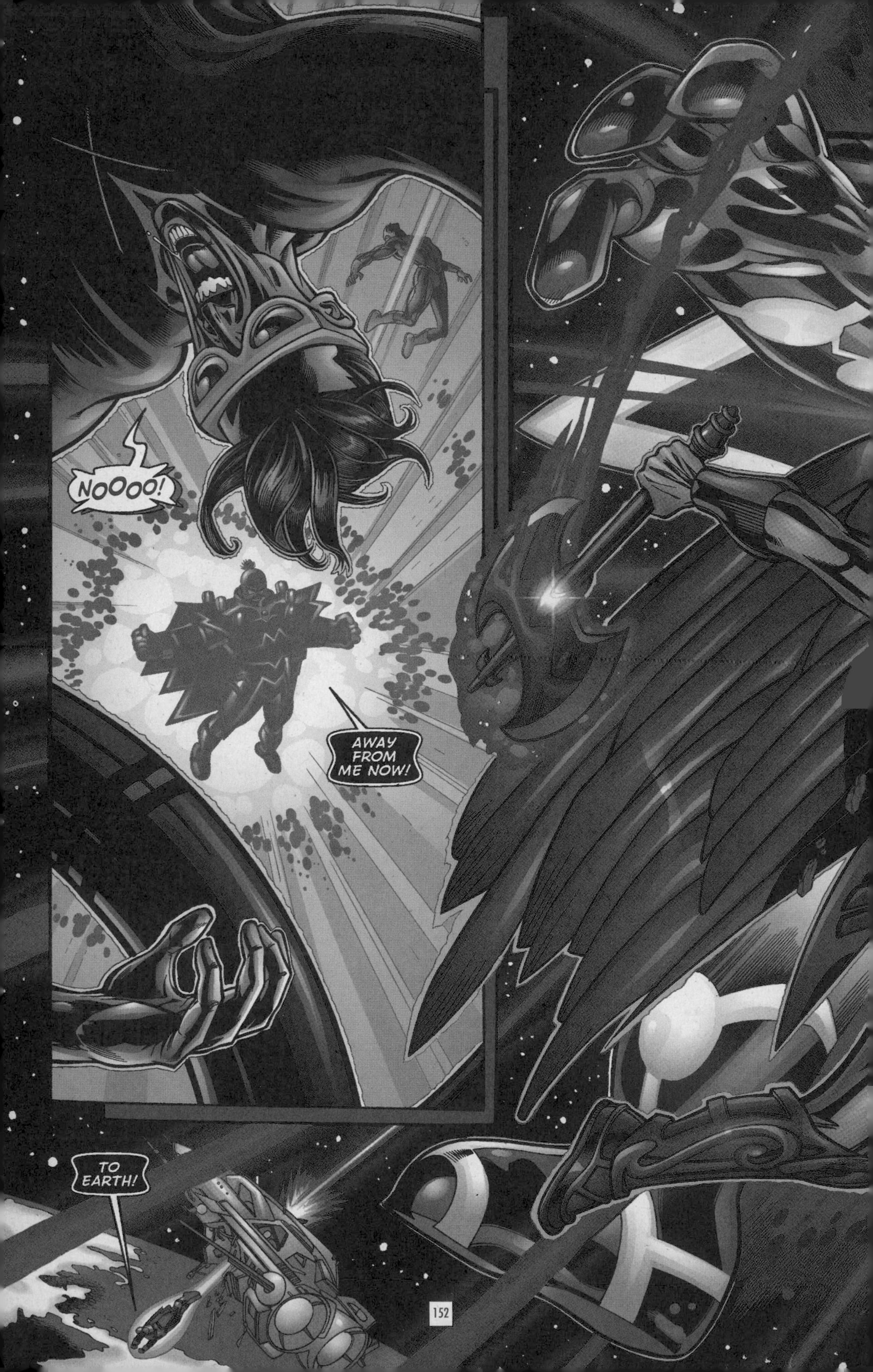
NOOOO!
AWAY FROM ME NOW!
TO EARTH!

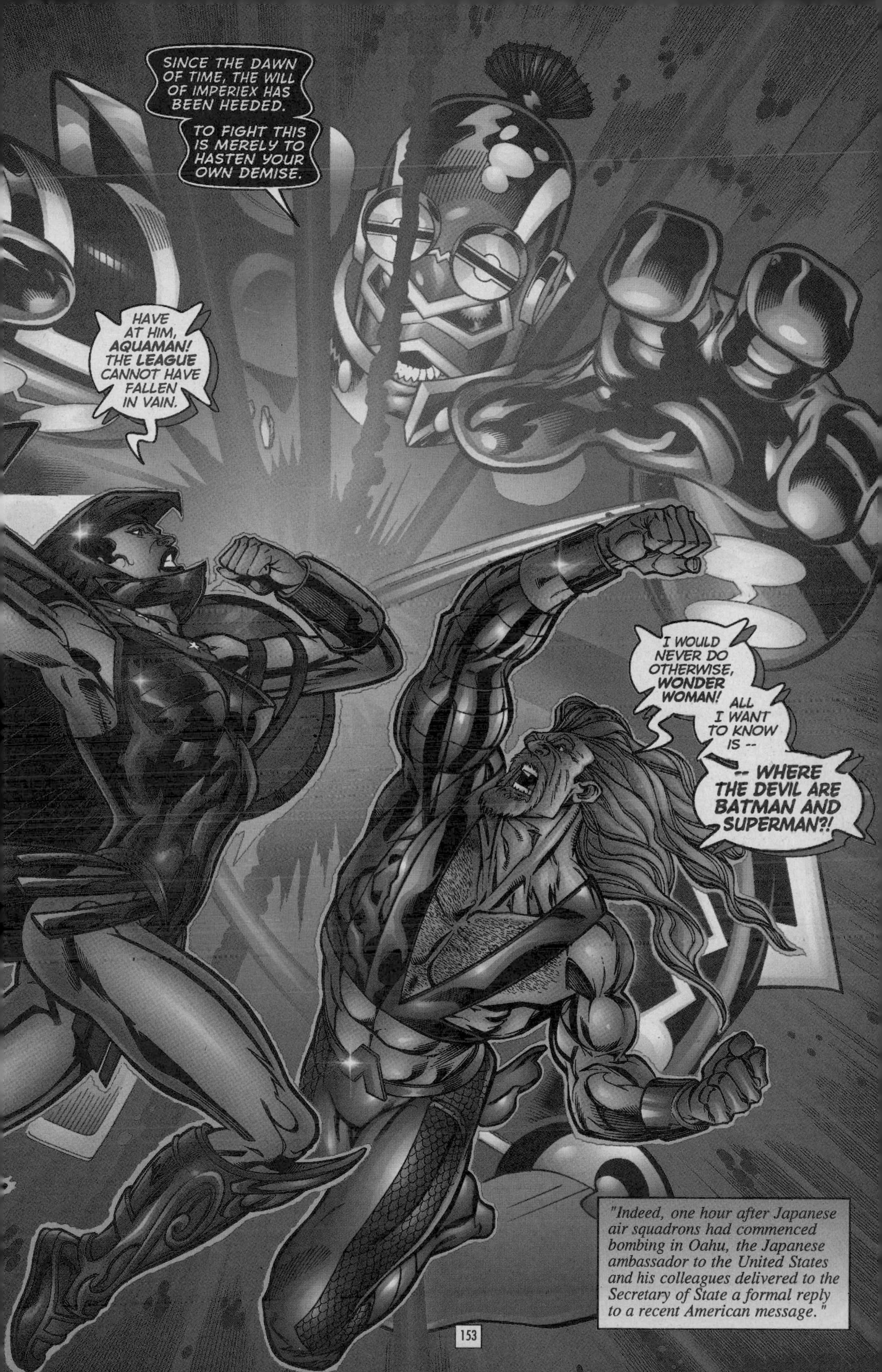
SINCE THE DAWN OF TIME, THE WILL OF IMPERIEX HAS BEEN HEEDED.
TO FIGHT THIS IS MERELY TO HASTEN YOUR OWN DEMISE.
HAVE AT HIM, AQUAMAN! THE LEAGUE CANNOT HAVE FALLEN IN VAIN.
I WOULD NEVER DO OTHERWISE, WONDER WOMAN!
ALL I WANT TO KNOW IS --
-- WHERE THE DEVIL ARE BATMAN AND SUPERMAN?!
"Indeed, one hour after Japanese air squadrons had commenced bombing in Oahu, the Japanese ambassador to the United States and his colleagues delivered to the Secretary of State a formal reply to a recent American message."

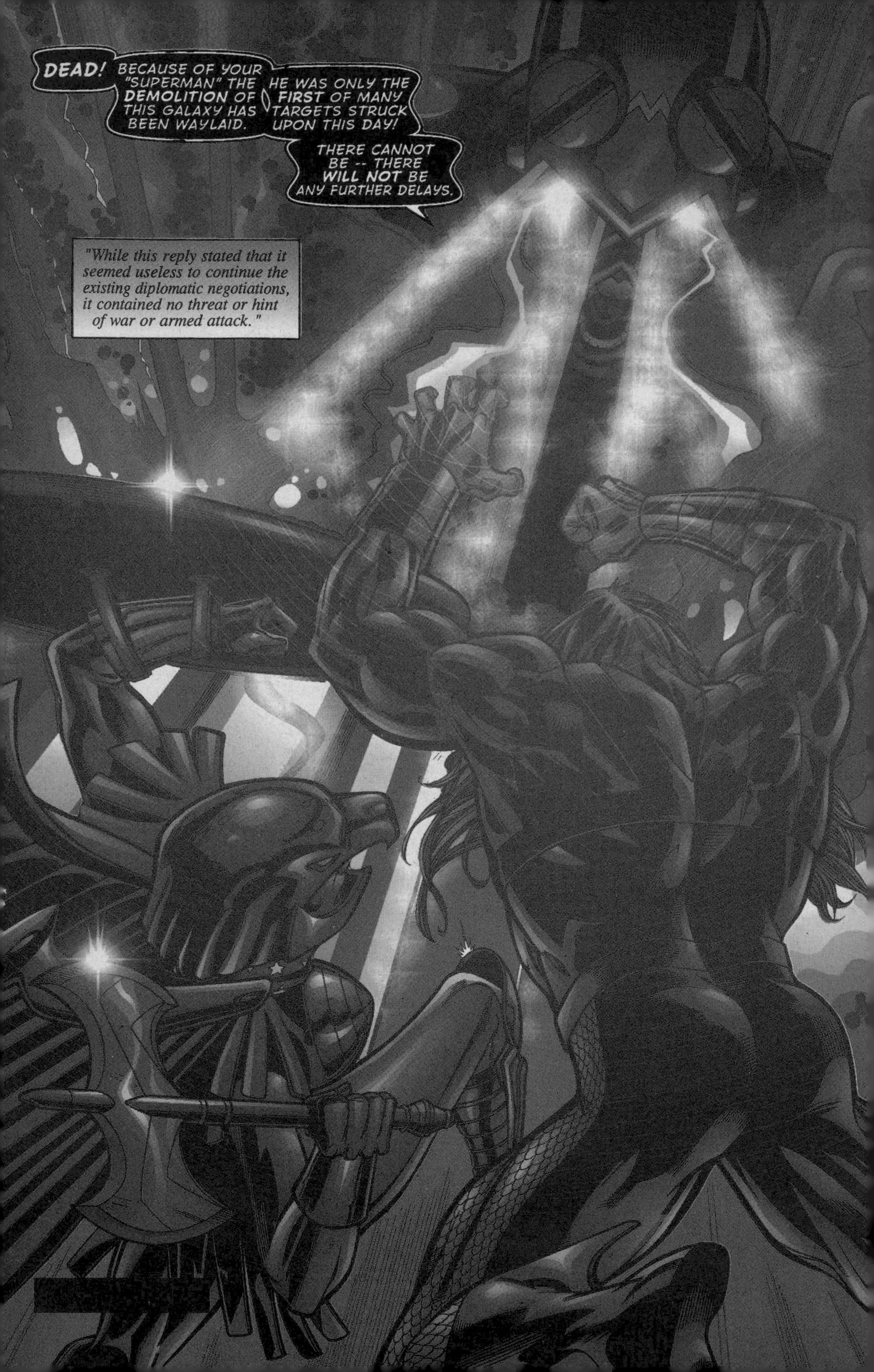
DEAD!
BECAUSE OF YOUR "SUPERMAN" THE DEMOLITION OF THIS GALAXY HAS BEEN WAYLAID.
HE WAS ONLY THE FIRST OF MANY TARGETS STRUCK UPON THIS DAY!
THERE CANNOT BE -- THERE WILL NOT BE ANY FURTHER DELAYS.
"While this reply stated that it seemed useless to continue the existing diplomatic negotiations, it contained no threat or hint of war or armed attack."

GOTHAM CITY. NOW.

ORACLE?

I'M ‡ZZTZZ‡ ONLINE ‡ZTZZ‡ BATMAN. ‡ZZTZ‡ APPARENTLY ‡ZTZZ‡ WE'RE NOT THE ONLY ‡ZTZZ‡ PLACE THAT'S ‡ZZTZZ‡ BEEN HIT.

SOMETHING TOOK ‡ZTZZ‡ TOPEKA, KANSAS OFF ‡ZTTZZ‡ THE MAP.

KANSAS...?

FIND NIGHTWING. ROBIN. BATGIRL. HUNTRESS, IF YOU HAVE TO.

AND CONTACT THE J.L.A. TELL THEM GOTHAM CITY HAS TO BE MY PRIORITY RIGHT NOW...

"It will be recorded that the distance of Hawaii from Japan makes it obvious that the attack was deliberately planned many days or even weeks ago."

SMALLVILLE, KANSAS. NOW.

THIS IS THE EMERGENCY BROADCASTING SYSTEM. WE ARE GETTING REPORTS NOW THAT A MASSIVE EXPLOSION HAS OCCURRED IN TOPEKA, KANSAS.

"During the intervening time, The Japanese Government has deliberately sought to deceive the United States by false statements and expressions of hope for continued peace."

AFTERSHOCKS HAVE BEEN FELT AS FAR WEST AS SALINA AND AS FAR SOUTH AS WICHITA. DAMAGE IS EXTREMELY HIGH.

STAY INDOORS. REPEAT. STAY INDOORS. THOSE OF YOU WITH TORNADO CELLARS, REMAIN THERE.

THIS IS THE EMERGENCY BROADCASTING SYSTEM.

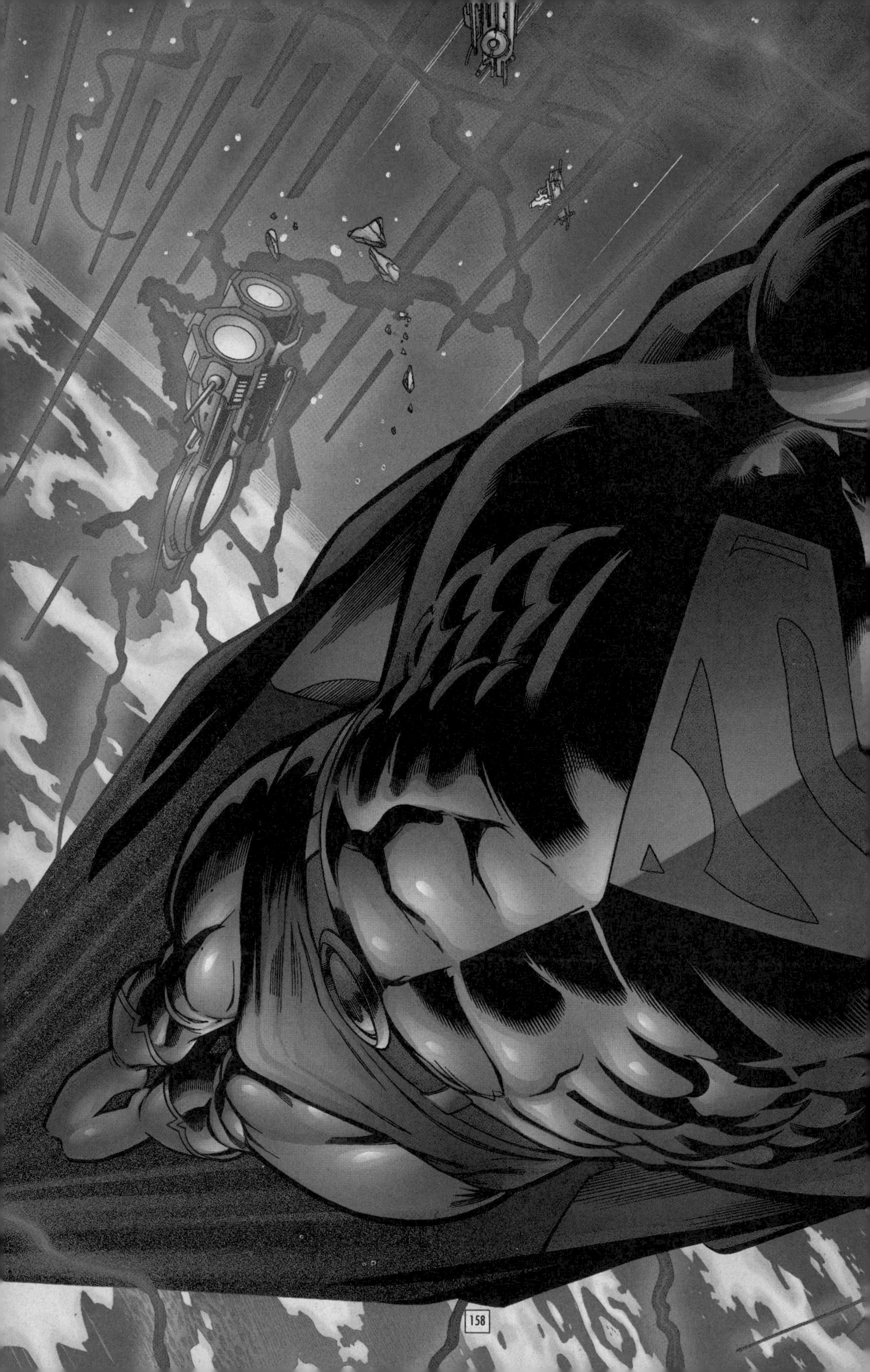

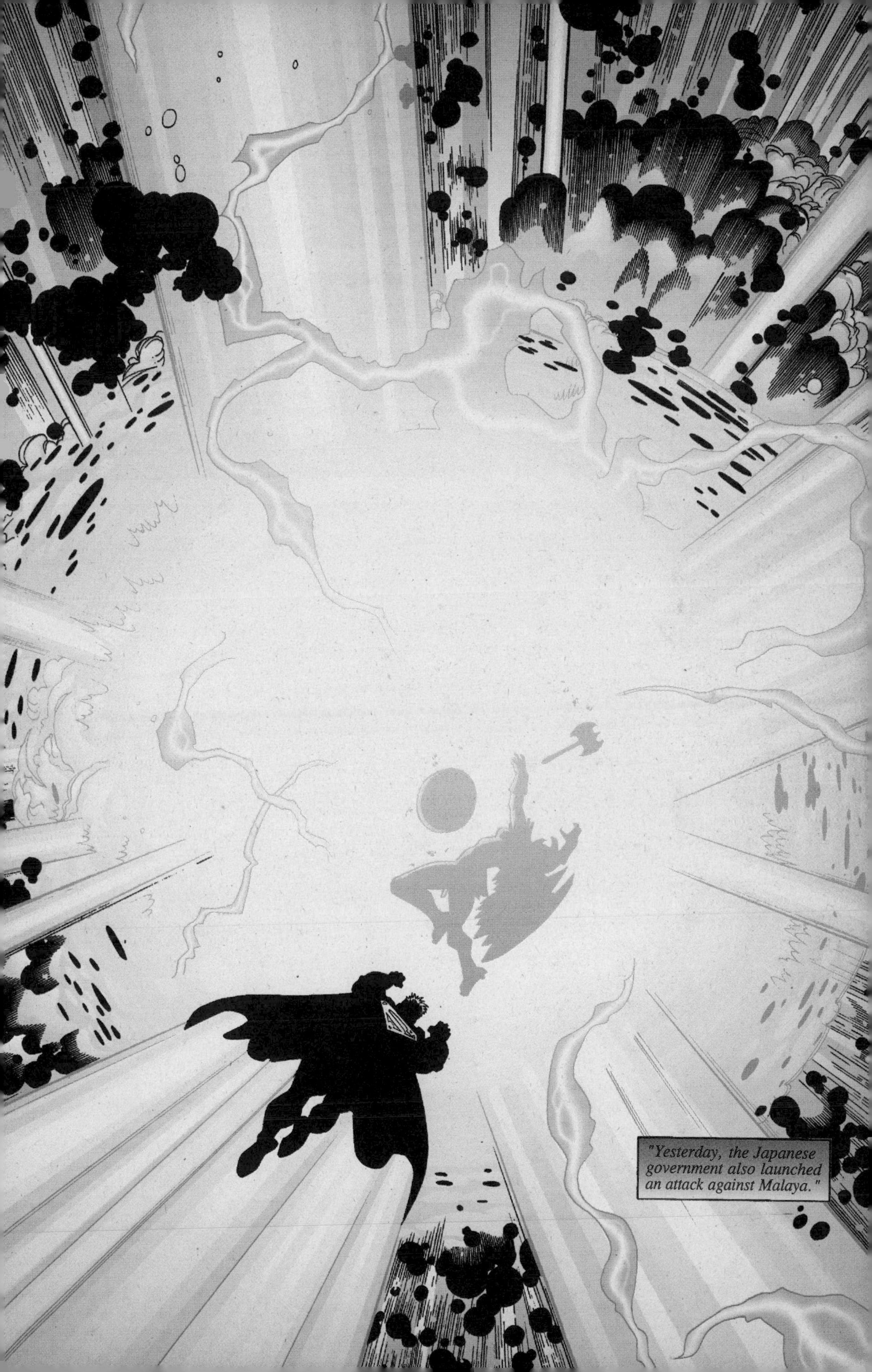
"Yesterday, the Japanese government also launched an attack against Malaya."

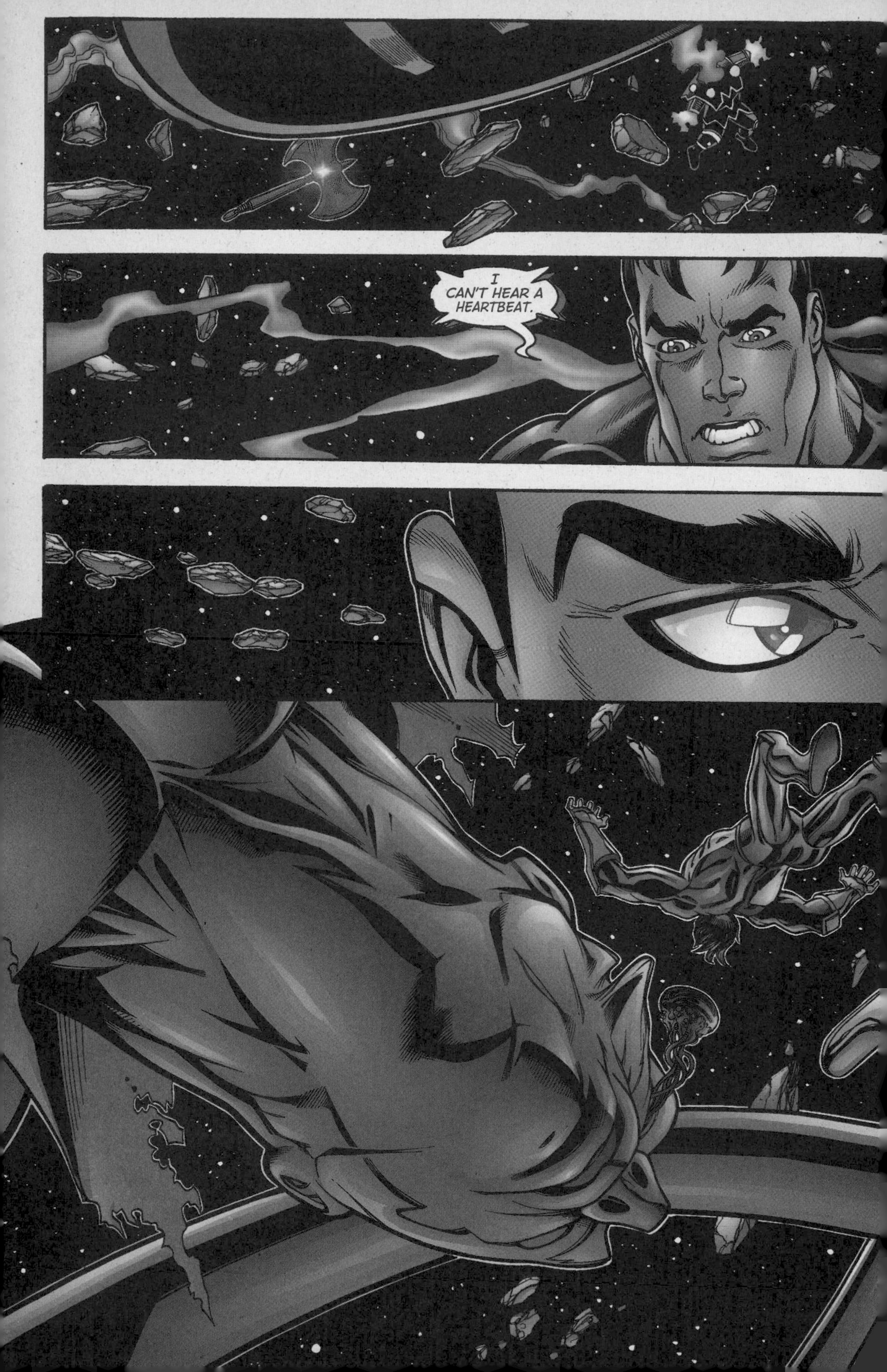
I CAN'T HEAR A HEARTBEAT.

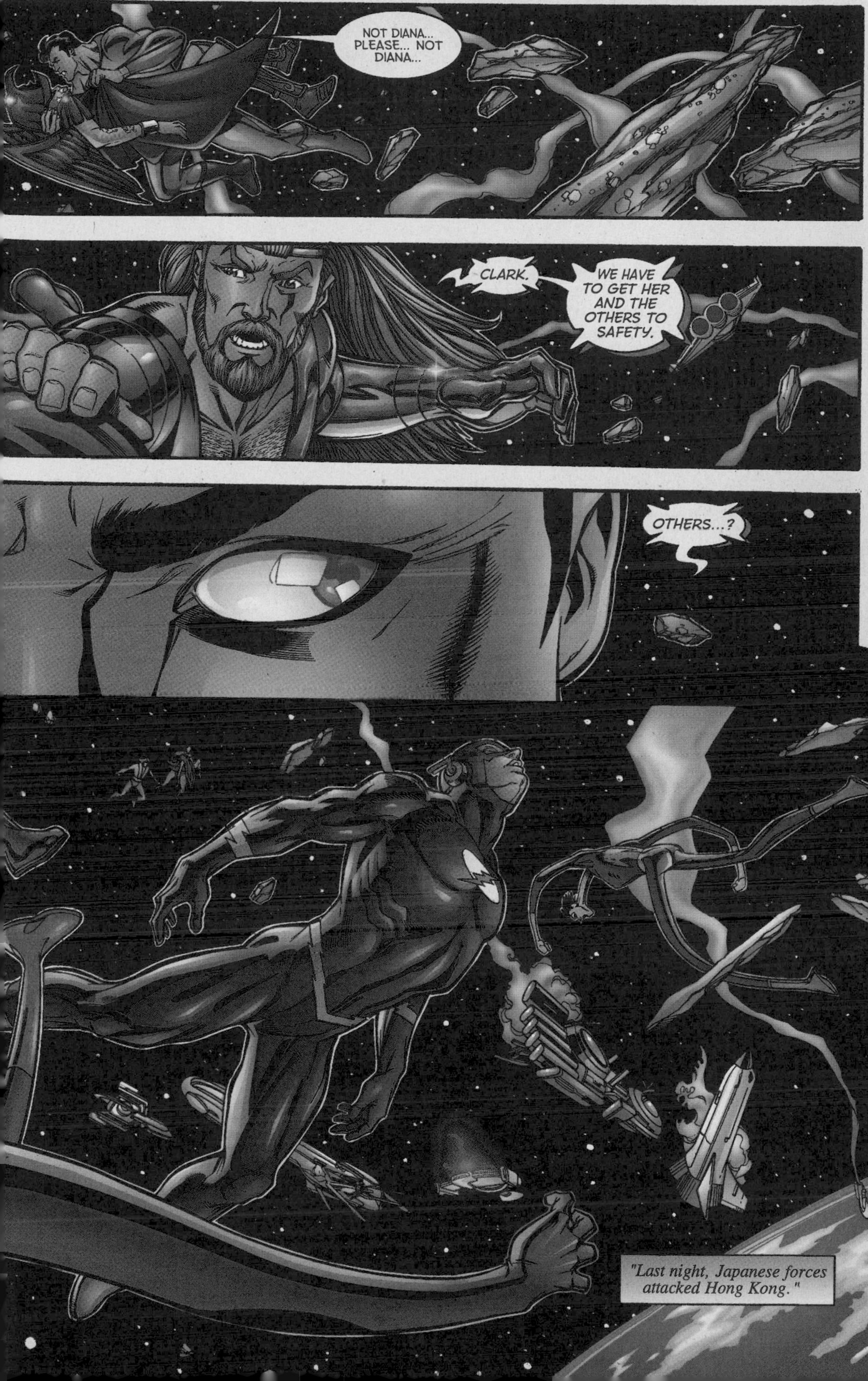
NOT DIANA... PLEASE... NOT DIANA...
CLARK.
WE HAVE TO GET HER AND THE OTHERS TO SAFETY.
OTHERS...?
"Last night, Japanese forces attacked Hong Kong."

"Last night, Japanese forces attacked Guam."

WE CAN HELP GET YOUR WOUNDED TO SAFETY.

A TRIAGE CENTER AND MEDICAL SERVICES ARE AVAILABLE ABOARD THE PARADOCS.

GOOD ENOUGH. I... SINCE WONDER WOMAN NEEDS THE MOST IMMEDIATE ATTENTION, I'LL TAKE HER IN FIRST.

MAXIMA AND STARFIRE. STRANGE ALLIANCES, INDEED.

I'LL BE BACK AS QUICKLY AS I CAN.

HE CARES FOR HER, THAT ONE.

OF COURSE, WE ALL CARE FOR DIANA.

AQUAMAN, I'M A LITTLE SURPRISED TO FIND YOU HERE WITH WHAT'S HAPPENED.

AN IMPERIEX PROBE HIT OUTSIDE THE CAPITAL CITY IN ATLANTIS.

WHAT? GET ME TO A JLA TELEPORTER.

AND REMIND SUPERMAN...

...THE OCEANS COVER THREE FOURTHS OF THE PLANET. IF ATLANTIS FALLS -- SO FALL THE REST OF YOU!

IS IT ARROGANCE TO SPEAK THE TRUTH?

IF SO, I LIKE THAT IN A MAN...

NOT TOO ARROGANT.

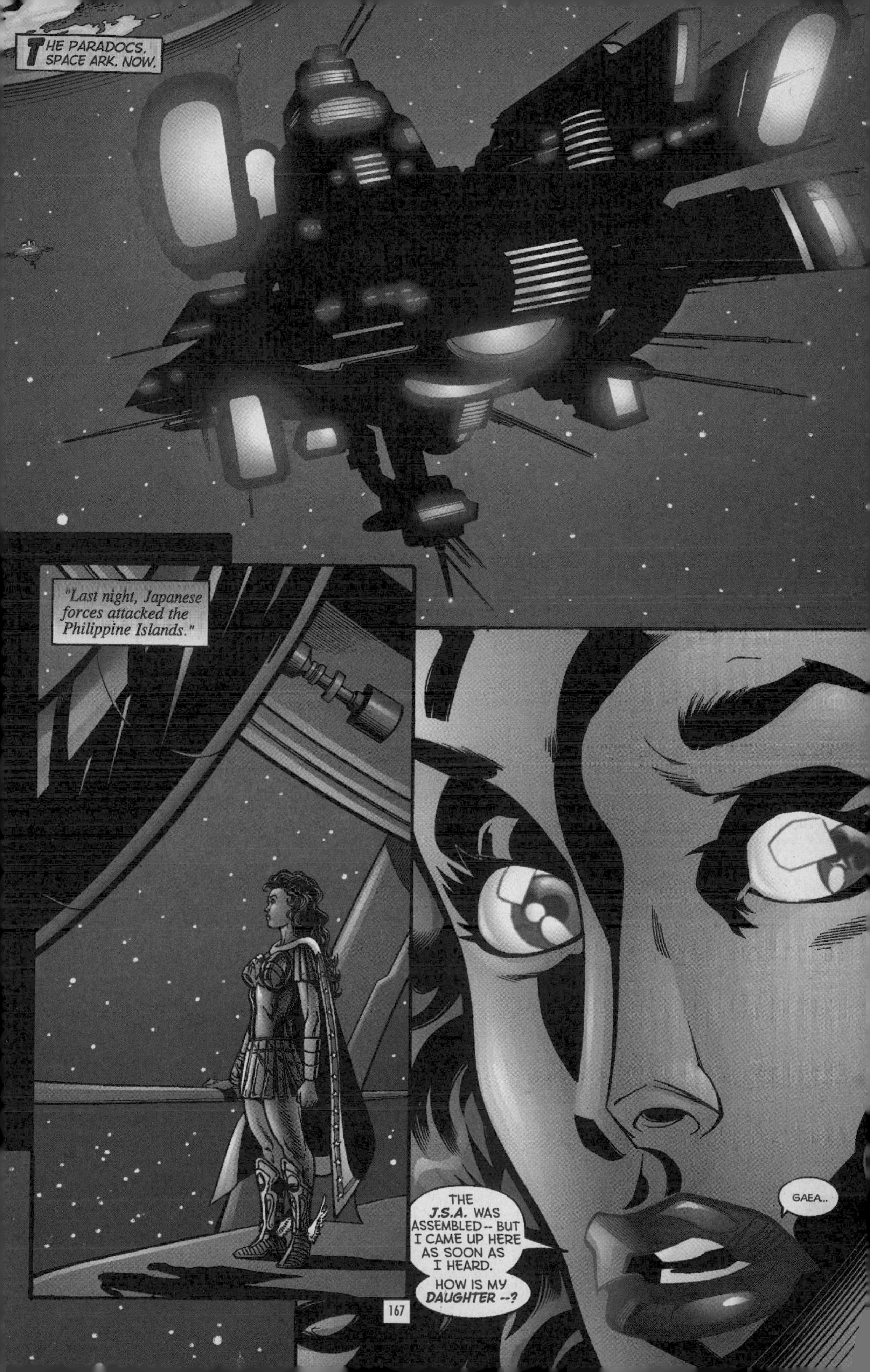
THE PARADOCS. SPACE ARK. NOW.
"Last night, Japanese forces attacked the Philippine Islands."
THE J.S.A. WAS ASSEMBLED -- BUT I CAME UP HERE AS SOON AS I HEARD.
HOW IS MY DAUGHTER --?
GAEA..

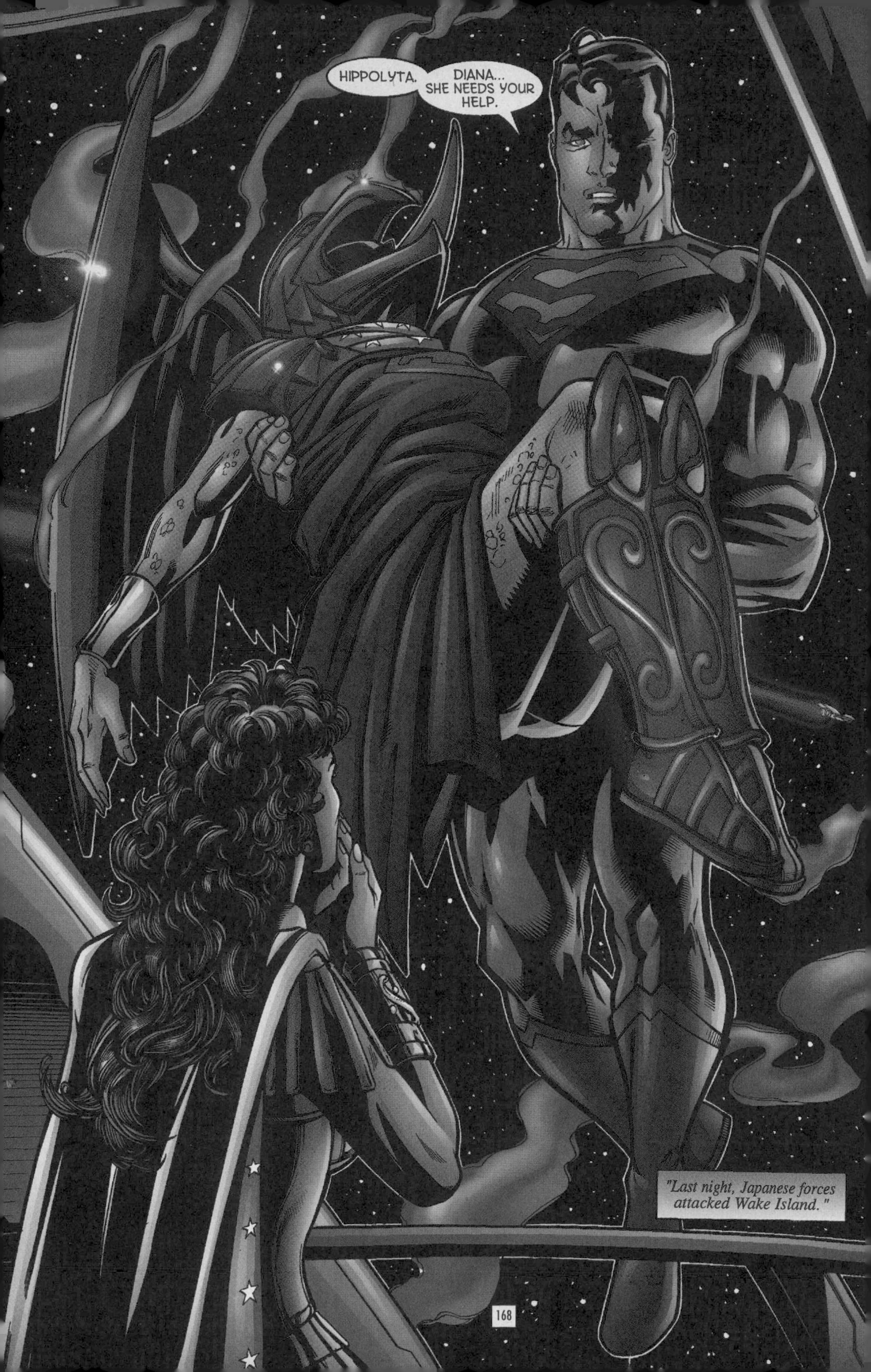
HIPPOLYTA.
DIANA... SHE NEEDS YOUR HELP.
"Last night, Japanese forces attacked Wake Island."

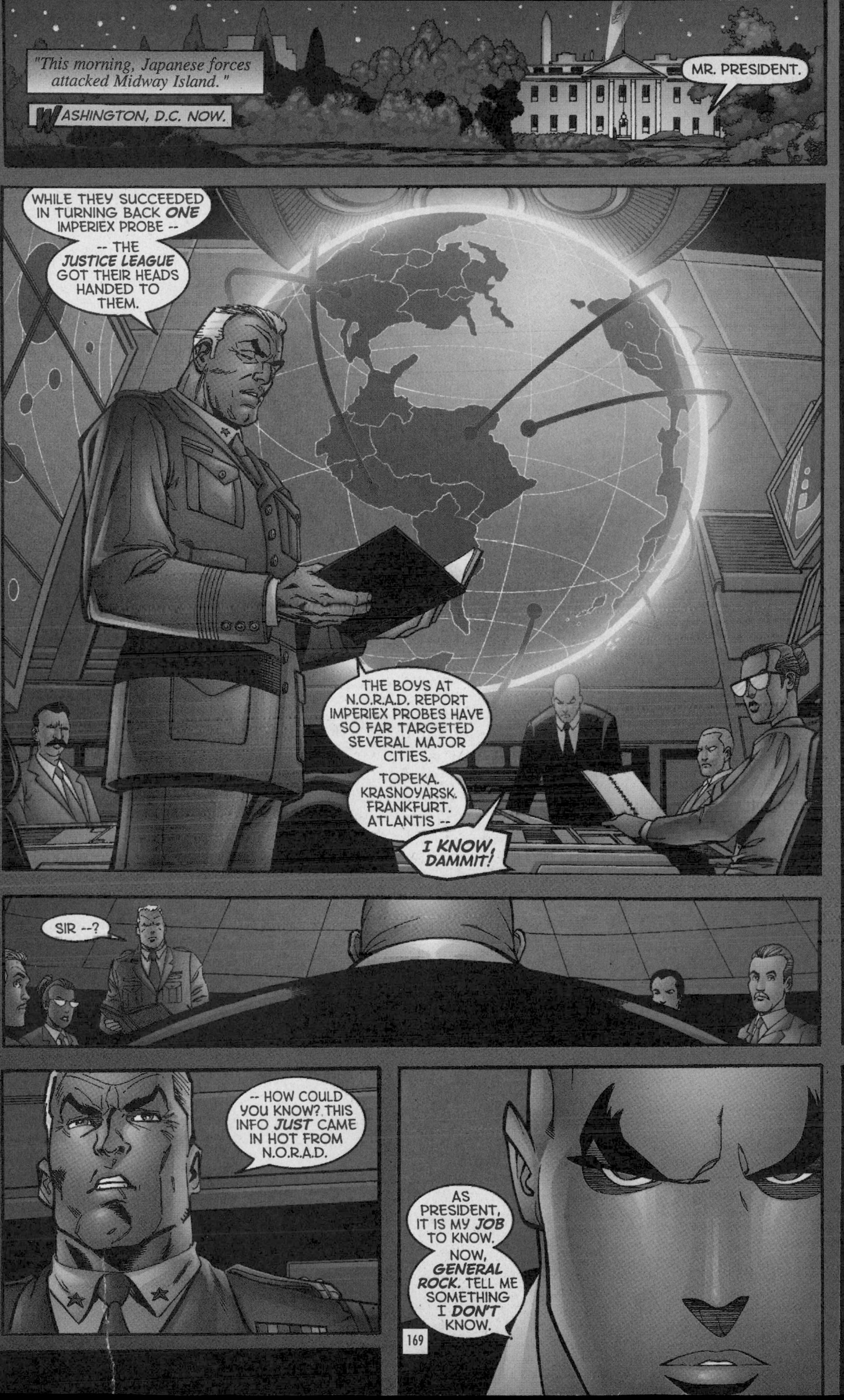
"This morning, Japanese forces attacked Midway Island."
WASHINGTON, D.C. NOW.
MR. PRESIDENT.
WHILE THEY SUCCEEDED IN TURNING BACK ONE IMPERIEX PROBE --
-- THE JUSTICE LEAGUE GOT THEIR HEADS HANDED TO THEM.
THE BOYS AT N.O.R.A.D. REPORT IMPERIEX PROBES HAVE SO FAR TARGETED SEVERAL MAJOR CITIES.
TOPEKA. KRASNOYARSK. FRANKFURT. ATLANTIS --
I KNOW, DAMMIT!
SIR --?
-- HOW COULD YOU KNOW? THIS INFO JUST CAME IN HOT FROM N.O.R.A.D.
AS PRESIDENT, IT IS MY JOB TO KNOW.
NOW, GENERAL ROCK. TELL ME SOMETHING I DON'T KNOW.

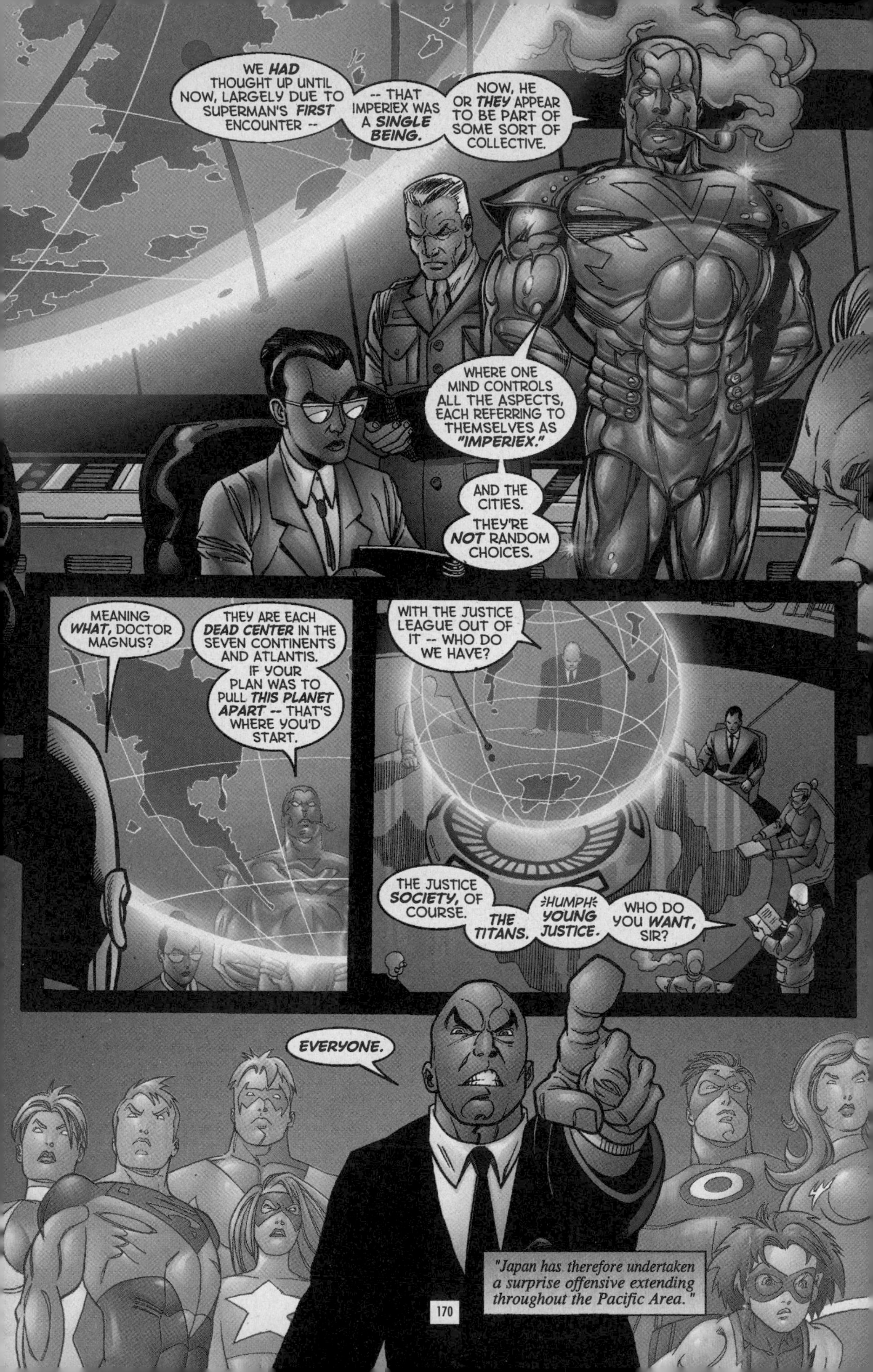
WE HAD THOUGHT UP UNTIL NOW, LARGELY DUE TO SUPERMAN'S FIRST ENCOUNTER --
-- THAT IMPERIEX WAS A SINGLE BEING.
NOW, HE OR THEY APPEAR TO BE PART OF SOME SORT OF COLLECTIVE.
WHERE ONE MIND CONTROLS ALL THE ASPECTS, EACH REFERRING TO THEMSELVES AS "IMPERIEX."
AND THE CITIES.
THEY'RE NOT RANDOM CHOICES.
MEANING WHAT, DOCTOR MAGNUS?
THEY ARE EACH DEAD CENTER IN THE SEVEN CONTINENTS AND ATLANTIS. IF YOUR PLAN WAS TO PULL THIS PLANET APART -- THAT'S WHERE YOU'D START.
WITH THE JUSTICE LEAGUE OUT OF IT -- WHO DO WE HAVE?
THE JUSTICE SOCIETY, OF COURSE.
THE TITANS.
HUMPH YOUNG JUSTICE.
WHO DO YOU WANT, SIR?
EVERYONE.
"Japan has therefore undertaken a surprise offensive extending throughout the Pacific Area."

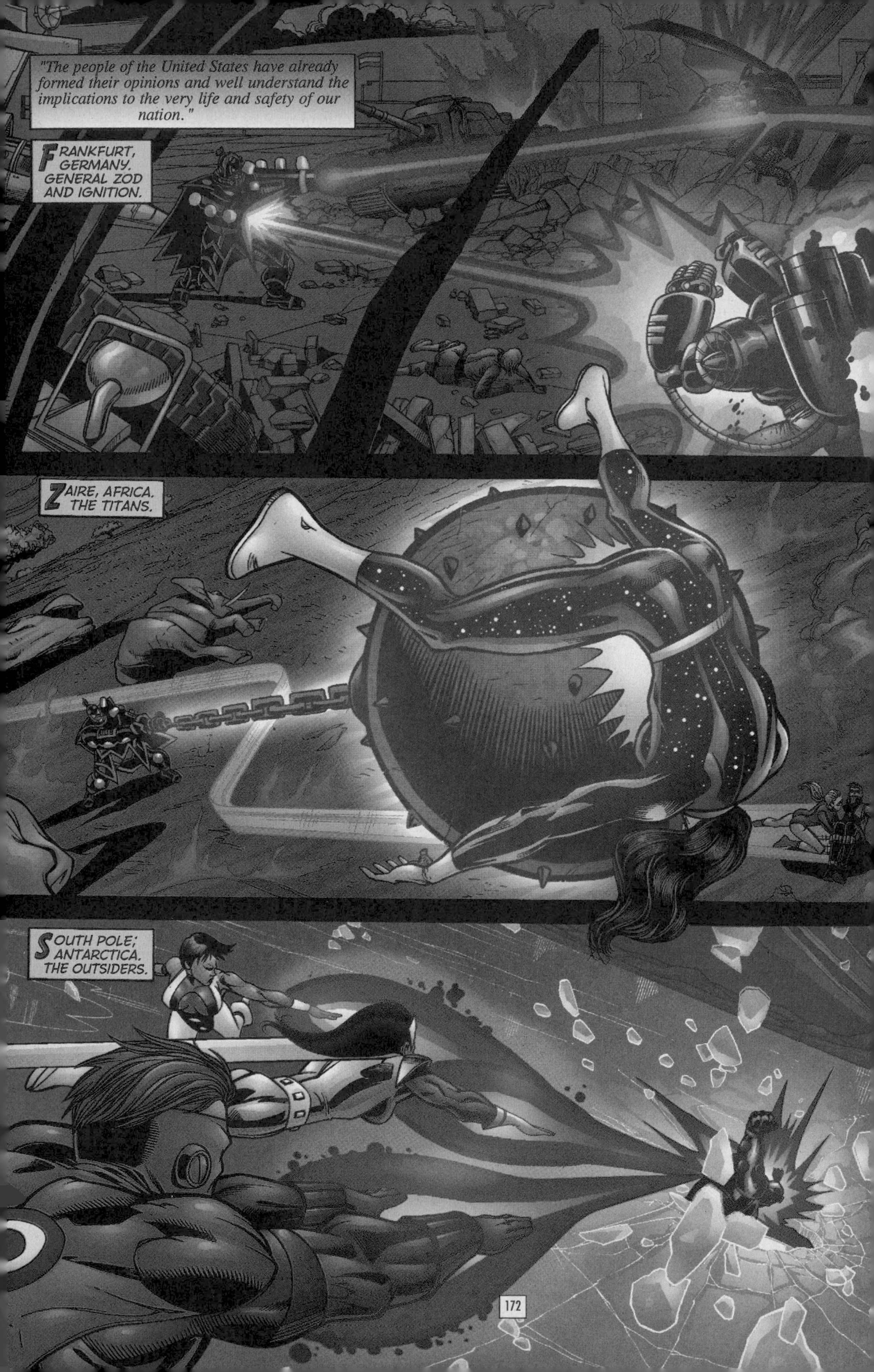
"The people of the United States have already formed their opinions and well understand the implications to the very life and safety of our nation."
FRANKFURT, GERMANY. GENERAL ZOD AND IGNITION.
ZAIRE, AFRICA. THE TITANS.
SOUTH POLE; ANTARCTICA. THE OUTSIDERS.

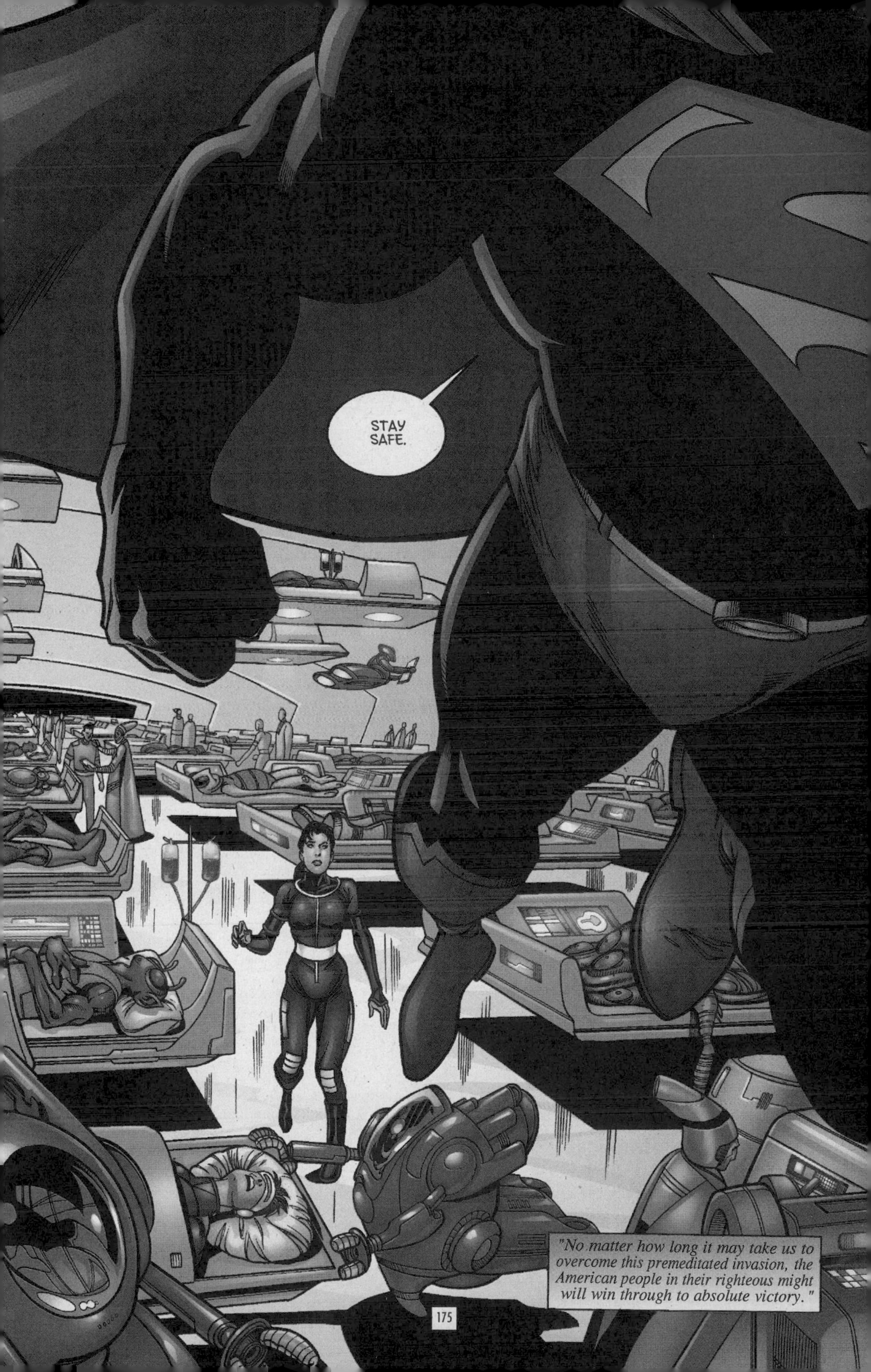
STAY SAFE.
"No matter how long it may take us to overcome this premeditated invasion, the American people in their righteous might will win through to absolute victory."

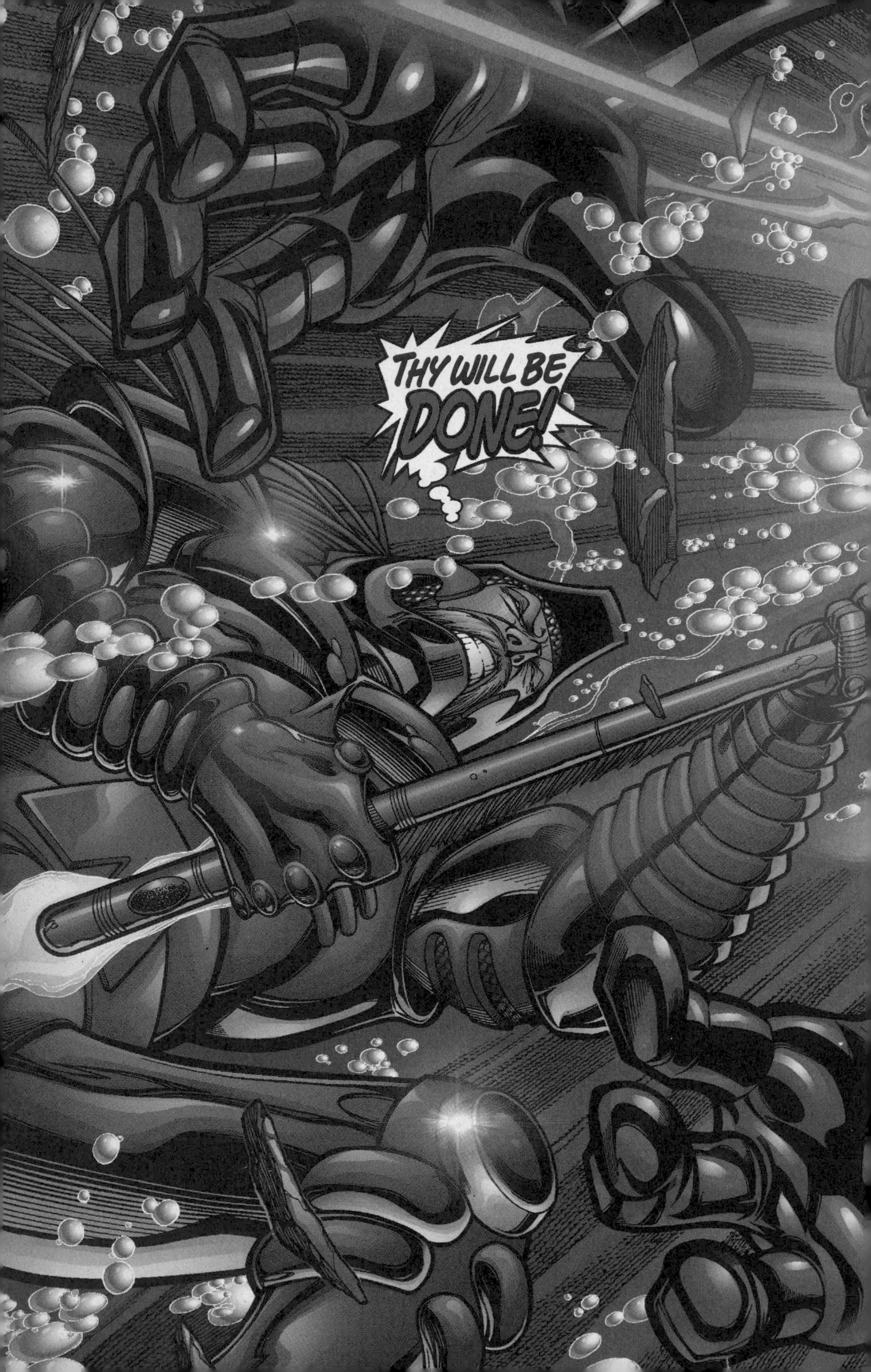
THY WILL BE DONE!

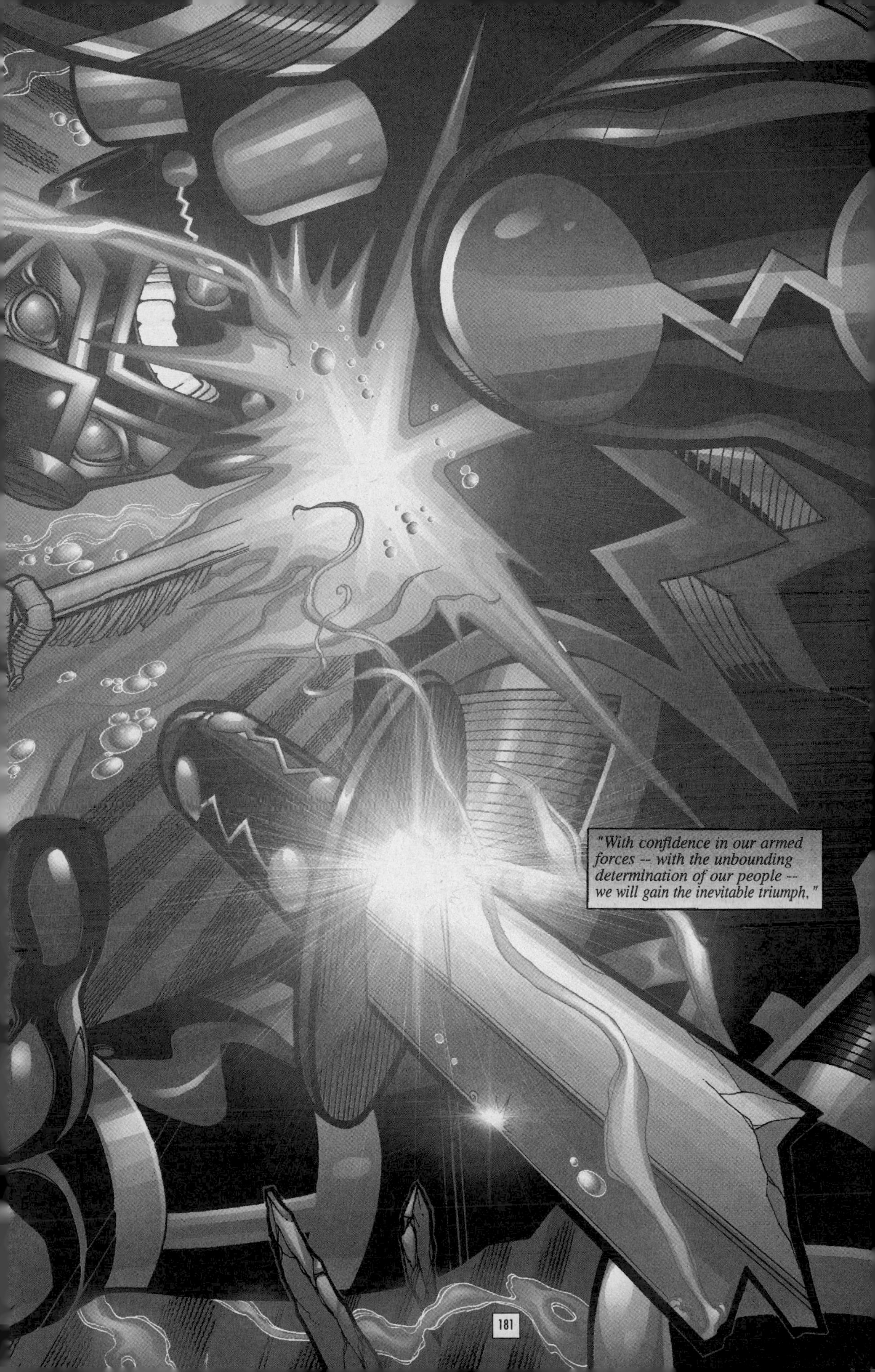
"With confidence in our armed forces -- with the unbounding determination of our people -- we will gain the inevitable triumph."

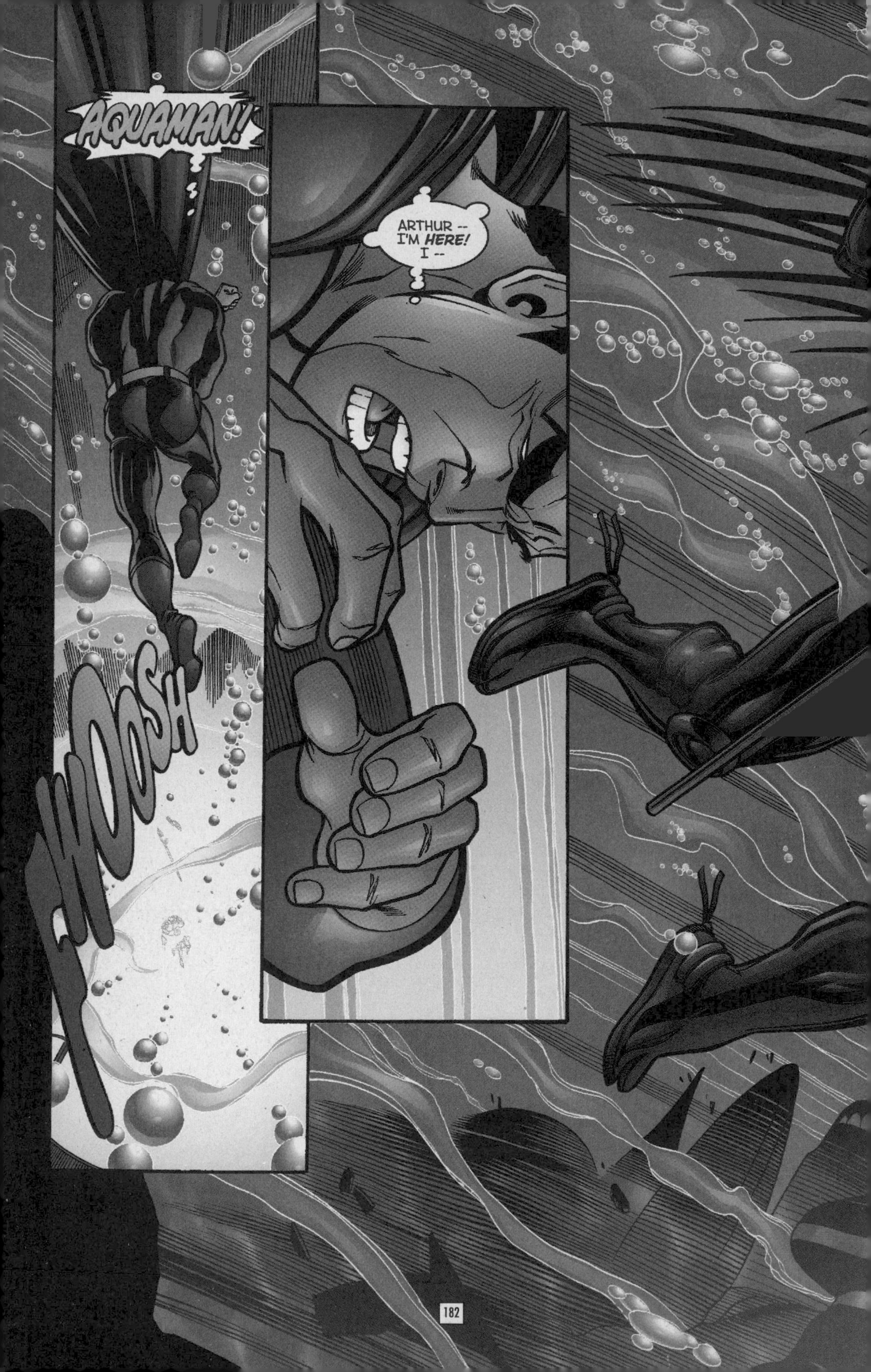
AQUAMAN!
ARTHUR -- I'M HERE! I --
WHOOSH

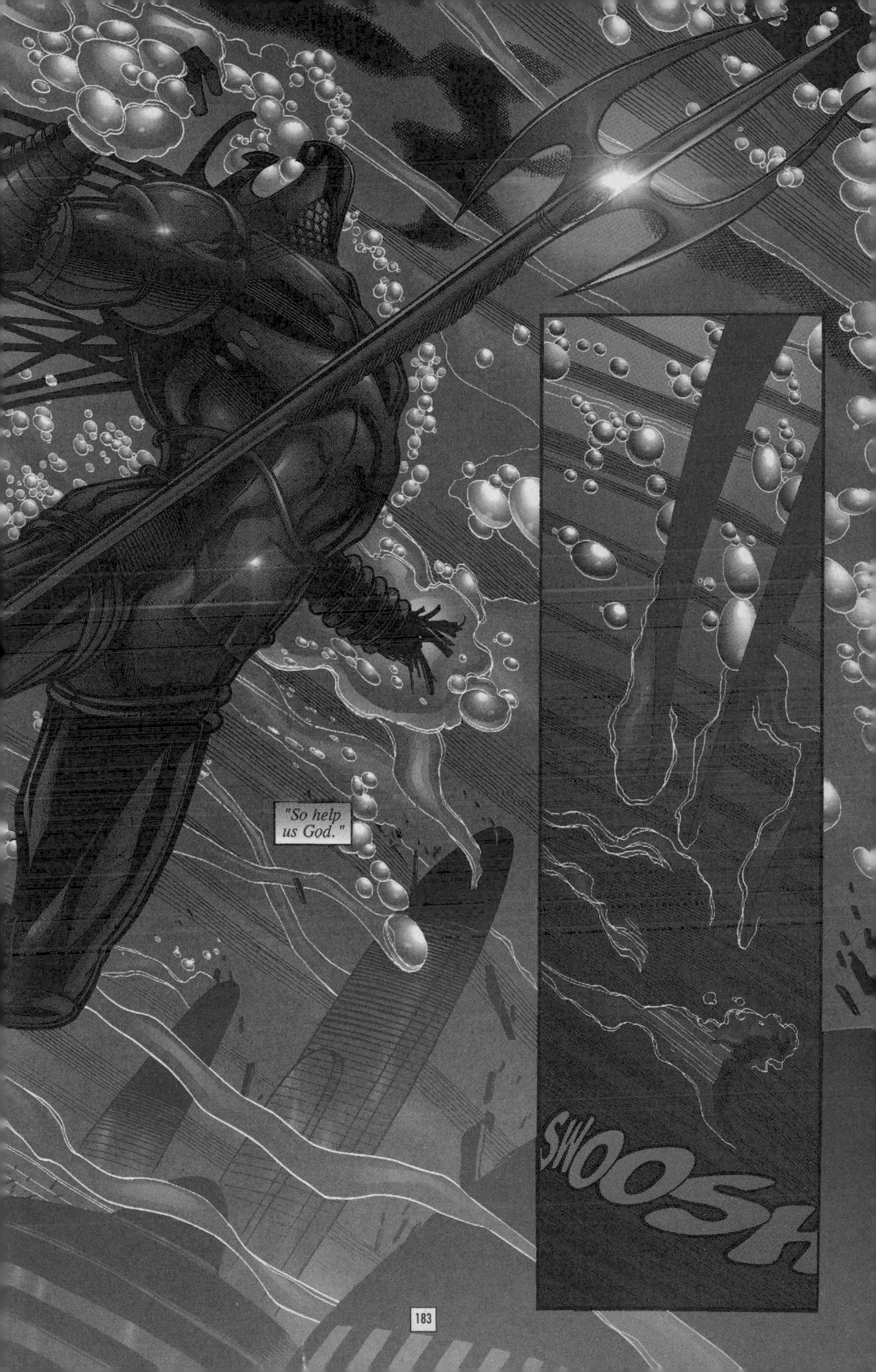
"So help us God."
SWOOSH

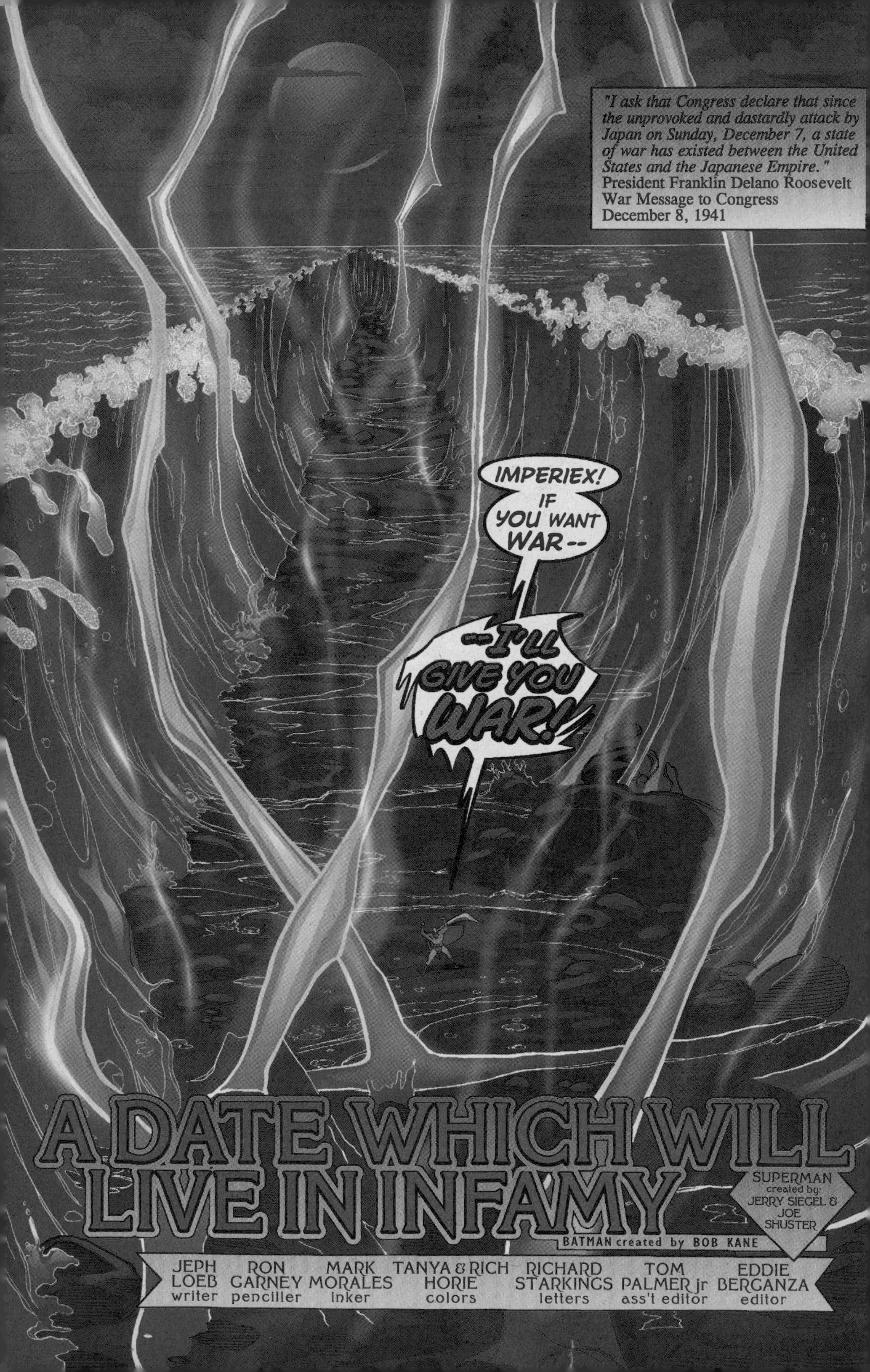

IMPERIEX! IF YOU WANT WAR --

-- I'LL GIVE YOU WAR!

A DATE WHICH WILL LIVE IN INFAMY

SUPERMAN created by: JERRY SIEGEL & JOE SHUSTER

BATMAN created by BOB KANE

JEPH LOEB writer

RON GARNEY penciller

MARK MORALES inker

TANYA & RICH HORIE colors

RICHARD STARKINGS letters

TOM PALMER jr ass't editor

EDDIE BERGANZA editor

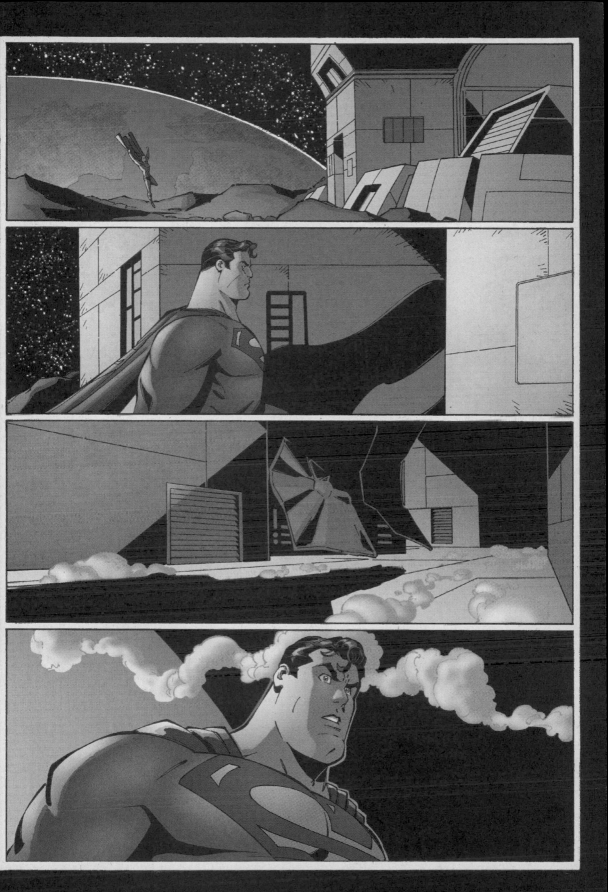

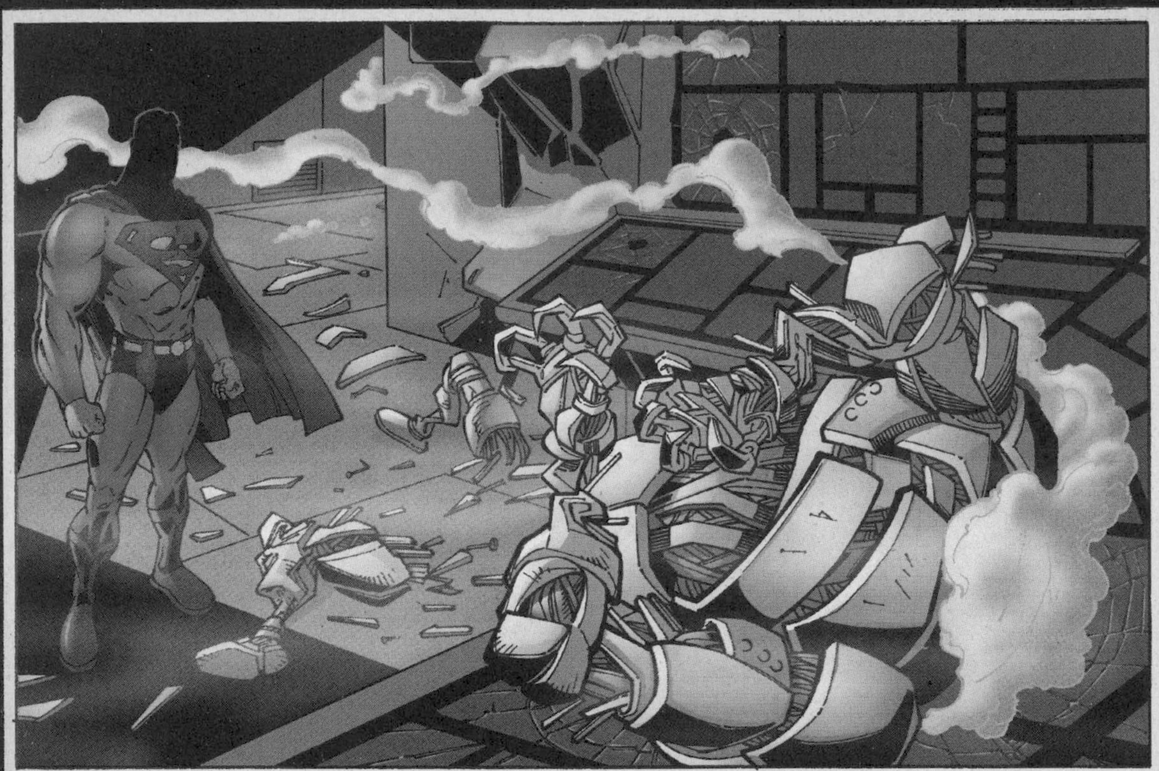

THE DOOMSDAY PROTOCOL

CASEY - WIERINGO - STUCKER - OAKLEY - WILDSTORM - PALMER JR. - BERGANZA

SUPERMAN CREATED BY JERRY SIEGEL & JOE SHUSTER

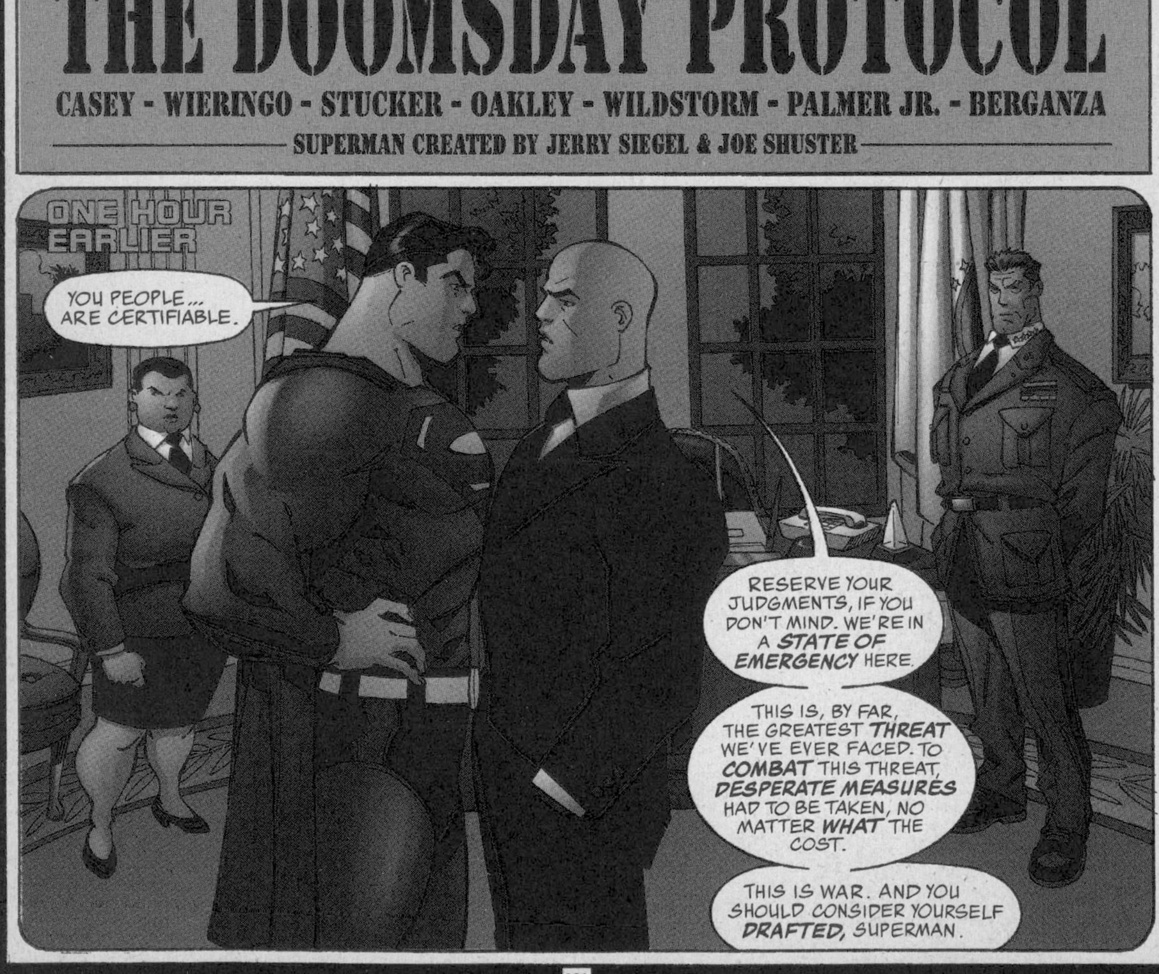
ONE HOUR EARLIER
YOU PEOPLE... ARE CERTIFIABLE.
RESERVE YOUR JUDGMENTS, IF YOU DON'T MIND. WE'RE IN A STATE OF EMERGENCY HERE.
THIS IS, BY FAR, THE GREATEST THREAT WE'VE EVER FACED. TO COMBAT THIS THREAT, DESPERATE MEASURES HAD TO BE TAKEN, NO MATTER WHAT THE COST.
THIS IS WAR. AND YOU SHOULD CONSIDER YOURSELF DRAFTED, SUPERMAN.

GENERAL ROCK, DO YOU MIND BRIEFING OUR GUEST...?

WE'VE LOST CONTACT WITH THE MOON. OUR TEAM IS COMPLETELY CUT OFF.

YOUR "TEAM"?

PROJECT: SUICIDE SQUAD WAS A MISTAKE FROM DAY ONE. WHAT MADE YOU THINK YOU COULD POSSIBLY CONTROL THEM--?!

HAVE YOU EVER SERVED IN A FORWARD AREA, SON?!

YOU'VE GOT THE NERVE TO QUESTION OUR TACTICS?! DON'T CONCERN YOURSELF WITH THE CONTROL ISSUE, SUPERMAN. WE'VE GOT ONE OF YOUR CRONIES BABYSITTING!

WHO--?!

MISS WALLER... ENGAGING IN THIS DISCOURSE IS WASTING PRECIOUS MOMENTS. AFTER KANSAS... AFTER APOKOLIPS APPEARING IN OUR SOLAR SYSTEM... AFTER... YOUR FELLOW JUSTICE LEAGUER...

HASN'T THERE BEEN ENOUGH LOST IN THIS CONFLICT ALREADY?

AT THIS VERY MOMENT ... YOU ARE NEEDED...

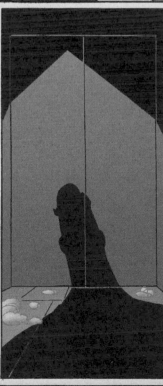

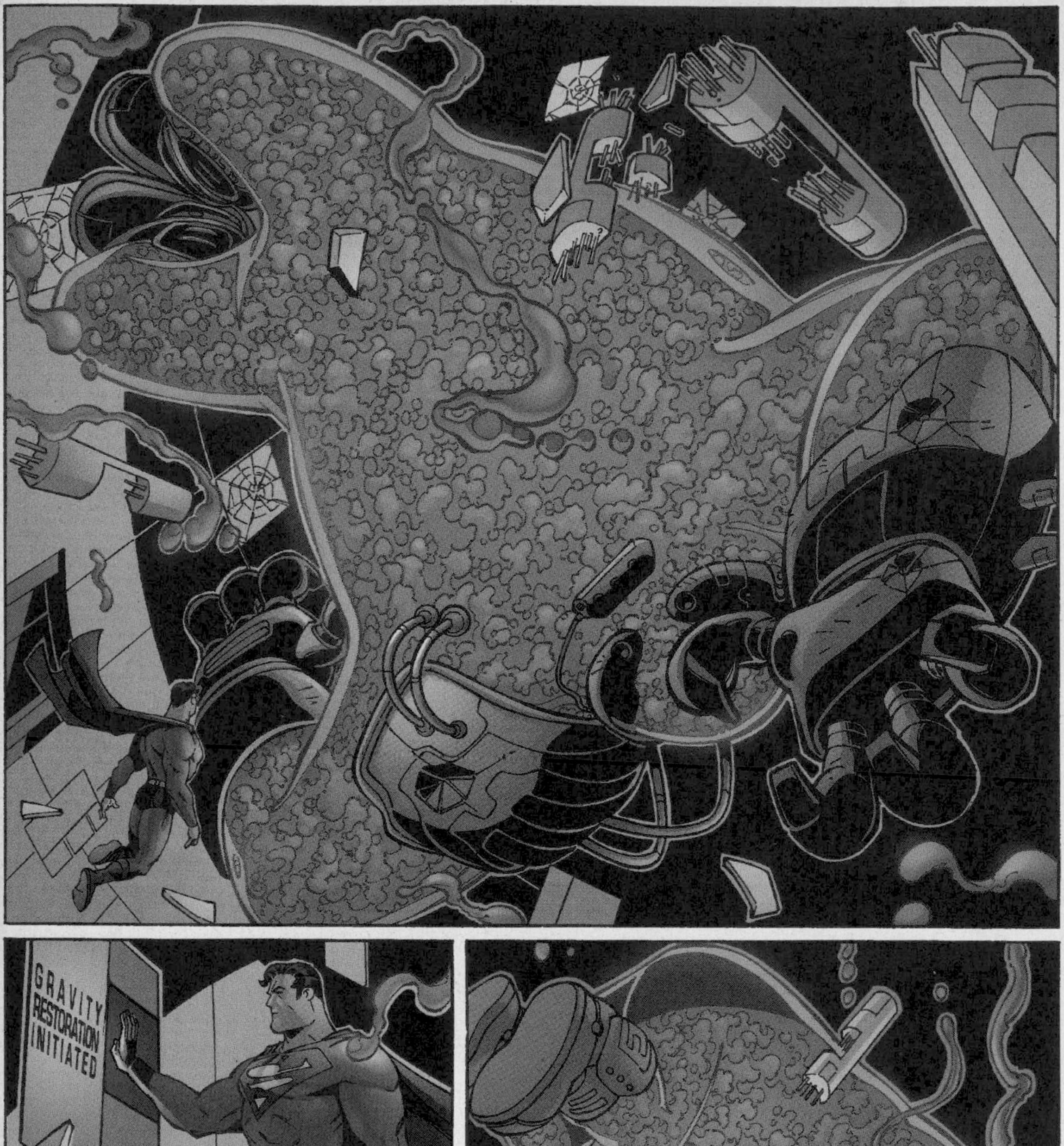

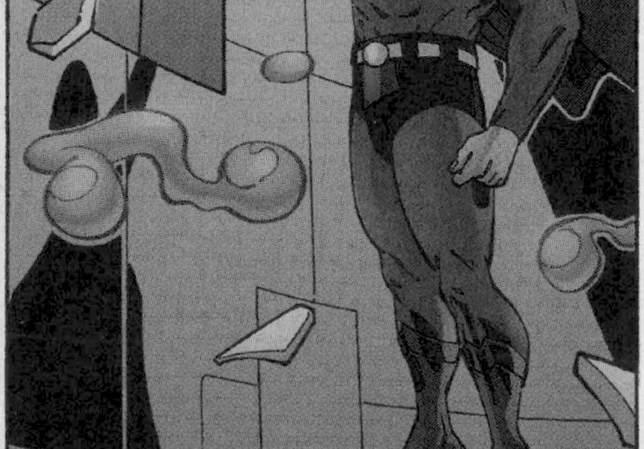
GRAVITY RESTORATION INITIATED

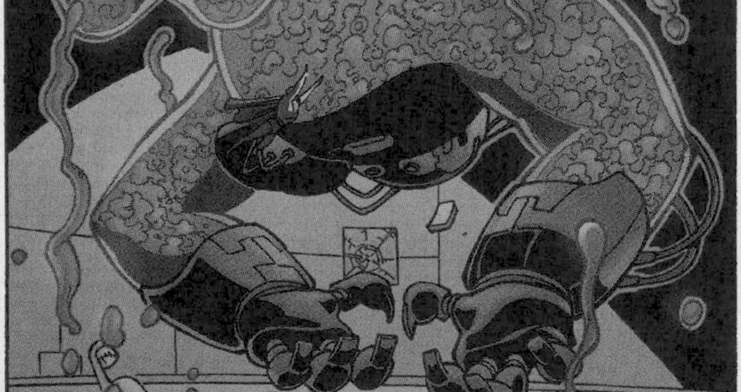

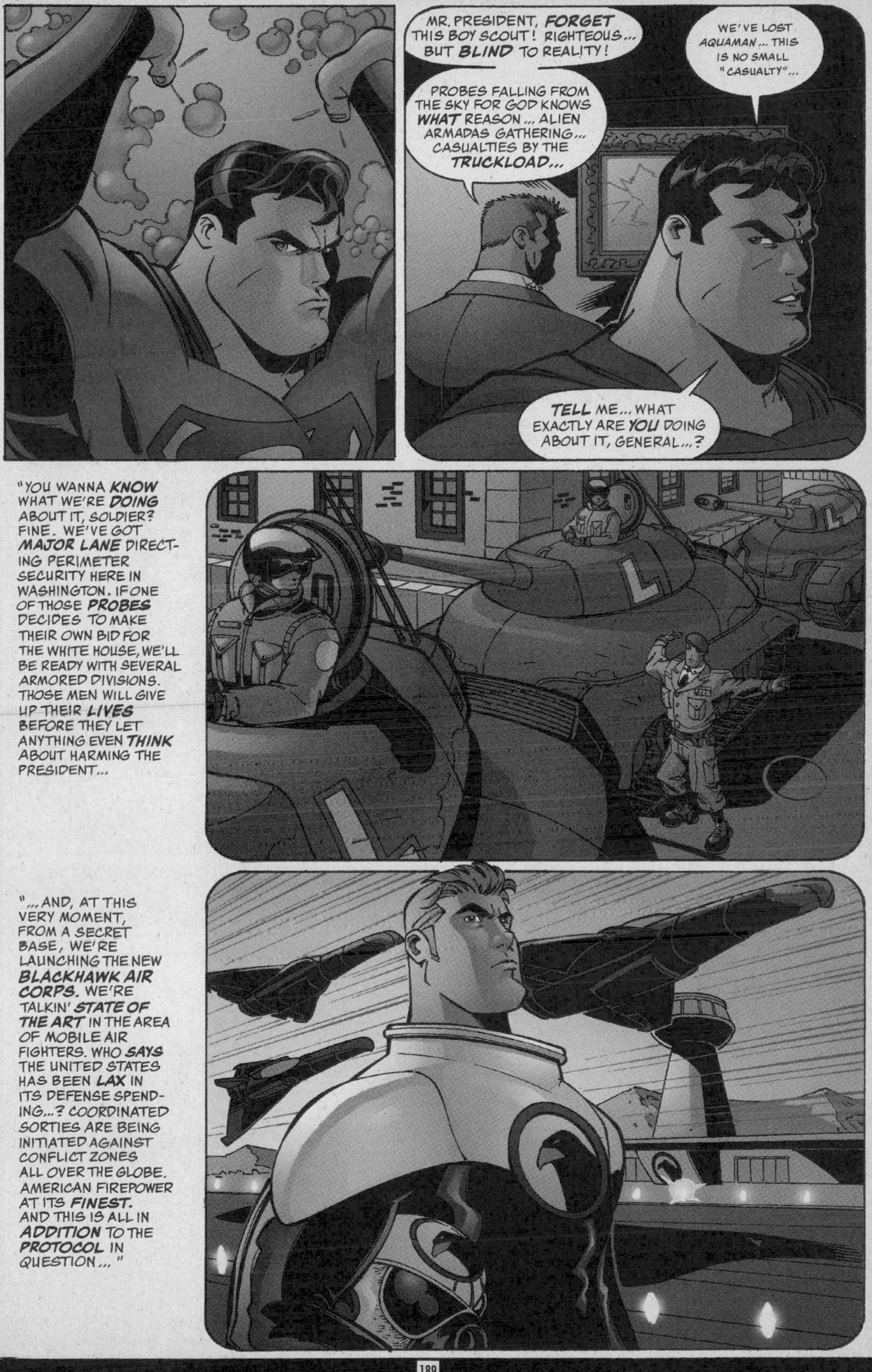
MR. PRESIDENT, FORGET THIS BOY SCOUT! RIGHTEOUS... BUT BLIND TO REALITY!
PROBES FALLING FROM THE SKY FOR GOD KNOWS WHAT REASON... ALIEN ARMADAS GATHERING... CASUALTIES BY THE TRUCKLOAD...
WE'VE LOST AQUAMAN... THIS IS NO SMALL "CASUALTY"...
TELL ME... WHAT EXACTLY ARE YOU DOING ABOUT IT, GENERAL...?
"YOU WANNA KNOW WHAT WE'RE DOING ABOUT IT, SOLDIER? FINE. WE'VE GOT MAJOR LANE DIRECTING PERIMETER SECURITY HERE IN WASHINGTON. IF ONE OF THOSE PROBES DECIDES TO MAKE THEIR OWN BID FOR THE WHITE HOUSE, WE'LL BE READY WITH SEVERAL ARMORED DIVISIONS. THOSE MEN WILL GIVE UP THEIR LIVES BEFORE THEY LET ANYTHING EVEN THINK ABOUT HARMING THE PRESIDENT...
"...AND, AT THIS VERY MOMENT, FROM A SECRET BASE, WE'RE LAUNCHING THE NEW BLACKHAWK AIR CORPS. WE'RE TALKIN' STATE OF THE ART IN THE AREA OF MOBILE AIR FIGHTERS. WHO SAYS THE UNITED STATES HAS BEEN LAX IN ITS DEFENSE SPENDING...? COORDINATED SORTIES ARE BEING INITIATED AGAINST CONFLICT ZONES ALL OVER THE GLOBE. AMERICAN FIREPOWER AT ITS FINEST. AND THIS IS ALL IN ADDITION TO THE PROTOCOL IN QUESTION..."

THIS IS A WASTE OF TIME.

I HATE TO *DISAGREE,* BUT I BELIEVE OUR DISTINGUISHED GUEST KNOWS *EXACTLY* WHAT THE STAKES ARE. I WOULD EXPECT NO LESS OF HIM.

THE *REAL* QUESTION IS... WILL HE BE *PREPARED* FOR WHAT HE MIGHT FIND IN THE JLA WATCHTOWER...? WE MUST *ASSUME* THAT THINGS HAVE GONE EXTREMELY *WRONG* WITH OUR ORIGINAL PLAN.

NONE OF US HAVE ANY CLEAR IDEA OF WHAT'S *HAP-PENED* UP THERE...

WE HAVE *GOT* TO STOP *MEETING* LIKE THIS, MATE.

I MEAN, WHAT ARE THE *ODDS*...?

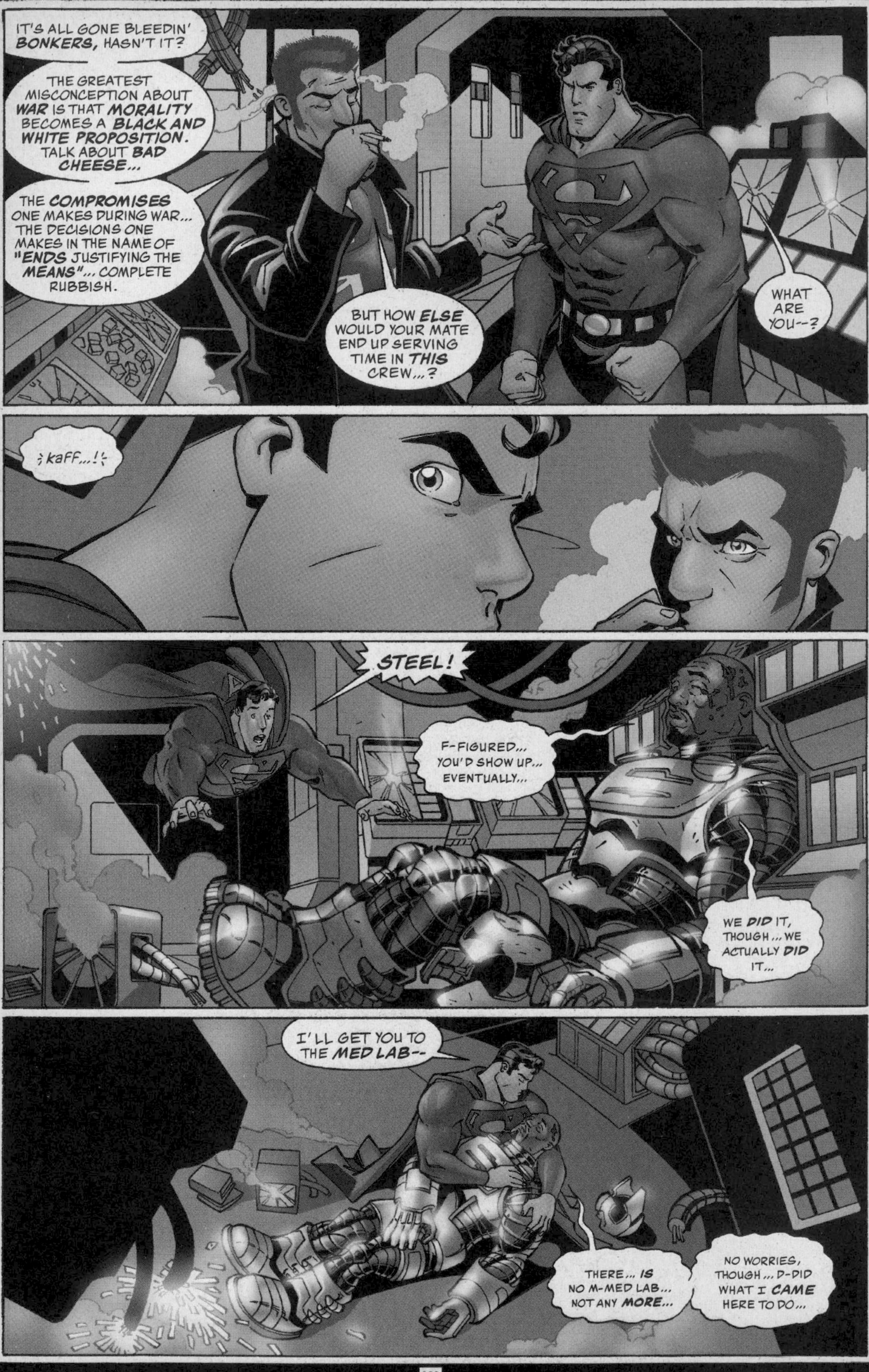
IT'S ALL GONE BLEEDIN' BONKERS, HASN'T IT?
THE GREATEST MISCONCEPTION ABOUT WAR IS THAT MORALITY BECOMES A BLACK AND WHITE PROPOSITION. TALK ABOUT BAD CHEESE...
THE COMPROMISES ONE MAKES DURING WAR... THE DECISIONS ONE MAKES IN THE NAME OF "ENDS JUSTIFYING THE MEANS"... COMPLETE RUBBISH.
BUT HOW ELSE WOULD YOUR MATE END UP SERVING TIME IN THIS CREW...?
WHAT ARE YOU--?
kaff...!
STEEL!
F-FIGURED... YOU'D SHOW UP... EVENTUALLY...
WE DID IT, THOUGH... WE ACTUALLY DID IT...
I'LL GET YOU TO THE MED LAB--
THERE... IS NO M-MED LAB... NOT ANY MORE...
NO WORRIES, THOUGH... D-DID WHAT I CAME HERE TO DO...

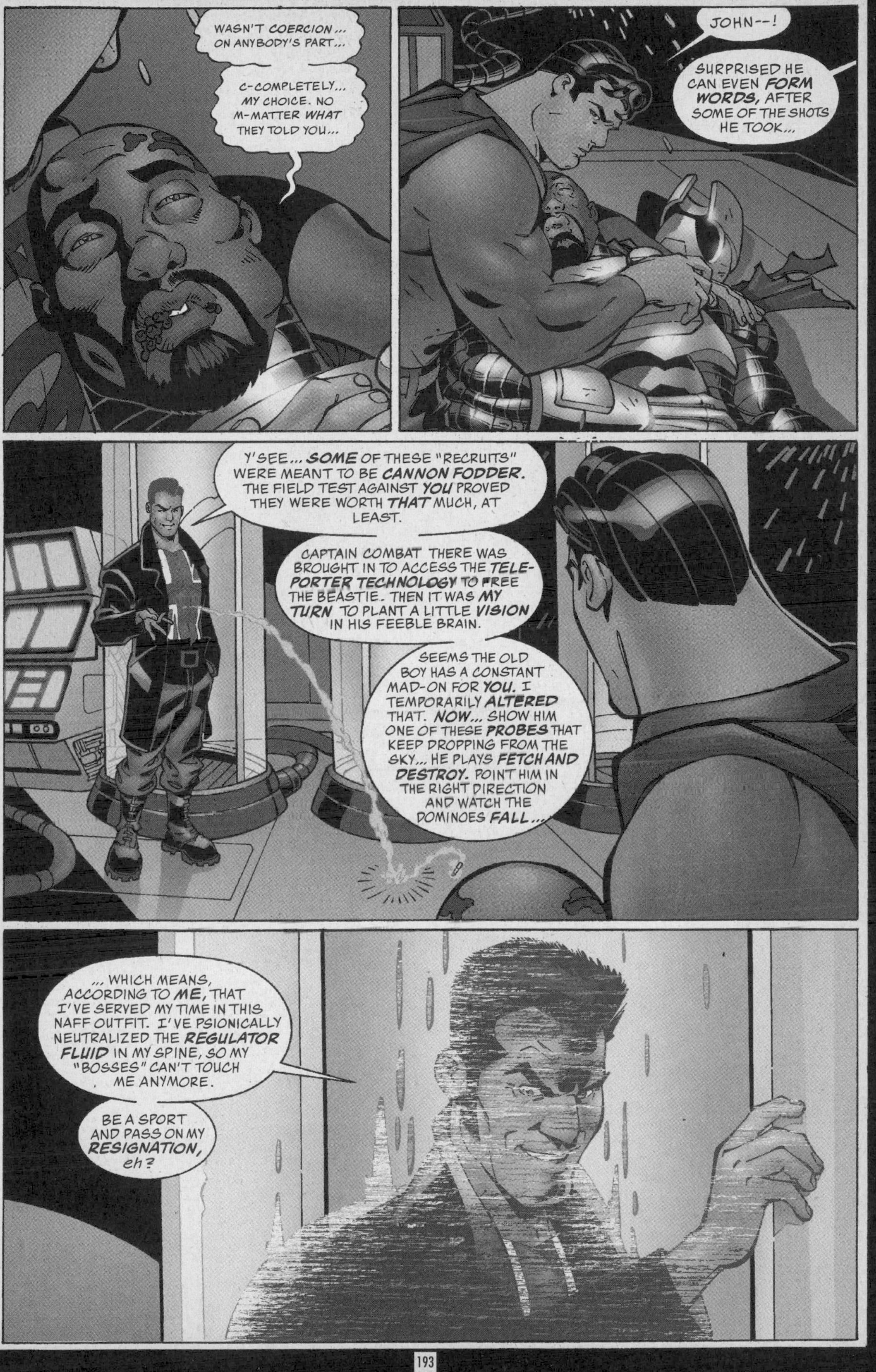
WASN'T COERCION... ON ANYBODY'S PART...
C-COMPLETELY... MY CHOICE. NO M-MATTER WHAT THEY TOLD YOU...
JOHN--!
SURPRISED HE CAN EVEN FORM WORDS, AFTER SOME OF THE SHOTS HE TOOK...
Y'SEE... SOME OF THESE "RECRUITS" WERE MEANT TO BE CANNON FODDER. THE FIELD TEST AGAINST YOU PROVED THEY WERE WORTH THAT MUCH, AT LEAST.
CAPTAIN COMBAT THERE WAS BROUGHT IN TO ACCESS THE TELE-PORTER TECHNOLOGY TO FREE THE BEASTIE. THEN IT WAS MY TURN TO PLANT A LITTLE VISION IN HIS FEEBLE BRAIN.
SEEMS THE OLD BOY HAS A CONSTANT MAD-ON FOR YOU. I TEMPORARILY ALTERED THAT. NOW... SHOW HIM ONE OF THESE PROBES THAT KEEP DROPPING FROM THE SKY... HE PLAYS FETCH AND DESTROY. POINT HIM IN THE RIGHT DIRECTION AND WATCH THE DOMINOES FALL...
...WHICH MEANS, ACCORDING TO ME, THAT I'VE SERVED MY TIME IN THIS NAFF OUTFIT. I'VE PSIONICALLY NEUTRALIZED THE REGULATOR FLUID IN MY SPINE, SO MY "BOSSES" CAN'T TOUCH ME ANYMORE.
BE A SPORT AND PASS ON MY RESIGNATION, eh?

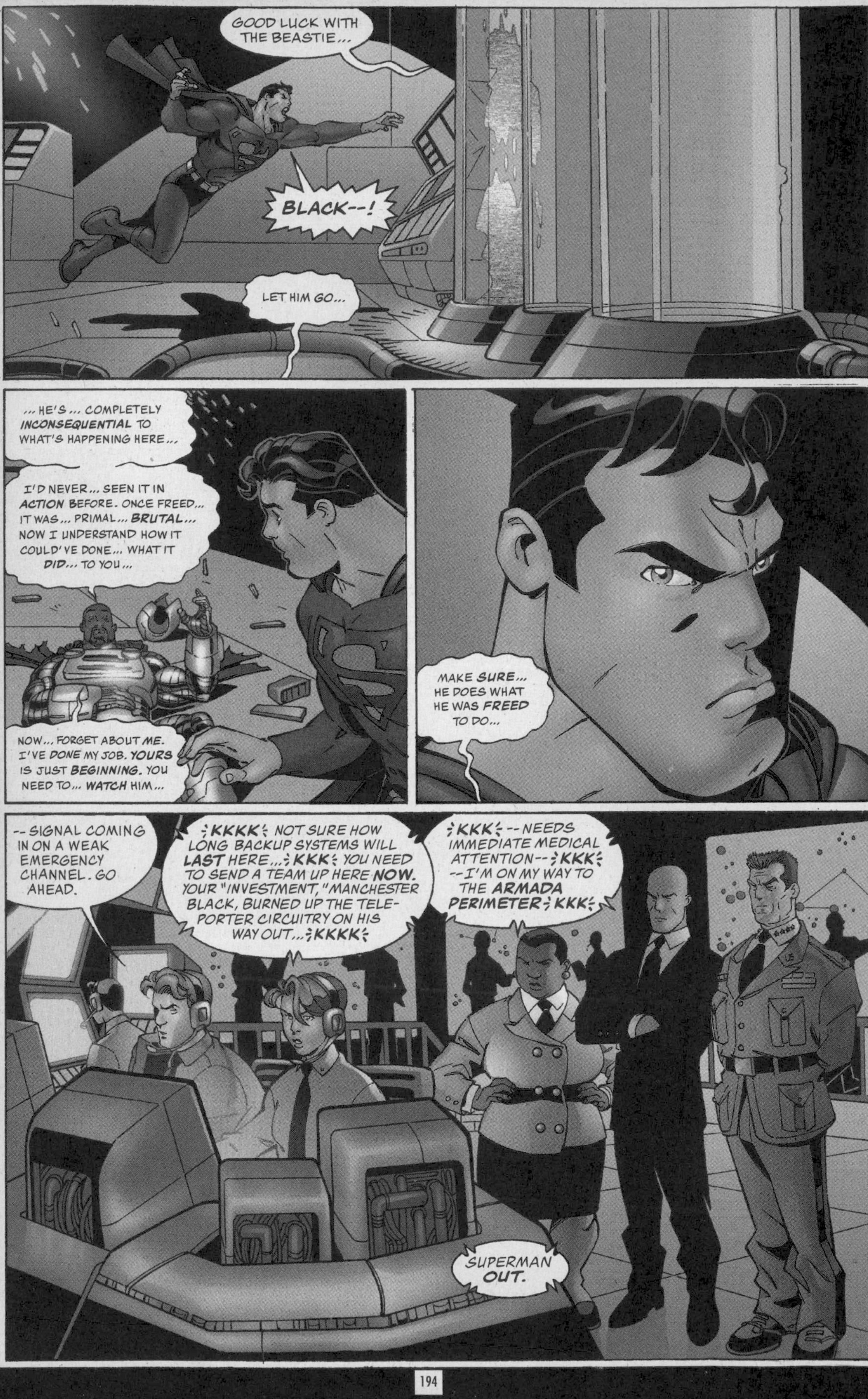
GOOD LUCK WITH THE BEASTIE...
BLACK--!
LET HIM GO...
...HE'S... COMPLETELY INCONSEQUENTIAL TO WHAT'S HAPPENING HERE...
I'D NEVER... SEEN IT IN ACTION BEFORE. ONCE FREED... IT WAS... PRIMAL... BRUTAL... NOW I UNDERSTAND HOW IT COULD'VE DONE... WHAT IT DID... TO YOU...
NOW... FORGET ABOUT ME. I'VE DONE MY JOB. YOURS IS JUST BEGINNING. YOU NEED TO... WATCH HIM...
MAKE SURE... HE DOES WHAT HE WAS FREED TO DO...
--SIGNAL COMING IN ON A WEAK EMERGENCY CHANNEL. GO AHEAD.
KKKK NOT SURE HOW LONG BACKUP SYSTEMS WILL LAST HERE... KKK YOU NEED TO SEND A TEAM UP HERE NOW. YOUR "INVESTMENT," MANCHESTER BLACK, BURNED UP THE TELEPORTER CIRCUITRY ON HIS WAY OUT... KKKK
KKK --NEEDS IMMEDIATE MEDICAL ATTENTION-- KKK --I'M ON MY WAY TO THE ARMADA PERIMETER KKK
SUPERMAN OUT.

HE'D FOUGHT A WAR ONCE **BEFORE.** IN THE STREETS OF METROPOLIS. IT WAS A WAR HE ULTIMATELY **LOST** AS HE SUCCUMBED TO THE SHEER **BRUTALITY** OF HIS OPPONENT... AND FOR THE FIRST TIME, HE FELT THE COLD HAND OF **DEATH** GRIPPED AROUND HIS HEART. AND IN THAT MOMENT, HE DID NOT RESIST. HE DID NOT DENY ITS PULL. HIS OPPONENT HAD BECOME... HIS **KILLER.**

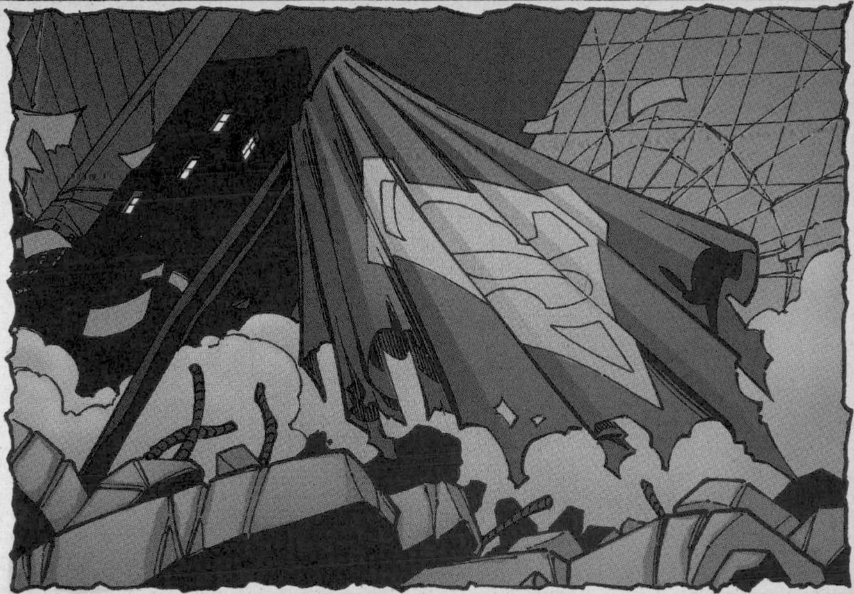

BUT HE HAD **RETURNED** FROM NOTHINGNESS. DEATH COULD NOT KEEP HIM FROM THOSE HE LOVED. NOW WAR HAS FOUND HIM ONCE AGAIN... AND ON A SCALE HE HAD RARELY EVEN HAD **NIGHTMARES** ABOUT. FACING NOT ONLY **DEATH,** BUT THE COMPLETE AND TOTAL **END OF EVERY-THING.** HERE, IN THE OUTER REACHES OF THE SOLAR SYSTEM, HE WAS **WITNESSING** IT FIRSTHAND. THIS WAR HAD ALREADY CLAIMED **LIVES.** AN **ALIEN ARMADA** FOUGHT TILL THEIR LAST BREATH.

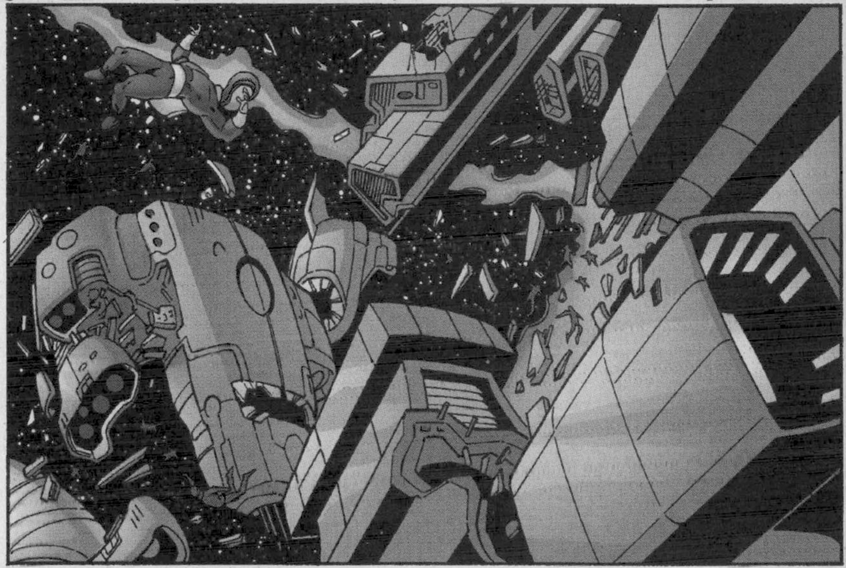

SO MANY CHOICES MADE, JUST IN THE PAST FEW DAYS, THAT HAVE **TESTED** HIS OWN MORAL COMPASS. SO MANY DECISIONS HE WONDERS IF HE'LL LIVE TO **REGRET.** SO MANY ALREADY **FALLEN,** SO MANY ALREADY **LOST,** AND THE GREATEST BATTLES HAVE YET TO BE **FOUGHT.** HE TRIES NOT TO **THINK** TOO MUCH ABOUT IT, AS MORE **IMMEDIATE** CONCERNS WEIGH ON HIS MIND. AND VIOLENT **MEMORIES** PREY UPON HIS JUDGMENT...

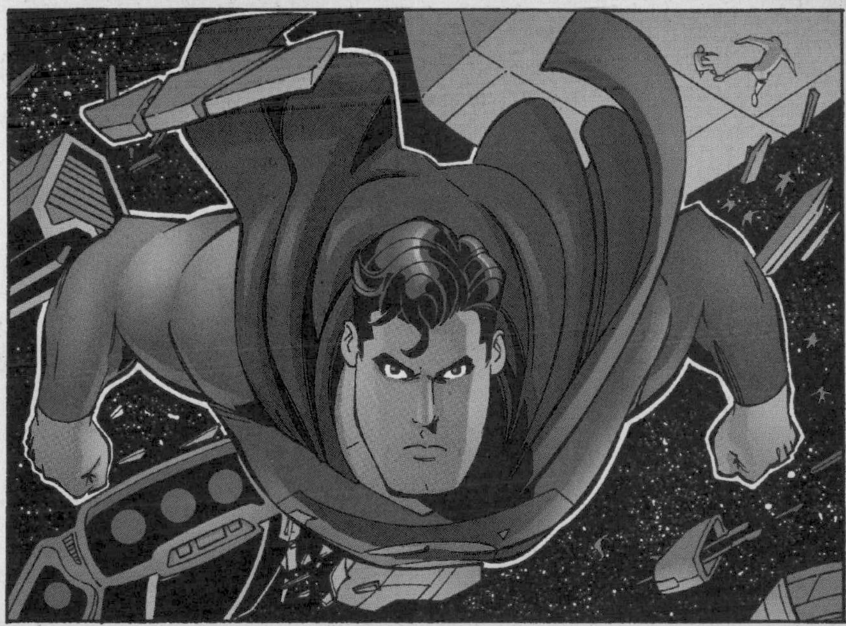

HE HAD CERTAINLY FELT **PAIN** BEFORE, BUT NEVER LIKE **THIS**. THE MEMORY OF EACH AND EVERY BLOW RINGS LIKE BELLS WITHIN HIS BRAIN. THE **TASTE** OF HIS OWN **BLOOD**. THE STINK OF UNSTOPPABLE **RAGE** RAINING DOWN CALCIFIED **FURY** UPON HIS HEAD. TRUTH BE TOLD... A SMALL PART OF HIM HAD ACTUALLY **WELCOMED** THE PEACEFUL EMBRACE OF DEATH. HE SAW IT AS THE ONLY TRUE **ESCAPE** FROM WHAT HE STILL FEARED WAS AN **INESCAPABLE** TRUTH...

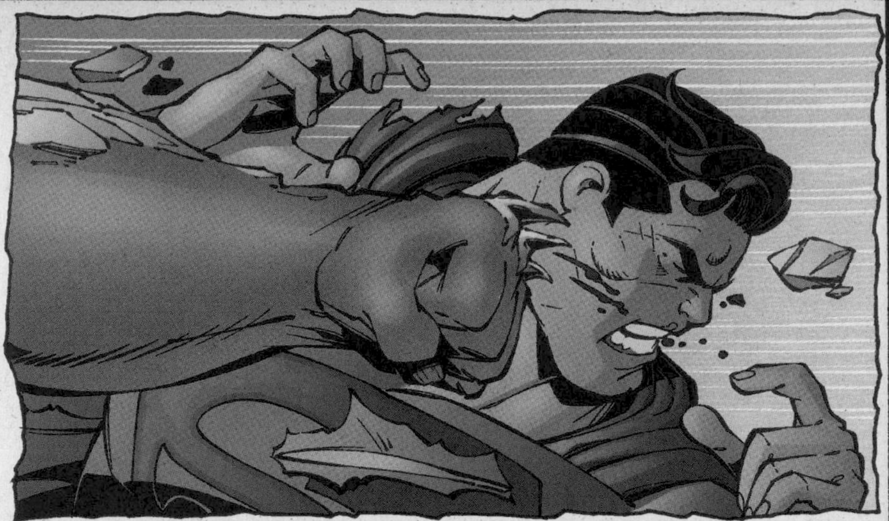

...THIS WAS A TRUE **ANOMALY** IN THE UNIVERSE. THIS WAS A BEING OF SUCH IMMEASURABLE **POWER** THAT ITS **NAME**, IN ANY TRANSLATION--BE IT A RECOGNIZABLE OR WHOLLY ALIEN TONGUE--STRUCK UNHOLY TERROR INTO THE HEARTS OF THOSE WHO HEARD IT. NO **MERCY** INVOLVED. NO **CRACKS** IN THE VENEER OF INDESTRUCTIBILITY. IT HAD NEVER HAD AN **EARTHLY** NAME UNTIL **RECENTLY**, EARNING IT RIGHTLY WITH THE **MURDER** OF THE GREATEST HERO OF THE AGE. IT WAS A NAME THAT PARENTS FRIGHTENED THEIR CHILDREN WITH. IT WAS A NAME THAT HAD BECOME **MYTH**.

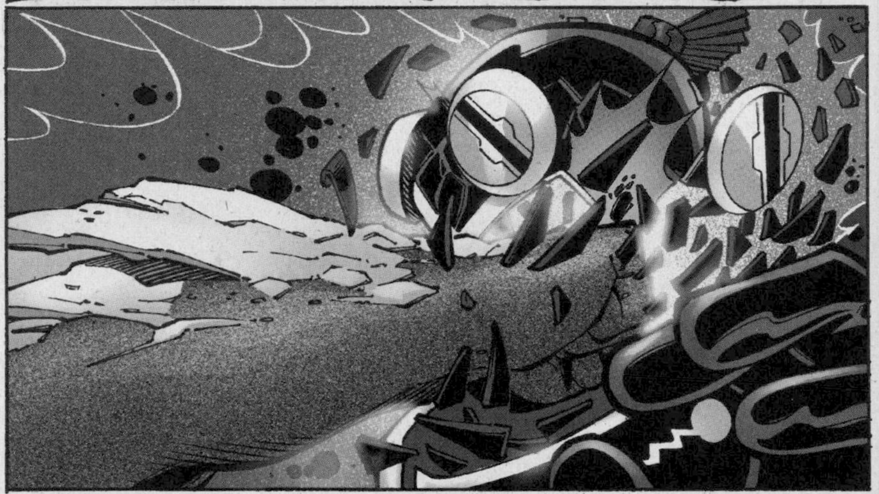

DOOMSDAY.

THE CREATURE THAT HAD **KILLED SUPERMAN**. AND NOW IT LIVED **AGAIN**. HE COULD ENGAGE IT ONCE AGAIN. EVERY FIBER IN HIS BODY SCREAMED OUT TO **DESTROY** THIS... ENGINE OF PURE DESTRUCTION. HE COULD **MAKE** THAT CHOICE RIGHT **NOW**. AND WHO WOULD **BLAME** HIM? BUT, WITH THE **UNIVERSE** HELD HOSTAGE... ONLY **ONE** CHOICE WAS CLEAR. ANOTHER **COMPROMISE**. ANOTHER DECISION HE FEARED HE WOULD LIVE TO **REGRET**...

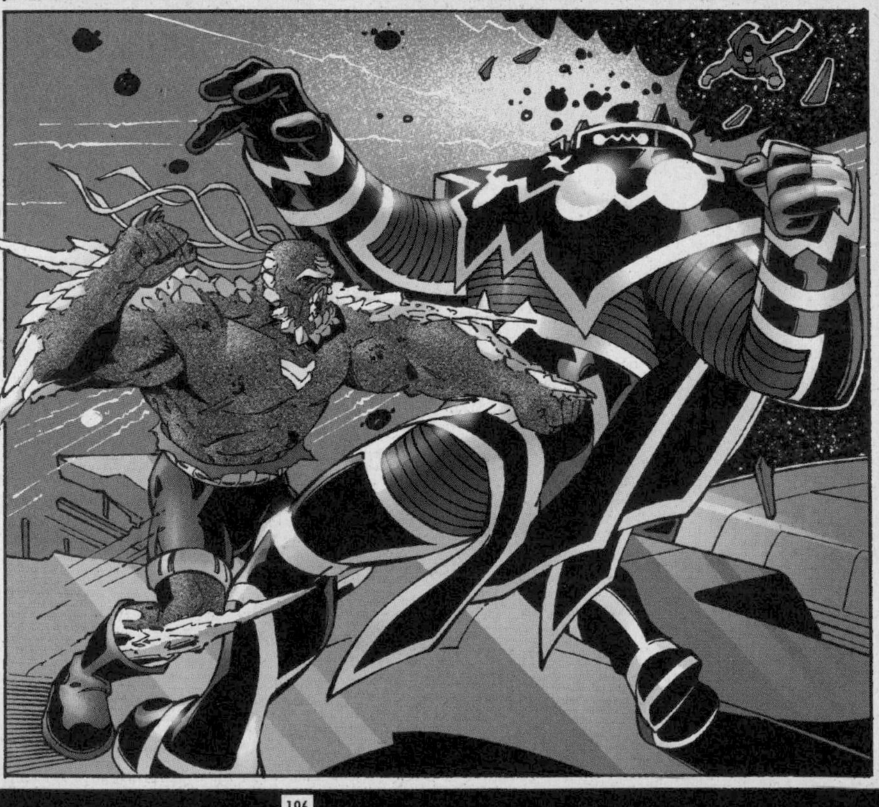

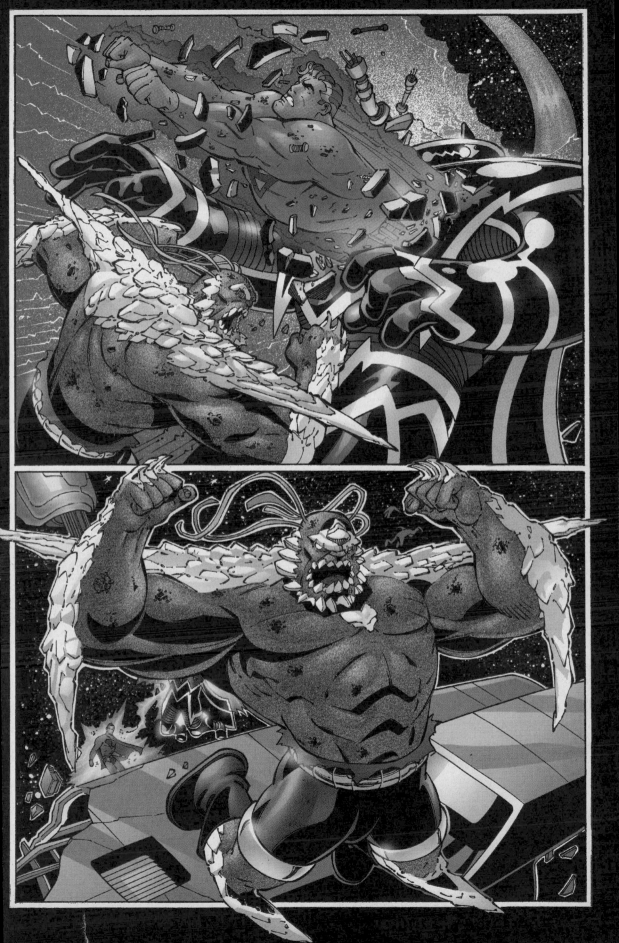

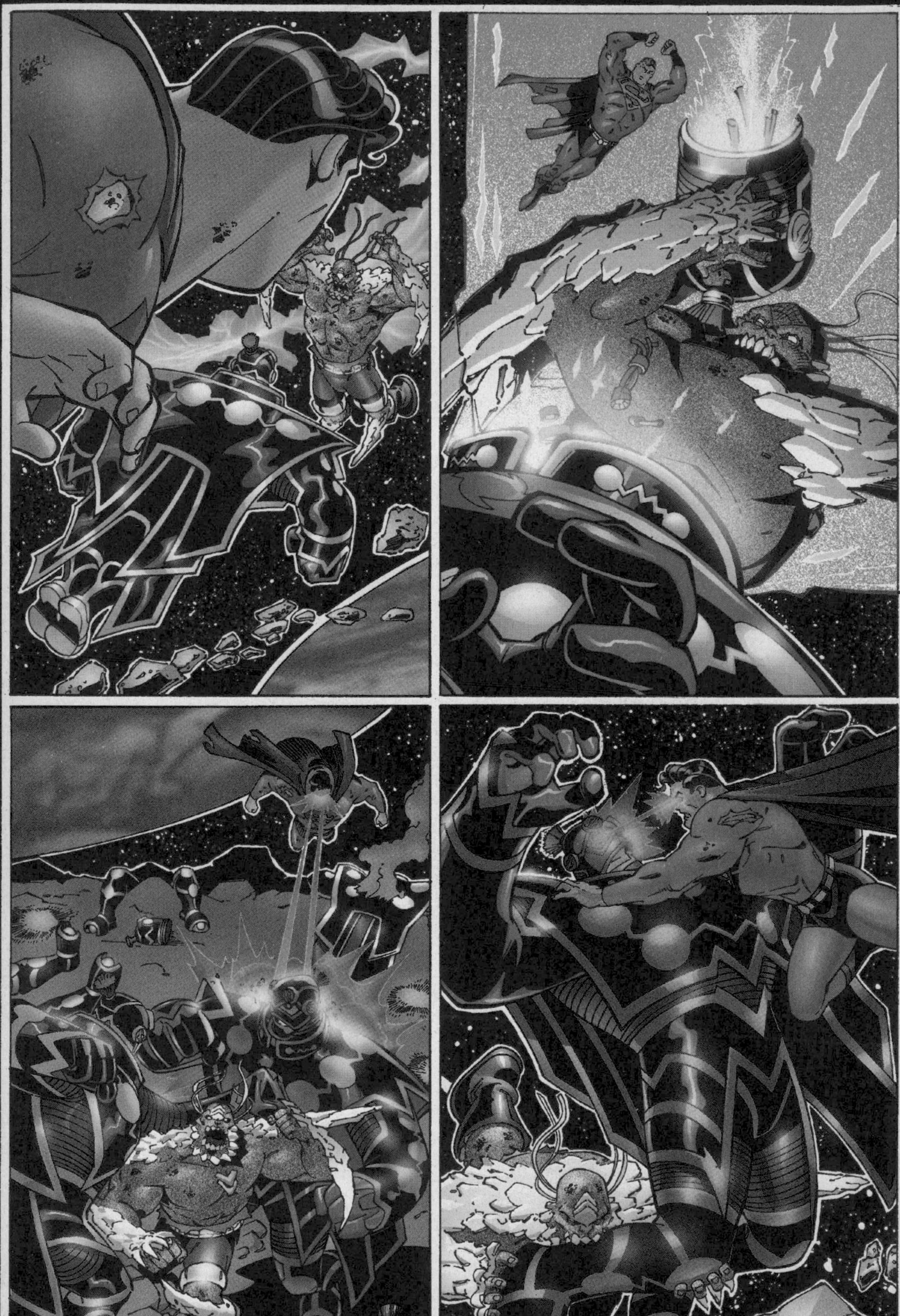

IT HAS BECOME **PRIMAL.** IT HAS BECOME SECOND NATURE. **TIME** HAS LOST ALL MEANING, HERE IN THE DEPTHS OF SPACE. HOW LONG HAVE THEY BEEN MAKING THIS TREK? HOURS? DAYS? HE HAS **NO IDEA.** NOR DOES HE **CARE,** AS THIS **ALLIANCE** WITH ONE OF HIS DEADLIEST ADVERSARIES HAS PUT HIM AT WAR WITH HIS OWN **CONSCIENCE** THIS BEING A WAR HE CANNOT AFFORD TO **FIGHT** AT THE MOMENT, HE HAS PUT THOSE THOUGHTS ASIDE, **NUMBING HIMSELF** INTO THE NECESSARY STATE OF **VIOLENCE.** THE DESTRUCTION OF SO MANY **PROBES** HAS DEMONSTRATED AN **IMPORTANT LESSON** TO HIM... THAT, IN WAR, **EMOTION** CAN HINDER THE ULTIMATE GOAL... TO **WIN.**

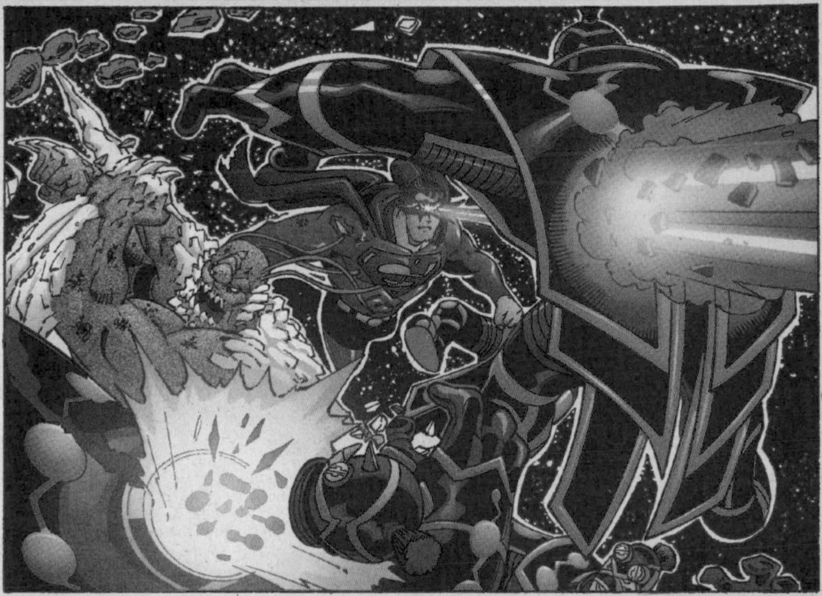

AS HIS "PARTNER" IS TRULY DESTRUCTION **PERSONIFIED,** SO HAS **HE** BECOME. AND FROM THAT TRANSFORMATION... **SUCCESS.** FAR AWAY FROM THE HUMANITY HE HOLDS IN SUCH HIGH MEASURE, WHERE THE PROBES SEEMED FAR MORE **DEADLY,** HE HAS **CUT LOOSE.** SUBSEQUENTLY, THE PROBES HAVE OFFERED LITTLE RESISTANCE. HE CAN'T HELP BUT THINK... IF ONLY HE'D COME TO THIS CONCLUSION ON **EARTH,** HOW MANY MIGHT'VE BEEN **SAVED...?** IS THIS HOW MEN LIKE **LUTHOR** CAN WALK BETWEEN THE RAINDROPS...? BY CULTIVATING THEIR INHERENT **RUTHLESSNESS...** THEIR **LACK OF CONSCIENCE...?**

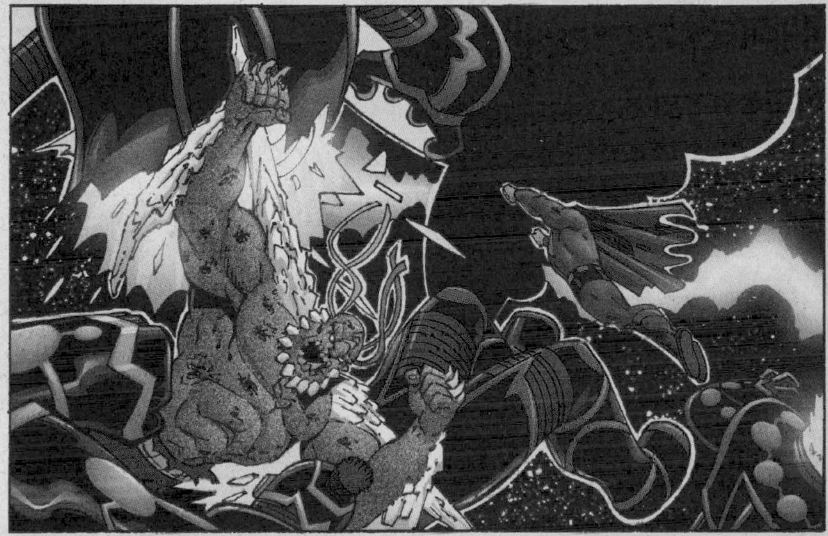

SO HE PLOWS **AHEAD,** CONFIDENT IN HIS POWERS. CONFIDENT IN HIS MINDSET AND HIS DECISIONS. READY TO STARE INTO THE ABYSS WITHOUT BLINKING. FOR A MOMENT, HE THINKS OF **LOIS.** HE THINKS OF HIS **PARENTS.** BUT ONLY FOR A MOMENT. SUCH THOUGHTS ARE **DANGEROUS.** HE **KNOWS** THAT NOW. HE IS READY TO FACE THE **TRUE** THREAT OF THIS CONFLICT... THE TRUE **ENEMY...**

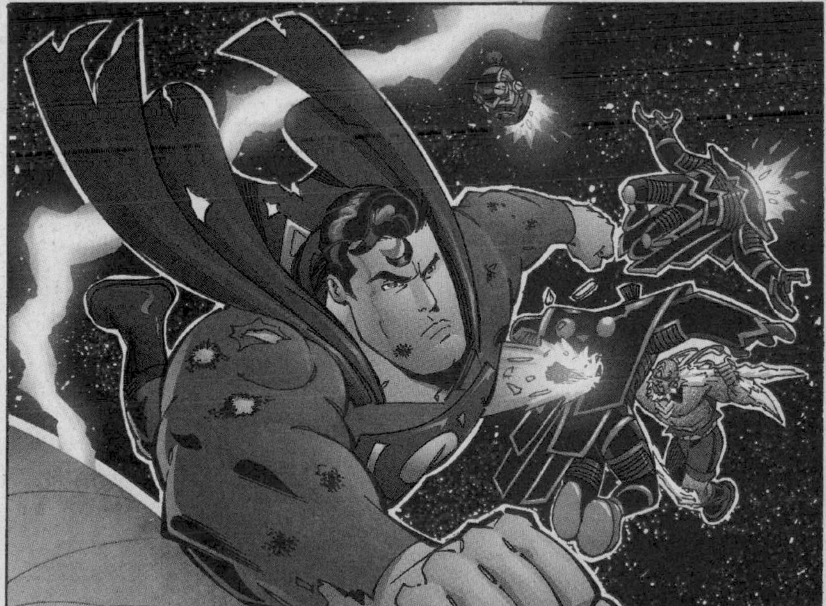

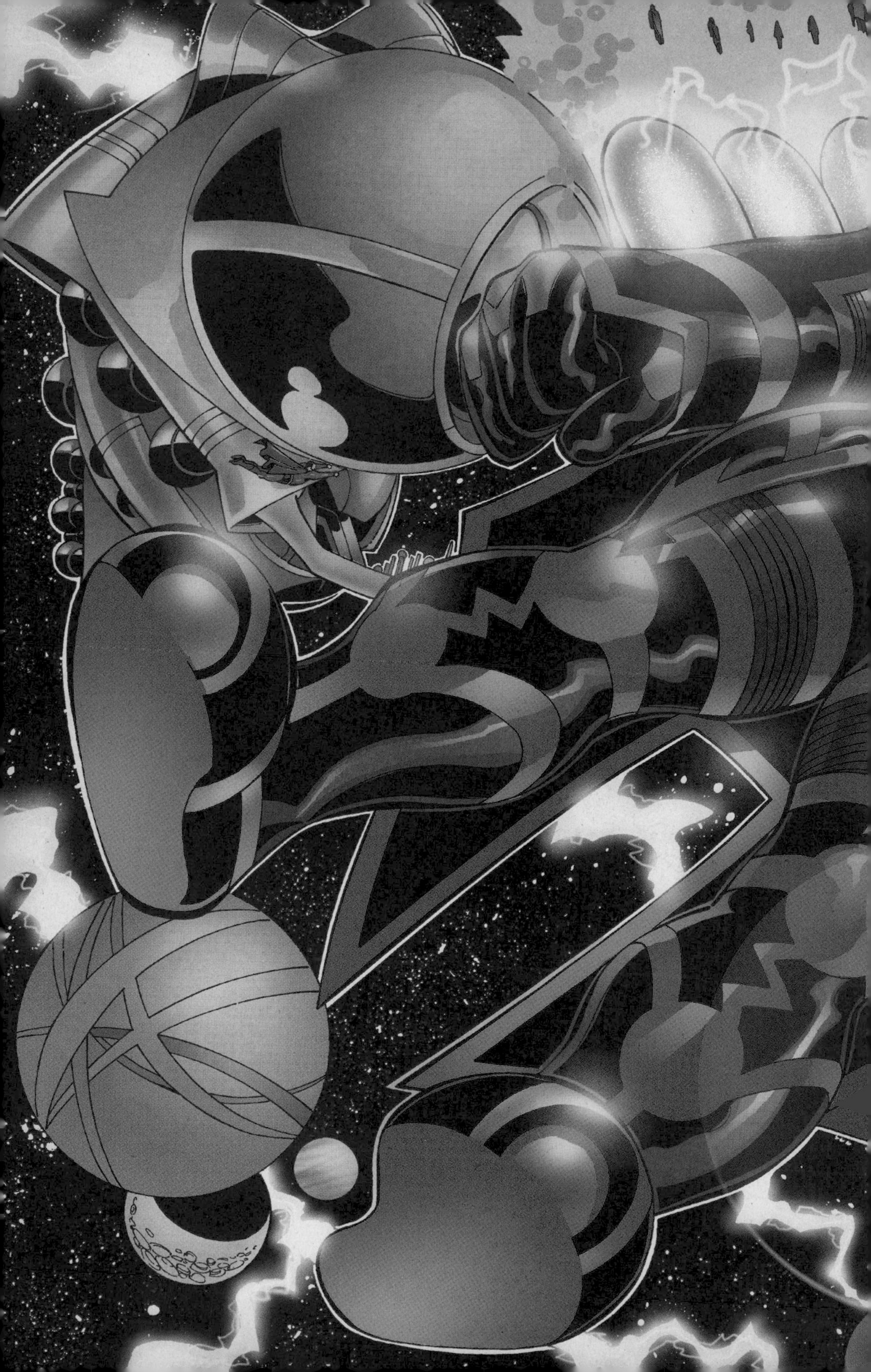

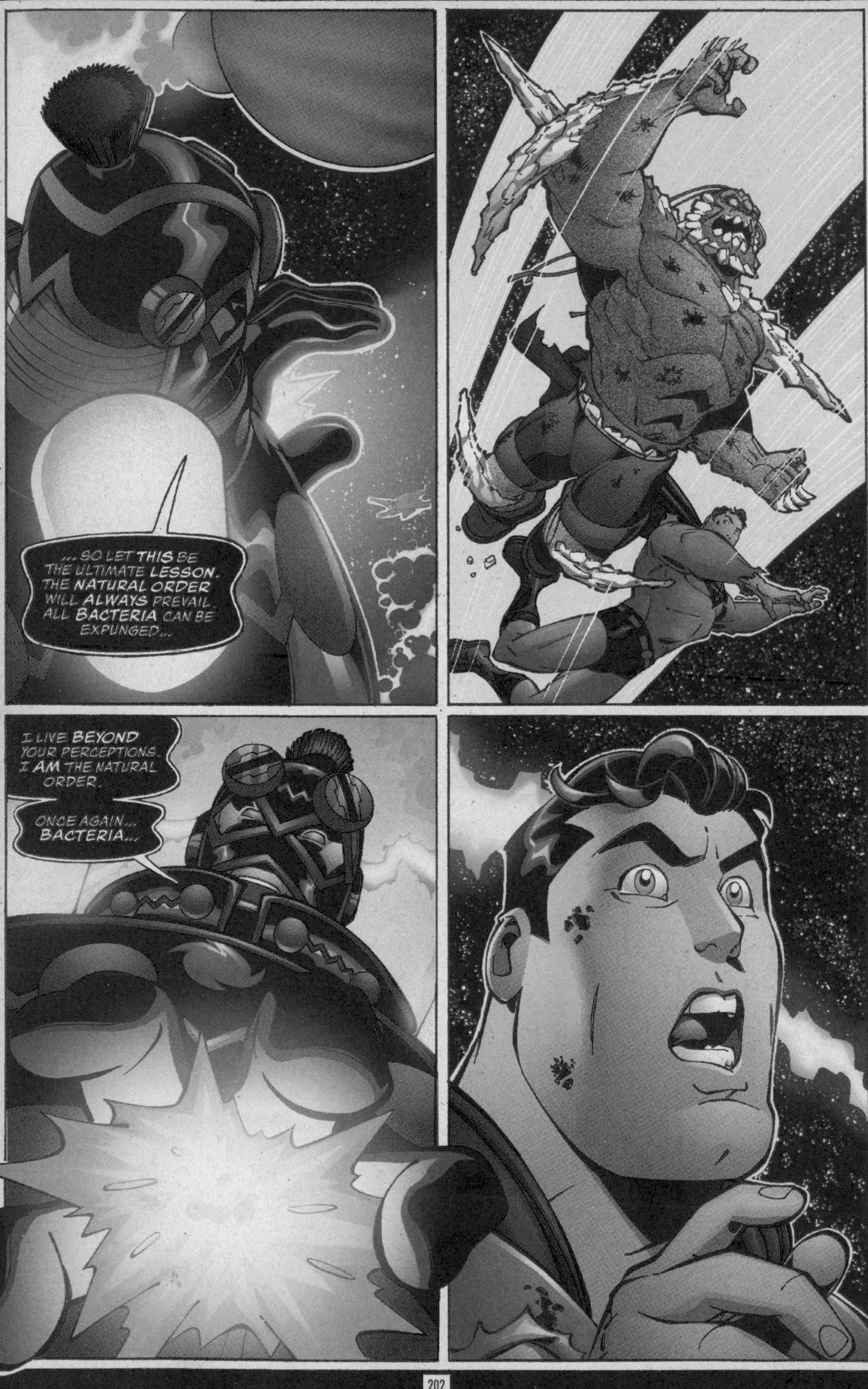
...SO LET THIS BE THE ULTIMATE LESSON. THE NATURAL ORDER WILL ALWAYS PREVAIL. ALL BACTERIA CAN BE EXPUNGED...
I LIVE BEYOND YOUR PERCEPTIONS. I AM THE NATURAL ORDER.
ONCE AGAIN... BACTERIA...

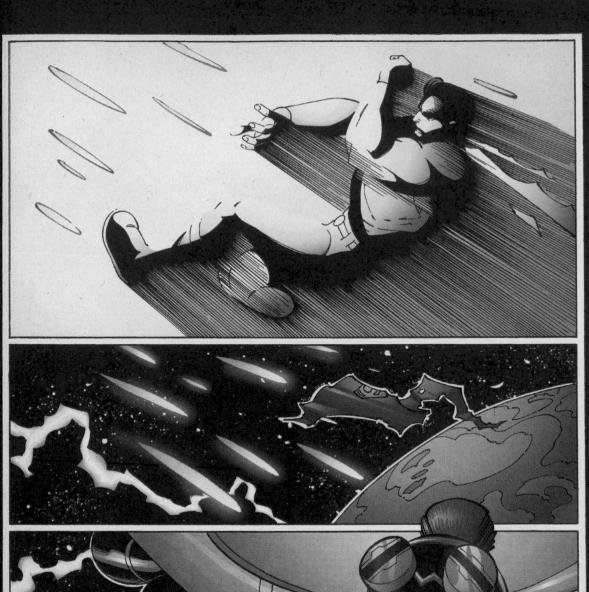

VERY WELL.

THE DESTINY OF **IMPERIEX** IS WRITTEN IN THE STARS. LET NATURE PROCEED.

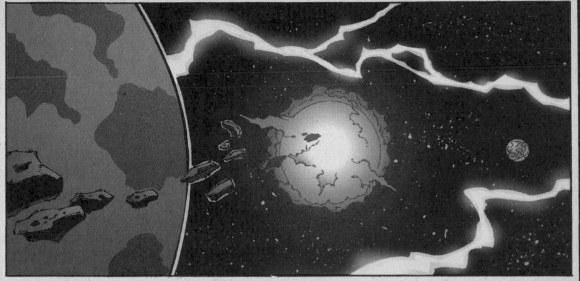

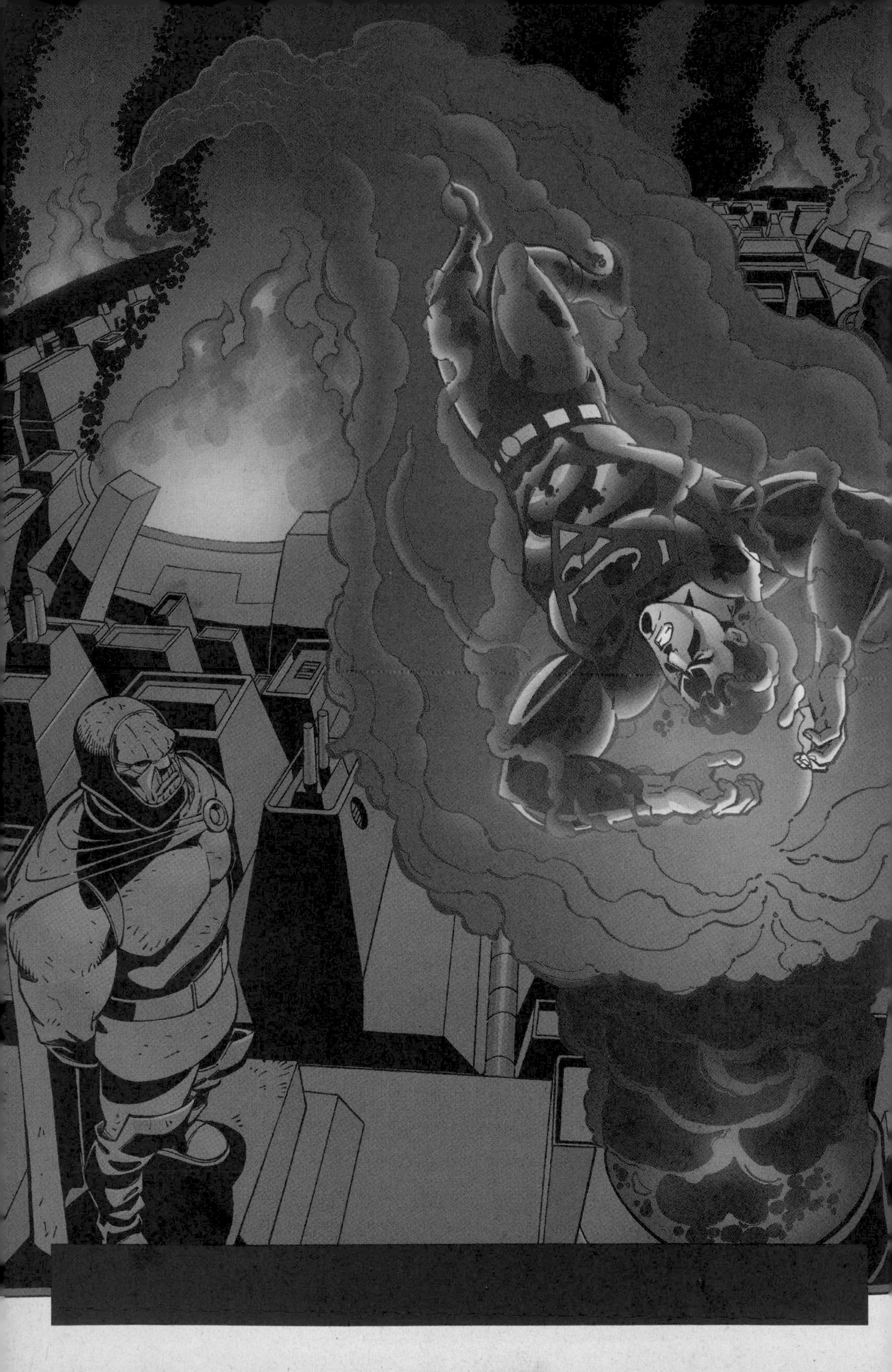

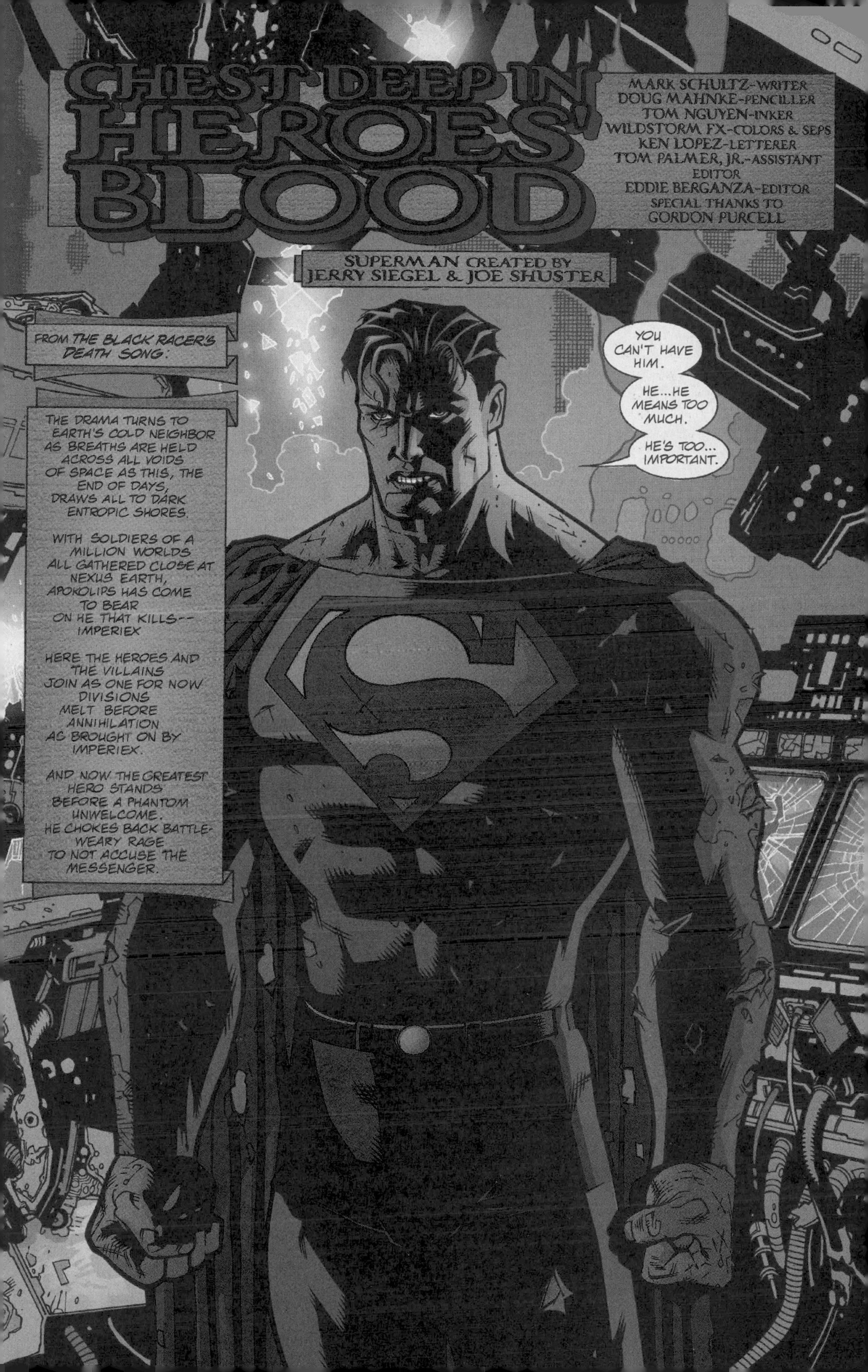
CHEST DEEP IN HEROES' BLOOD
MARK SCHULTZ-WRITER
DOUG MAHNKE-PENCILLER
TOM NGUYEN-INKER
WILDSTORM FX-COLORS & SEPS
KEN LOPEZ-LETTERER
TOM PALMER, JR.-ASSISTANT EDITOR
EDDIE BERGANZA-EDITOR
SPECIAL THANKS TO GORDON PURCELL
SUPERMAN CREATED BY JERRY SIEGEL & JOE SHUSTER
FROM THE BLACK RACER'S DEATH SONG:
THE DRAMA TURNS TO EARTH'S COLD NEIGHBOR AS BREATHS ARE HELD ACROSS ALL VOIDS OF SPACE AS THIS, THE END OF DAYS, DRAWS ALL TO DARK ENTROPIC SHORES.
WITH SOLDIERS OF A MILLION WORLDS ALL GATHERED CLOSE AT NEXUS EARTH, APOKOLIPS HAS COME TO BEAR ON HE THAT KILLS-- IMPERIEX
HERE THE HEROES AND THE VILLAINS JOIN AS ONE FOR NOW DIVISIONS MELT BEFORE ANNIHILATION AS BROUGHT ON BY IMPERIEX.
AND NOW THE GREATEST HERO STANDS BEFORE A PHANTOM UNWELCOME. HE CHOKES BACK BATTLE-WEARY RAGE TO NOT ACCUSE THE MESSENGER.
YOU CAN'T HAVE HIM.
HE...HE MEANS TOO MUCH.
HE'S TOO... IMPORTANT.

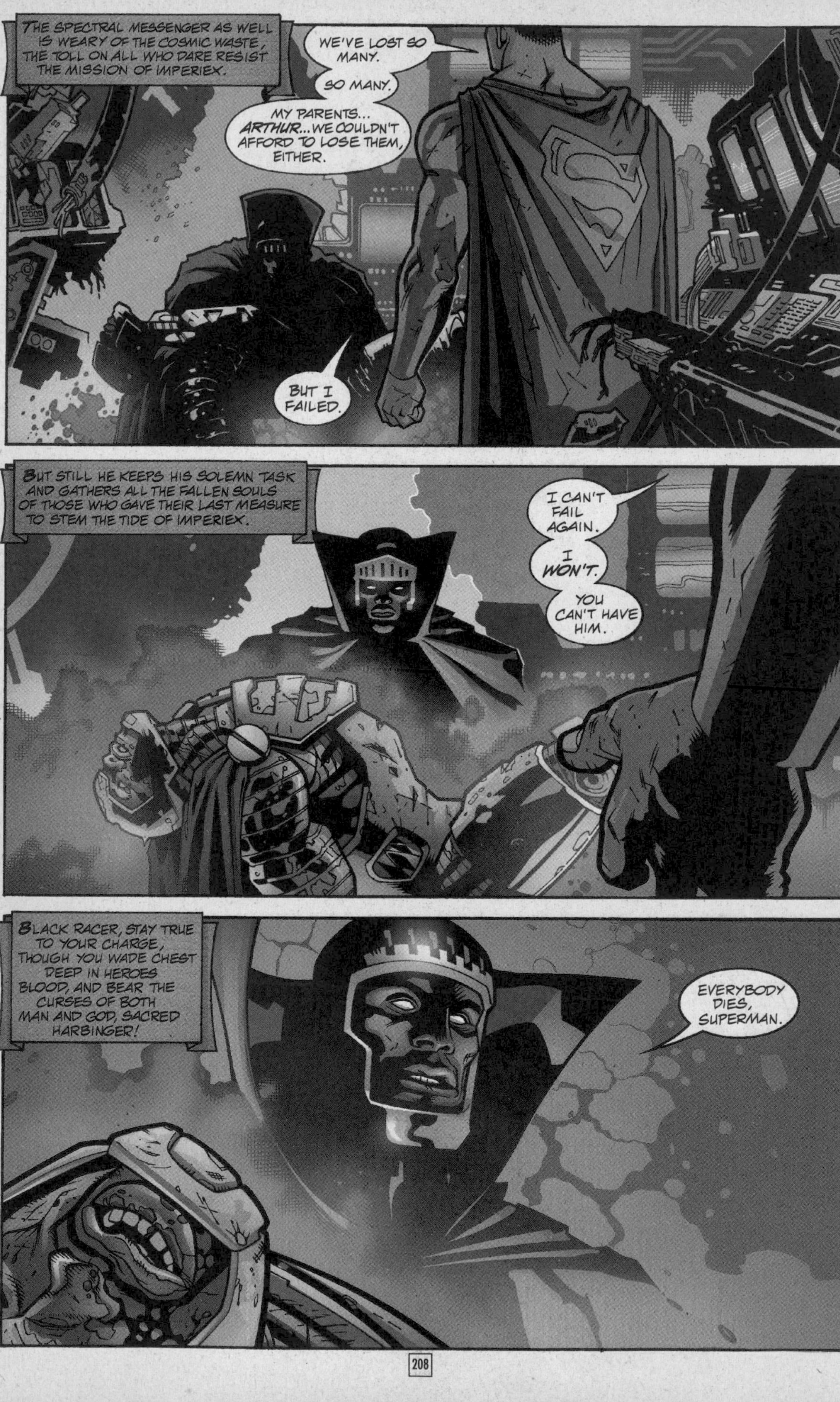
THE SPECTRAL MESSENGER AS WELL IS WEARY OF THE COSMIC WASTE, THE TOLL ON ALL WHO DARE RESIST THE MISSION OF IMPERIEX.
WE'VE LOST SO MANY.
SO MANY.
MY PARENTS... ARTHUR... WE COULDN'T AFFORD TO LOSE THEM, EITHER.
BUT I FAILED.
BUT STILL HE KEEPS HIS SOLEMN TASK AND GATHERS ALL THE FALLEN SOULS OF THOSE WHO GAVE THEIR LAST MEASURE TO STEM THE TIDE OF IMPERIEX.
I CAN'T FAIL AGAIN.
I WON'T.
YOU CAN'T HAVE HIM.
BLACK RACER, STAY TRUE TO YOUR CHARGE, THOUGH YOU WADE CHEST DEEP IN HEROES BLOOD, AND BEAR THE CURSES OF BOTH MAN AND GOD, SACRED HARBINGER!
EVERYBODY DIES, SUPERMAN.

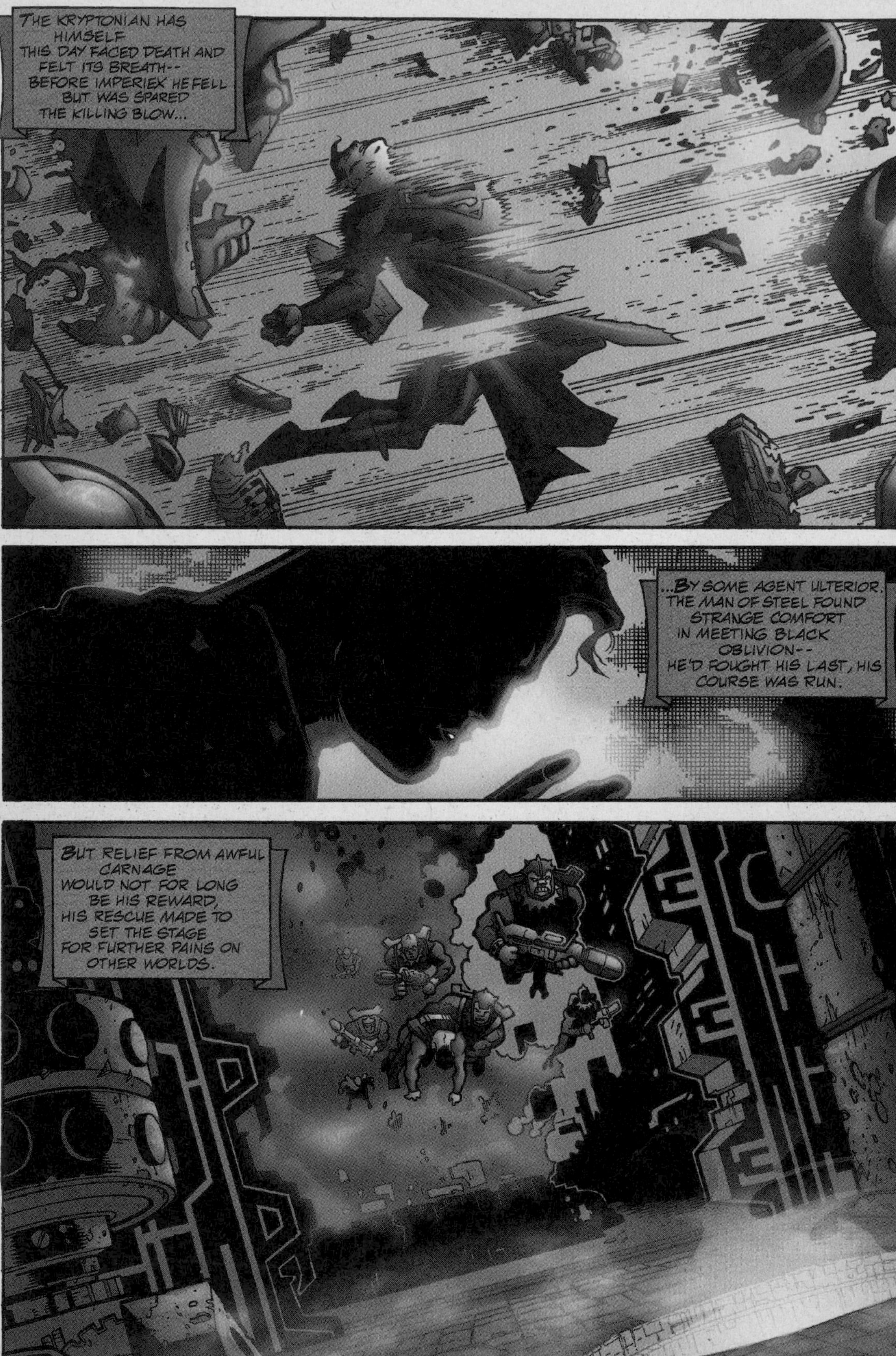
THE KRYPTONIAN HAS HIMSELF THIS DAY FACED DEATH AND FELT ITS BREATH-- BEFORE IMPERIEX HE FELL BUT WAS SPARED THE KILLING BLOW...
...BY SOME AGENT ULTERIOR. THE MAN OF STEEL FOUND STRANGE COMFORT IN MEETING BLACK OBLIVION-- HE'D FOUGHT HIS LAST, HIS COURSE WAS RUN.
BUT RELIEF FROM AWFUL CARNAGE WOULD NOT FOR LONG BE HIS REWARD, HIS RESCUE MADE TO SET THE STAGE FOR FURTHER PAINS ON OTHER WORLDS.

BRAVE THE BATTLE, SKILLED THE COMBAT...
SO MUCH FOR TRUST.
SO MUCH FOR THE ALLIANCE.
I GUESS NOT EVEN THE COMMON DANGER OF UNIVERSAL ANNIHILATION...
THE MAN OF STEEL COULD NOT BE HELD--
...CAN KEEP APOKOLIPS FROM HER TREACHEROUS WAYS!
--BY MINIONS OF A LESSER NATURE--
FWOOOM
NOT SO, ALIEN CUR!
--UNTIL THE FIEND HIMSELF APPEARED.
DARKSEID TRANSPORTED YOU FROM YOUR FATE AT THE HAND OF IMPERIEX'S MATTER COLLAPSE AND ENERGY NULL...
...FOR A HIGHER PURPOSE!

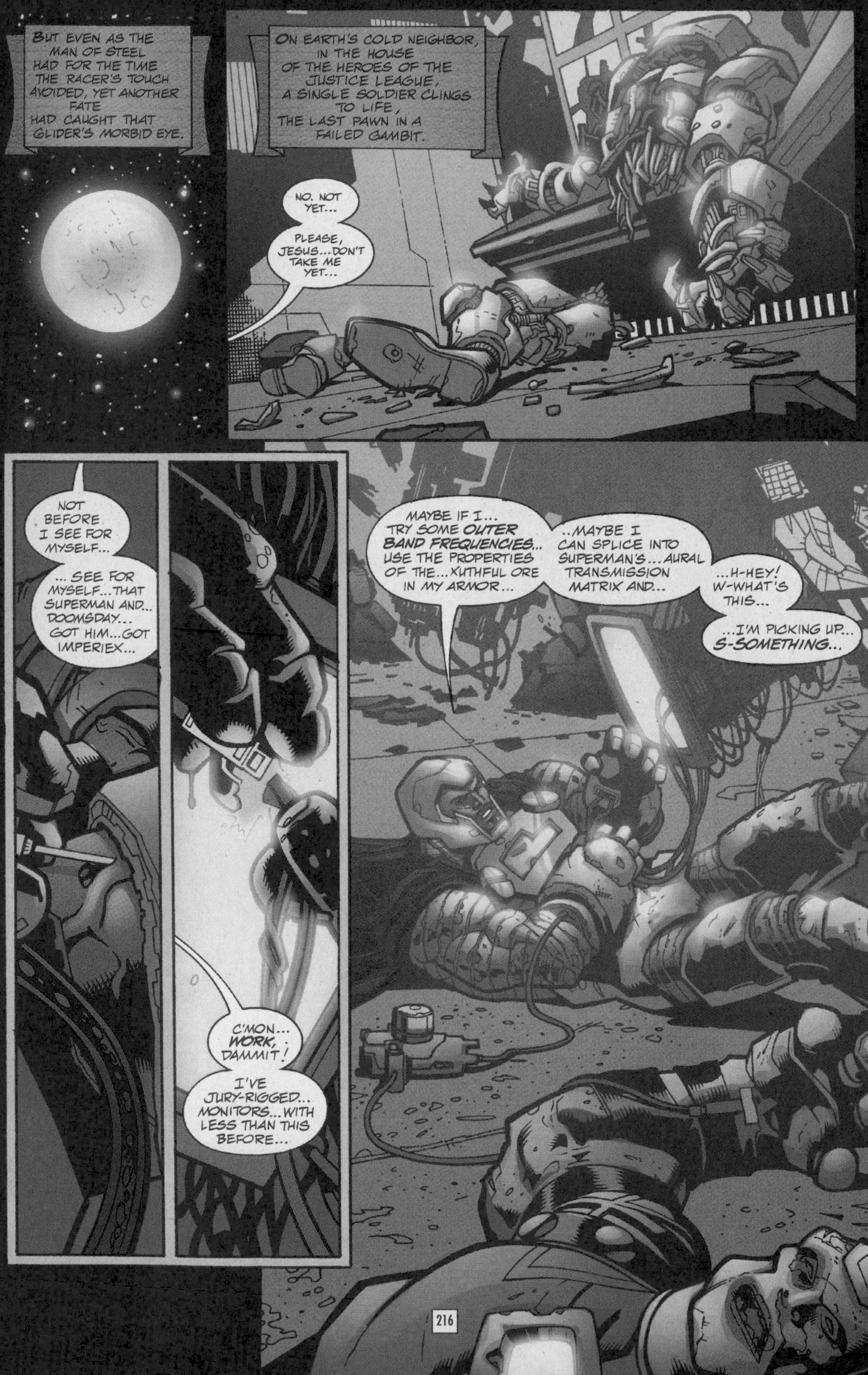

BUT EVEN AS THE MAN OF STEEL HAD FOR THE TIME THE RACER'S TOUCH AVOIDED, YET ANOTHER FATE HAD CAUGHT THAT GLIDER'S MORBID EYE.
ON EARTH'S COLD NEIGHBOR, IN THE HOUSE OF THE HEROES OF THE JUSTICE LEAGUE, A SINGLE SOLDIER CLINGS TO LIFE, THE LAST PAWN IN A FAILED GAMBIT.
NO. NOT YET...
PLEASE, JESUS...DON'T TAKE ME YET...
NOT BEFORE I SEE FOR MYSELF...
... SEE FOR MYSELF...THAT SUPERMAN AND... DOOMSDAY... GOT HIM...GOT IMPERIEX...
C'MON... WORK, DAMMIT!
I'VE JURY-RIGGED... MONITORS...WITH LESS THAN THIS BEFORE...
MAYBE IF I... TRY SOME OUTER BAND FREQUENCIES... USE THE PROPERTIES OF THE...XUTHFUL ORE IN MY ARMOR...
..MAYBE I CAN SPLICE INTO SUPERMAN'S...AURAL TRANSMISSION MATRIX AND...
...H-HEY! W-WHAT'S THIS...
...I'M PICKING UP... S-SOMETHING...

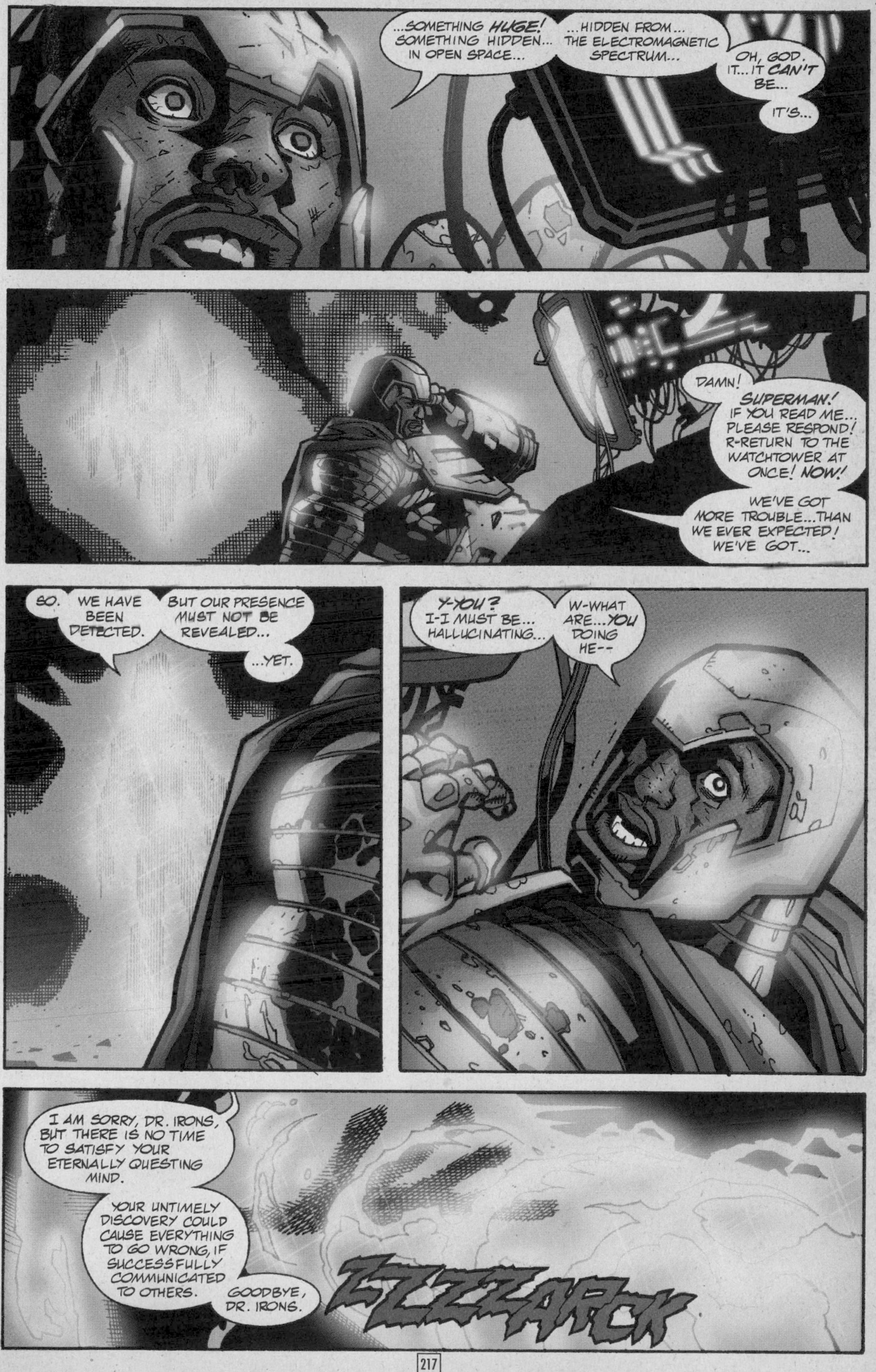

...SOMETHING HUGE! SOMETHING HIDDEN... IN OPEN SPACE...
...HIDDEN FROM... THE ELECTROMAGNETIC SPECTRUM...
OH, GOD. IT... IT CAN'T BE...
IT'S...
DAMN!
SUPERMAN! IF YOU READ ME... PLEASE RESPOND! R-RETURN TO THE WATCHTOWER AT ONCE! NOW!
WE'VE GOT MORE TROUBLE...THAN WE EVER EXPECTED! WE'VE GOT...
SO. WE HAVE BEEN DETECTED.
BUT OUR PRESENCE MUST NOT BE REVEALED...
...YET.
Y-YOU? I-I MUST BE... HALLUCINATING...
W-WHAT ARE...YOU DOING HE--
I AM SORRY, DR. IRONS, BUT THERE IS NO TIME TO SATISFY YOUR ETERNALLY QUESTING MIND.
YOUR UNTIMELY DISCOVERY COULD CAUSE EVERYTHING TO GO WRONG, IF SUCCESSFULLY COMMUNICATED TO OTHERS.
GOODBYE, DR. IRONS.
ZZZZARCK

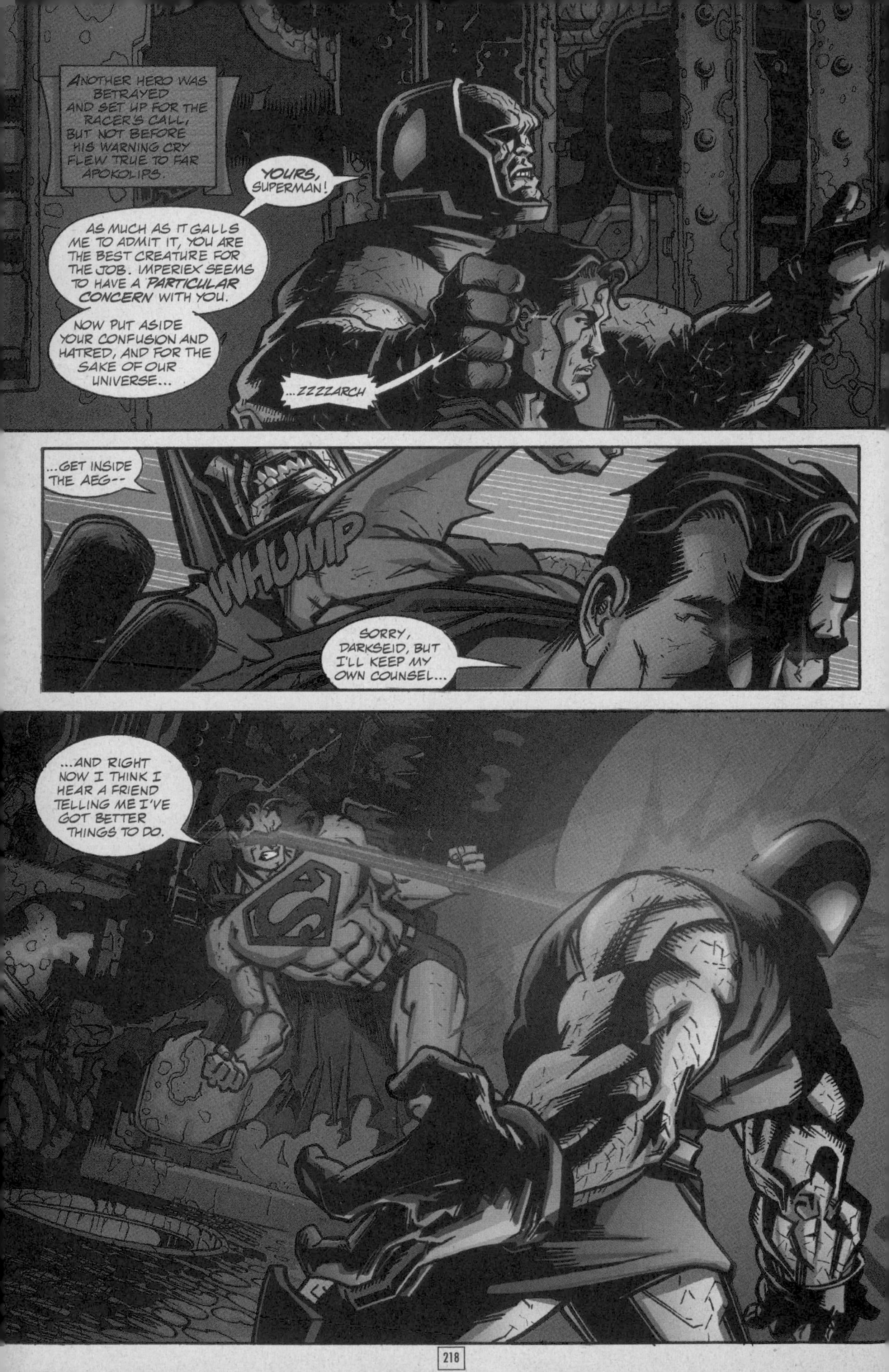
ANOTHER HERO WAS BETRAYED AND SET UP FOR THE RACER'S CALL, BUT NOT BEFORE HIS WARNING CRY FLEW TRUE TO FAR APOKOLIPS.
YOURS, SUPERMAN!
AS MUCH AS IT GALLS ME TO ADMIT IT, YOU ARE THE BEST CREATURE FOR THE JOB. IMPERIEX SEEMS TO HAVE A PARTICULAR CONCERN WITH YOU.
NOW PUT ASIDE YOUR CONFUSION AND HATRED, AND FOR THE SAKE OF OUR UNIVERSE...
...ZZZZARCH
...GET INSIDE THE AEG--
WHUMP
SORRY, DARKSEID, BUT I'LL KEEP MY OWN COUNSEL...
...AND RIGHT NOW I THINK I HEAR A FRIEND TELLING ME I'VE GOT BETTER THINGS TO DO.

FOOL! FOOL!! YOU ARE **NOT** BEING GIVEN A CHOICE! MY UNLEASHED **OMEGA EFFECT** WILL BRING EVEN YOU TO YOUR KNEES!

SHWA-POOOM

OH, NO, DEAR "ALLY."

NOT IF YOUR **ENTROPY AEGIS** IS AS STRONG AS YOU CLAIM...

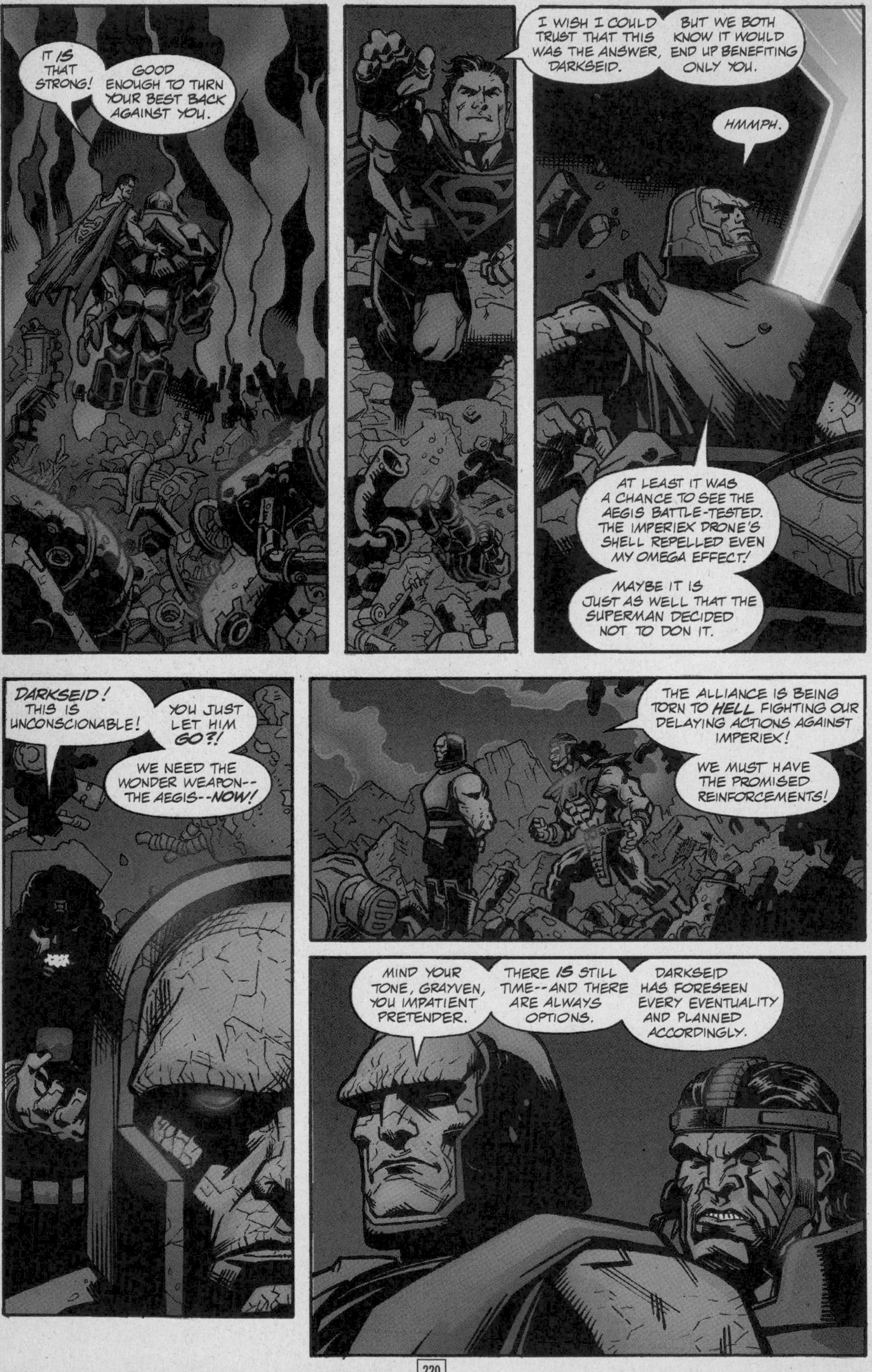
IT IS THAT STRONG!
GOOD ENOUGH TO TURN YOUR BEST BACK AGAINST YOU.
I WISH I COULD TRUST THAT THIS WAS THE ANSWER, DARKSEID.
BUT WE BOTH KNOW IT WOULD END UP BENEFITING ONLY YOU.
HMMPH.
AT LEAST IT WAS A CHANCE TO SEE THE AEGIS BATTLE-TESTED. THE IMPERIEX DRONE'S SHELL REPELLED EVEN MY OMEGA EFFECT!
MAYBE IT IS JUST AS WELL THAT THE SUPERMAN DECIDED NOT TO DON IT.
DARKSEID! THIS IS UNCONSCIONABLE!
YOU JUST LET HIM GO?!
WE NEED THE WONDER WEAPON-- THE AEGIS--NOW!
THE ALLIANCE IS BEING TORN TO HELL FIGHTING OUR DELAYING ACTIONS AGAINST IMPERIEX!
WE MUST HAVE THE PROMISED REINFORCEMENTS!
MIND YOUR TONE, GRAYVEN, YOU IMPATIENT PRETENDER.
THERE IS STILL TIME--AND THERE ARE ALWAYS OPTIONS.
DARKSEID HAS FORESEEN EVERY EVENTUALITY AND PLANNED ACCORDINGLY.

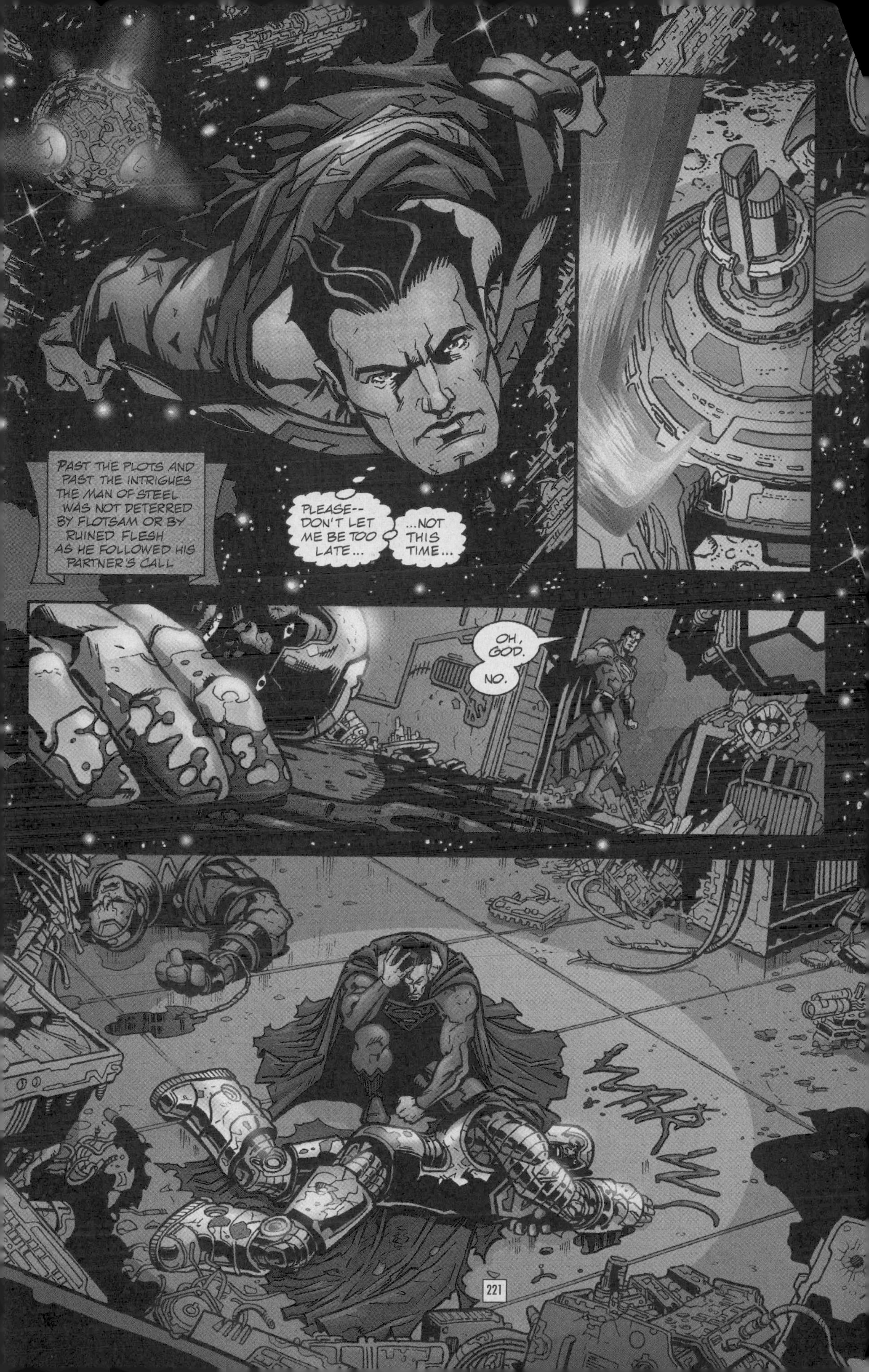
PAST THE PLOTS AND PAST THE INTRIGUES THE MAN OF STEEL WAS NOT DETERRED BY FLOTSAM OR BY RUINED FLESH AS HE FOLLOWED HIS PARTNER'S CALL
PLEASE-- DON'T LET ME BE TOO LATE...
...NOT THIS TIME...
OH, GOD.
NO.
WHAR

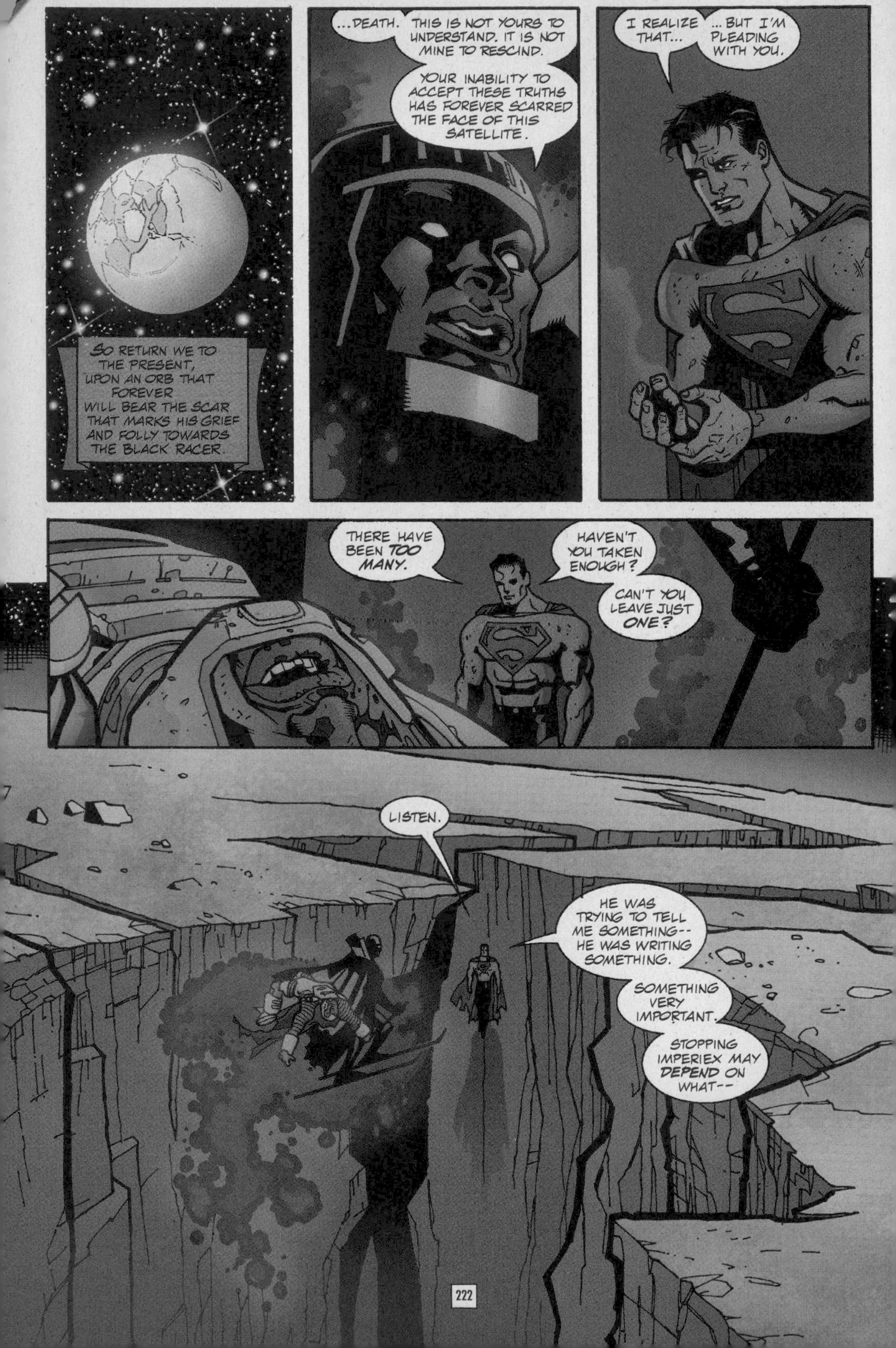

SO RETURN WE TO THE PRESENT, UPON AN ORB THAT FOREVER WILL BEAR THE SCAR THAT MARKS HIS GRIEF AND FOLLY TOWARDS THE BLACK RACER.
...DEATH.
THIS IS NOT YOURS TO UNDERSTAND. IT IS NOT MINE TO RESCIND.
YOUR INABILITY TO ACCEPT THESE TRUTHS HAS FOREVER SCARRED THE FACE OF THIS SATELLITE.
I REALIZE THAT...
...BUT I'M PLEADING WITH YOU.
THERE HAVE BEEN TOO MANY.
HAVEN'T YOU TAKEN ENOUGH?
CAN'T YOU LEAVE JUST ONE?
LISTEN.
HE WAS TRYING TO TELL ME SOMETHING-- HE WAS WRITING SOMETHING.
SOMETHING VERY IMPORTANT.
STOPPING IMPERIEX MAY DEPEND ON WHAT--

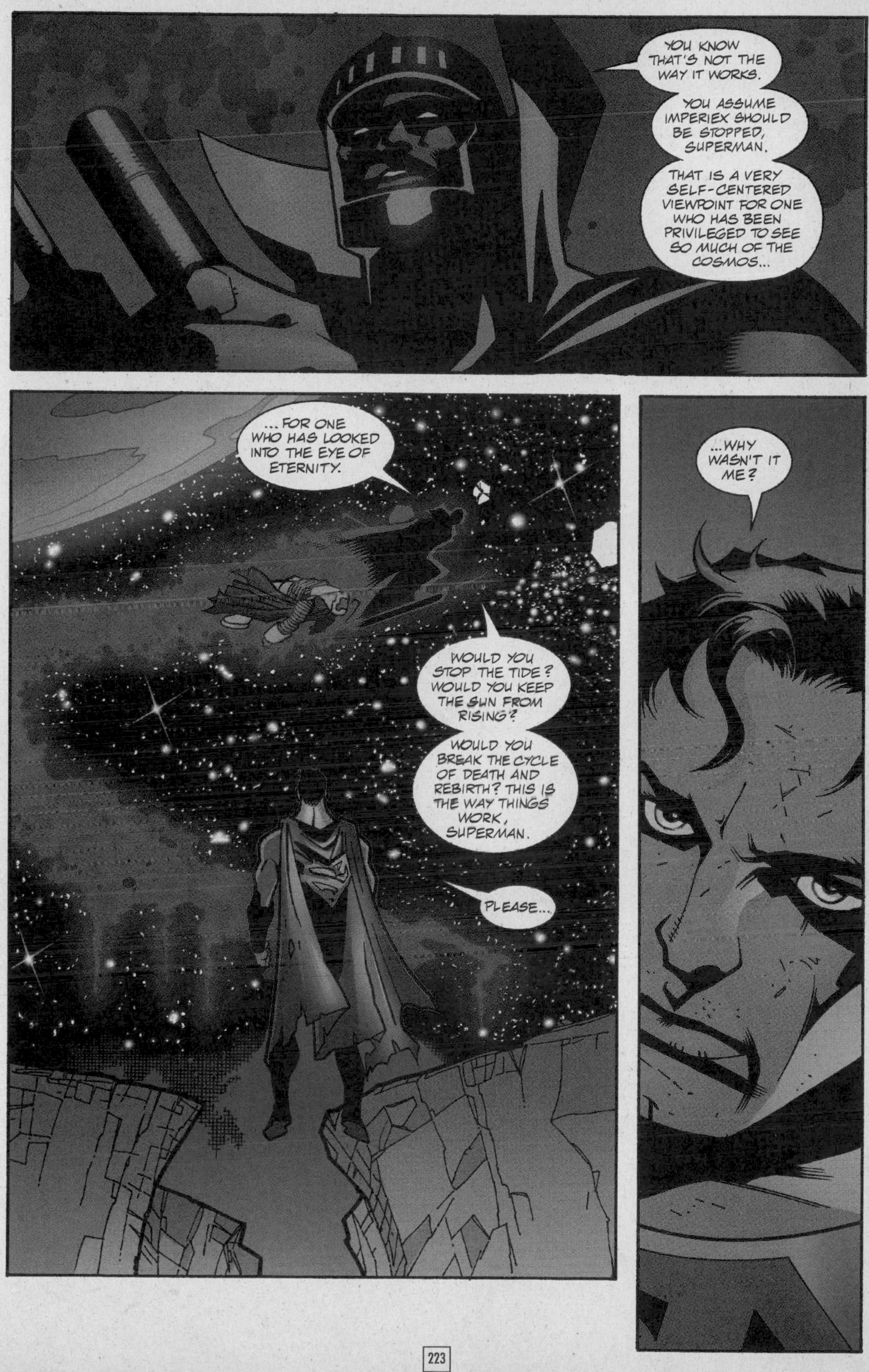
YOU KNOW THAT'S NOT THE WAY IT WORKS.
YOU ASSUME IMPERIEX SHOULD BE STOPPED, SUPERMAN.
THAT IS A VERY SELF-CENTERED VIEWPOINT FOR ONE WHO HAS BEEN PRIVILEGED TO SEE SO MUCH OF THE COSMOS...
...FOR ONE WHO HAS LOOKED INTO THE EYE OF ETERNITY.
WOULD YOU STOP THE TIDE? WOULD YOU KEEP THE SUN FROM RISING?
WOULD YOU BREAK THE CYCLE OF DEATH AND REBIRTH? THIS IS THE WAY THINGS WORK, SUPERMAN.
PLEASE...
...WHY WASN'T IT ME?

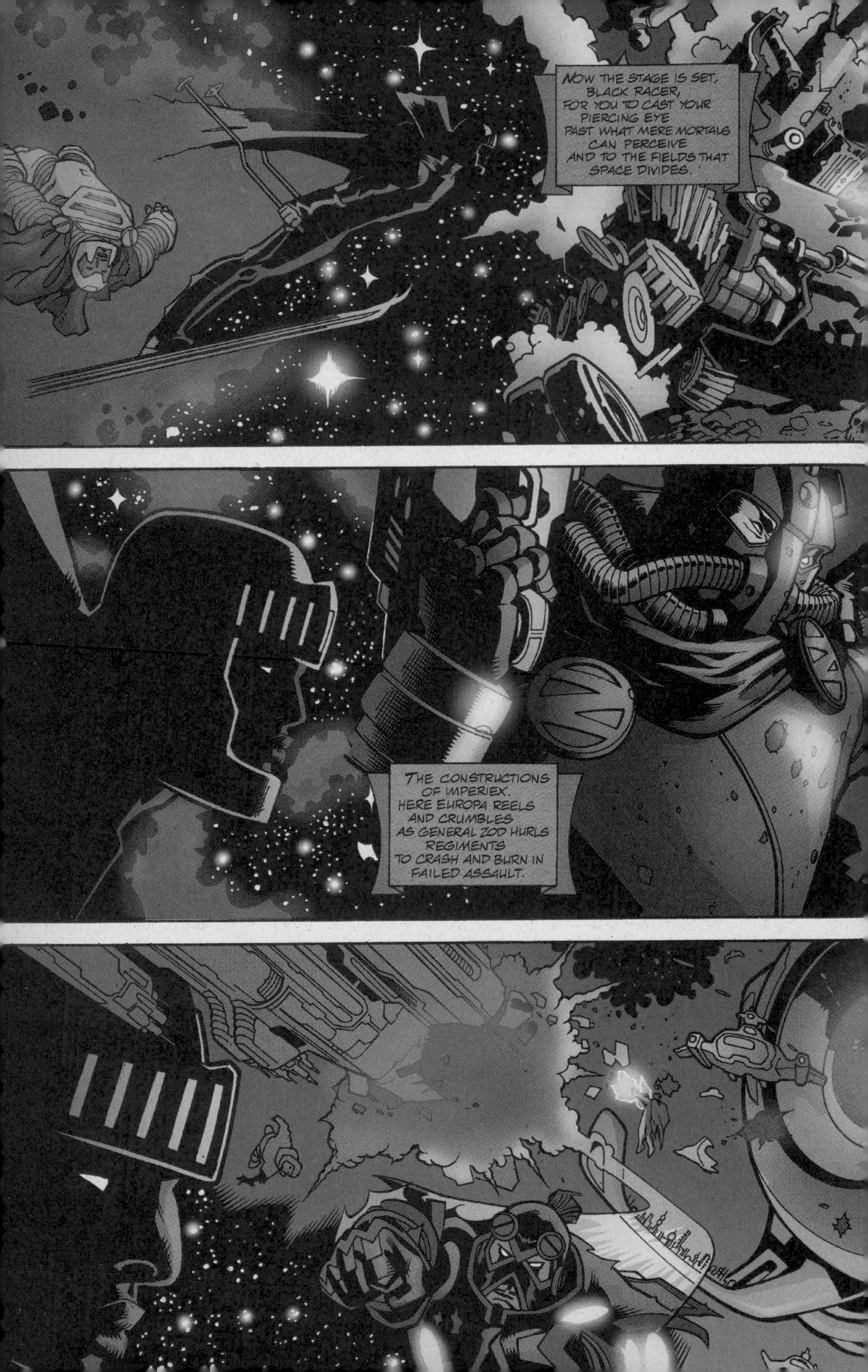
NOW THE STAGE IS SET, BLACK RACER, FOR YOU TO CAST YOUR PIERCING EYE PAST WHAT MERE MORTALS CAN PERCEIVE AND TO THE FIELDS THAT SPACE DIVIDES.
THE CONSTRUCTIONS OF IMPERIEX. HERE EUROPA REELS AND CRUMBLES AS GENERAL ZOD HURLS REGIMENTS TO CRASH AND BURN IN FAILED ASSAULT.

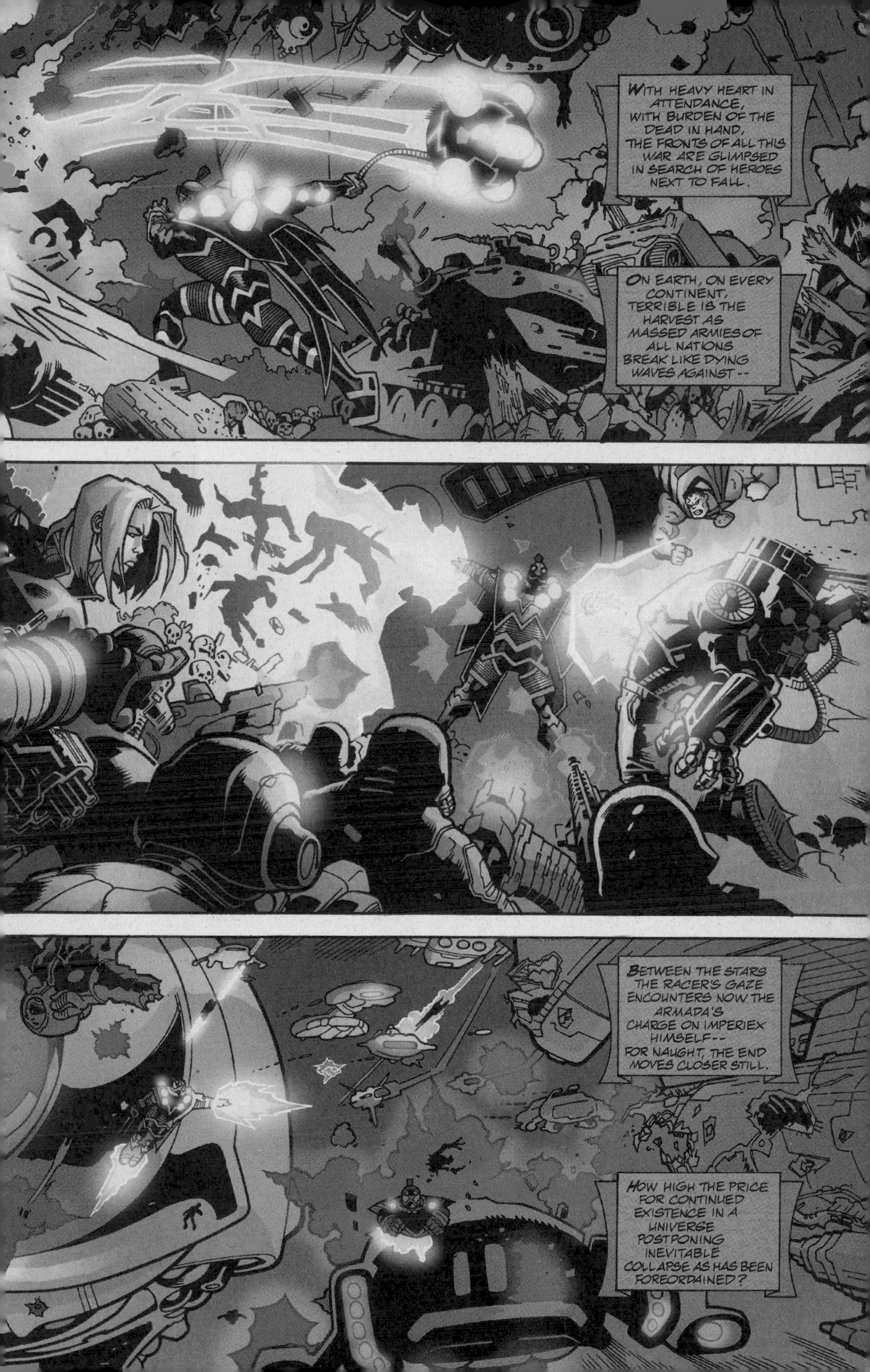
WITH HEAVY HEART IN ATTENDANCE, WITH BURDEN OF THE DEAD IN HAND, THE FRONTS OF ALL THIS WAR ARE GLIMPSED IN SEARCH OF HEROES NEXT TO FALL.
ON EARTH, ON EVERY CONTINENT, TERRIBLE IS THE HARVEST AS MASSED ARMIES OF ALL NATIONS BREAK LIKE DYING WAVES AGAINST --
BETWEEN THE STARS THE RACER'S GAZE ENCOUNTERS NOW THE ARMADA'S CHARGE ON IMPERIEX HIMSELF-- FOR NAUGHT, THE END MOVES CLOSER STILL.
HOW HIGH THE PRICE FOR CONTINUED EXISTENCE IN A UNIVERSE POSTPONING INEVITABLE COLLAPSE AS HAS BEEN FOREORDAINED?

THE DEAD PILE HIGH,
THE REST AWAIT
ATTENTION FROM THE
BLACK RACER.
THE LEGIONS OF THE
DAMNED MARCH ON,
AWARE NO ONE GETS
OUT ALIVE.

AND EVEN THIS THE
RACER SEES:
A CITY KNOWN IN
MEMORY
NOW UNDER SIEGE
AND FAILING FAST
BENEATH IMPERIEX'S
ATTACK.

WITHIN THAT TOWN HIS
MIND'S EYE FINDS
THE FACE OF ONE WHO
GAVE HIS ALL
IN DEFENSE OF WHAT
HE BELIEVED,
REWARDED WITH THE
GRIMMEST ROLE.

A SIMILARITY
PERCEIVED--
THE RACER'S JADED
HEART BEGINS
TO QUICKEN AS
AWAKENED IS
A TOUCH OF LOST
HUMANITY.

226

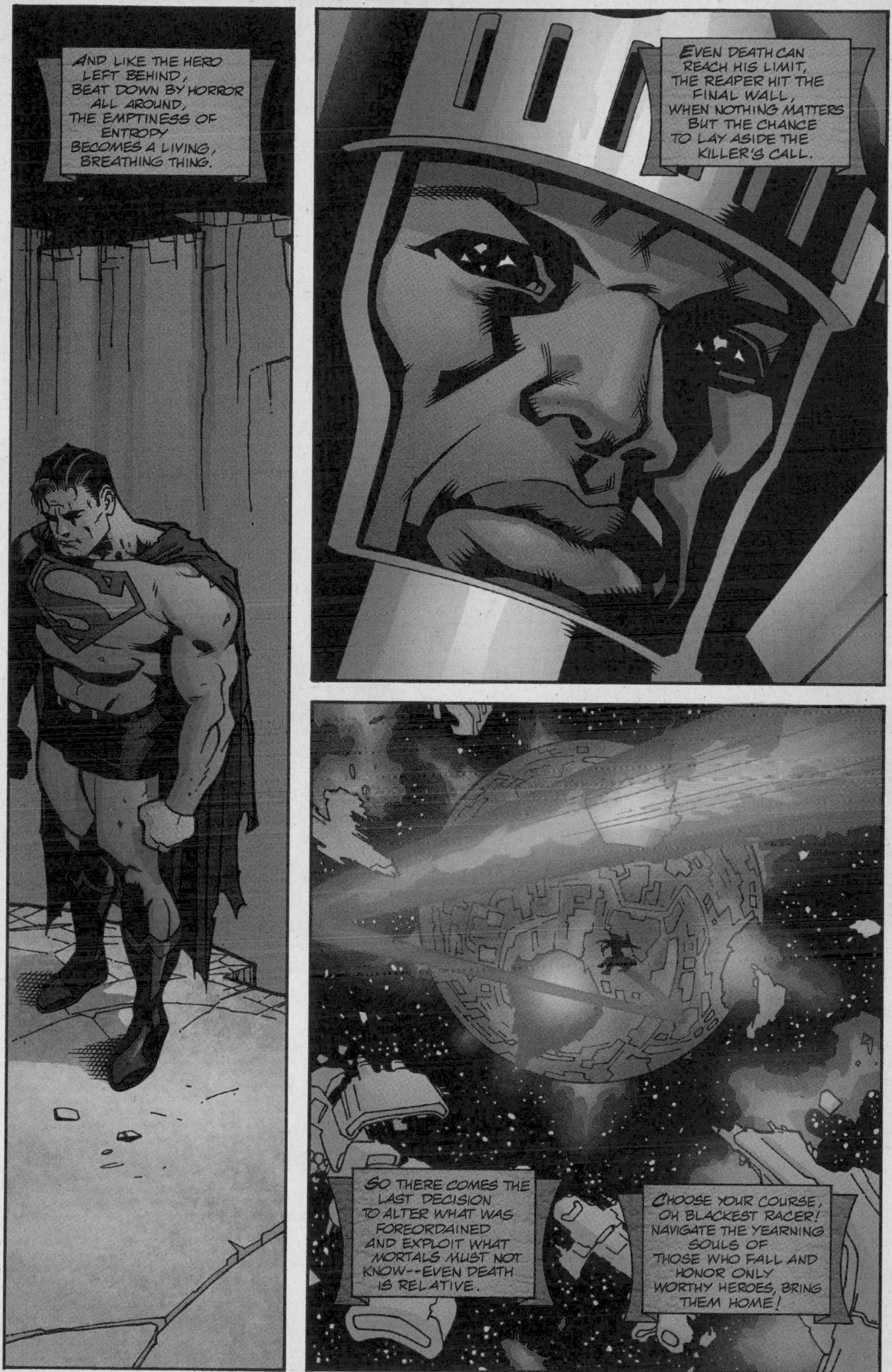
AND LIKE THE HERO LEFT BEHIND, BEAT DOWN BY HORROR ALL AROUND, THE EMPTINESS OF ENTROPY BECOMES A LIVING, BREATHING THING.
EVEN DEATH CAN REACH HIS LIMIT, THE REAPER HIT THE FINAL WALL, WHEN NOTHING MATTERS BUT THE CHANCE TO LAY ASIDE THE KILLER'S CALL.
SO THERE COMES THE LAST DECISION TO ALTER WHAT WAS FOREORDAINED AND EXPLOIT WHAT MORTALS MUST NOT KNOW--EVEN DEATH IS RELATIVE.
CHOOSE YOUR COURSE, OH BLACKEST RACER! NAVIGATE THE YEARNING SOULS OF THOSE WHO FALL AND HONOR ONLY WORTHY HEROES, BRING THEM HOME!

I'M HERE. AFRICA. CLOSEST ONE...
...THE DEVICE HAS ALREADY BROKEN THE CRUST. ENGAGING.
JOHN HENRY IRONS IS DEAD.
ARTHUR IS... I THINK HE'S DEAD TOO.
I... ARE YOU READING? WHAT AM I LOOKING FOR?
DIANA... IF I DIDN'T KNOW WHAT I WAS LOOKING AT... MEAT. MEAT THE COLOR OF RED CLAY.
IS THIS DOING ANYTHING?
JOHN'S HEART RUSTLED LIKE A LEATHER BAG UNDER ITS LAST BEAT.
THERE WAS NOTHING LEFT OF ARTHUR BUT THE SMELL AND A SLICK ON THE WATER. MACKEREL. NO... YELLOWTAIL.
MY PARENTS ARE MISSING.
I DON'T KNOW WHAT I'M DOING, AND I KEEP THINKING I'M FORGETTING SOMETHING.
NOW THERE'S A BUG IN MY EAR.

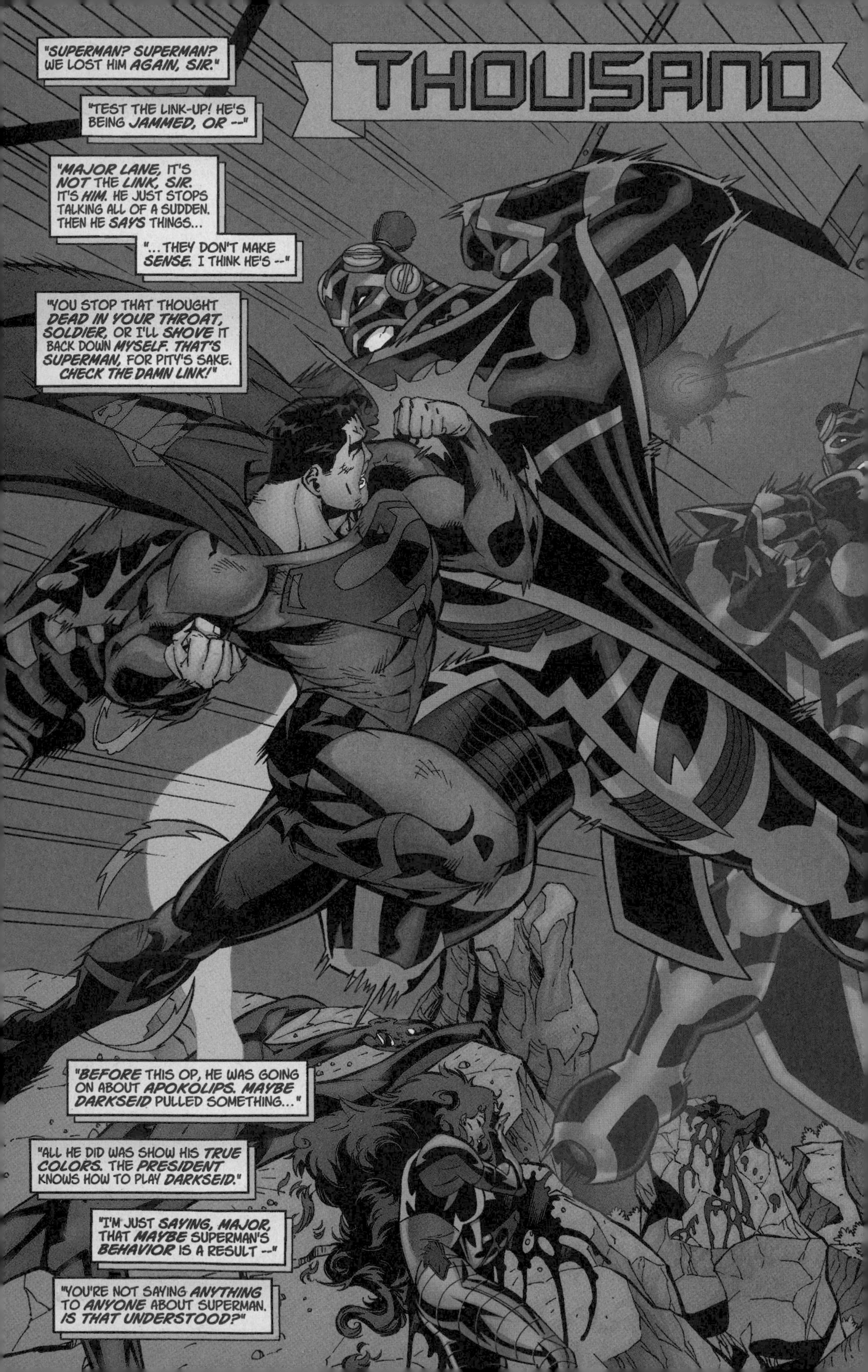
"SUPERMAN? SUPERMAN? WE LOST HIM AGAIN, SIR."
THOUSAND
"TEST THE LINK-UP! HE'S BEING JAMMED, OR --"
"MAJOR LANE, IT'S NOT THE LINK, SIR. IT'S HIM. HE JUST STOPS TALKING ALL OF A SUDDEN. THEN HE SAYS THINGS...
"... THEY DON'T MAKE SENSE. I THINK HE'S --"
"YOU STOP THAT THOUGHT DEAD IN YOUR THROAT, SOLDIER, OR I'LL SHOVE IT BACK DOWN MYSELF. THAT'S SUPERMAN, FOR PITY'S SAKE. CHECK THE DAMN LINK!"
"BEFORE THIS OP, HE WAS GOING ON ABOUT APOKOLIPS. MAYBE DARKSEID PULLED SOMETHING..."
"ALL HE DID WAS SHOW HIS TRUE COLORS. THE PRESIDENT KNOWS HOW TO PLAY DARKSEID."
"I'M JUST SAYING, MAJOR, THAT MAYBE SUPERMAN'S BEHAVIOR IS A RESULT --"
"YOU'RE NOT SAYING ANYTHING TO ANYONE ABOUT SUPERMAN. IS THAT UNDERSTOOD?"

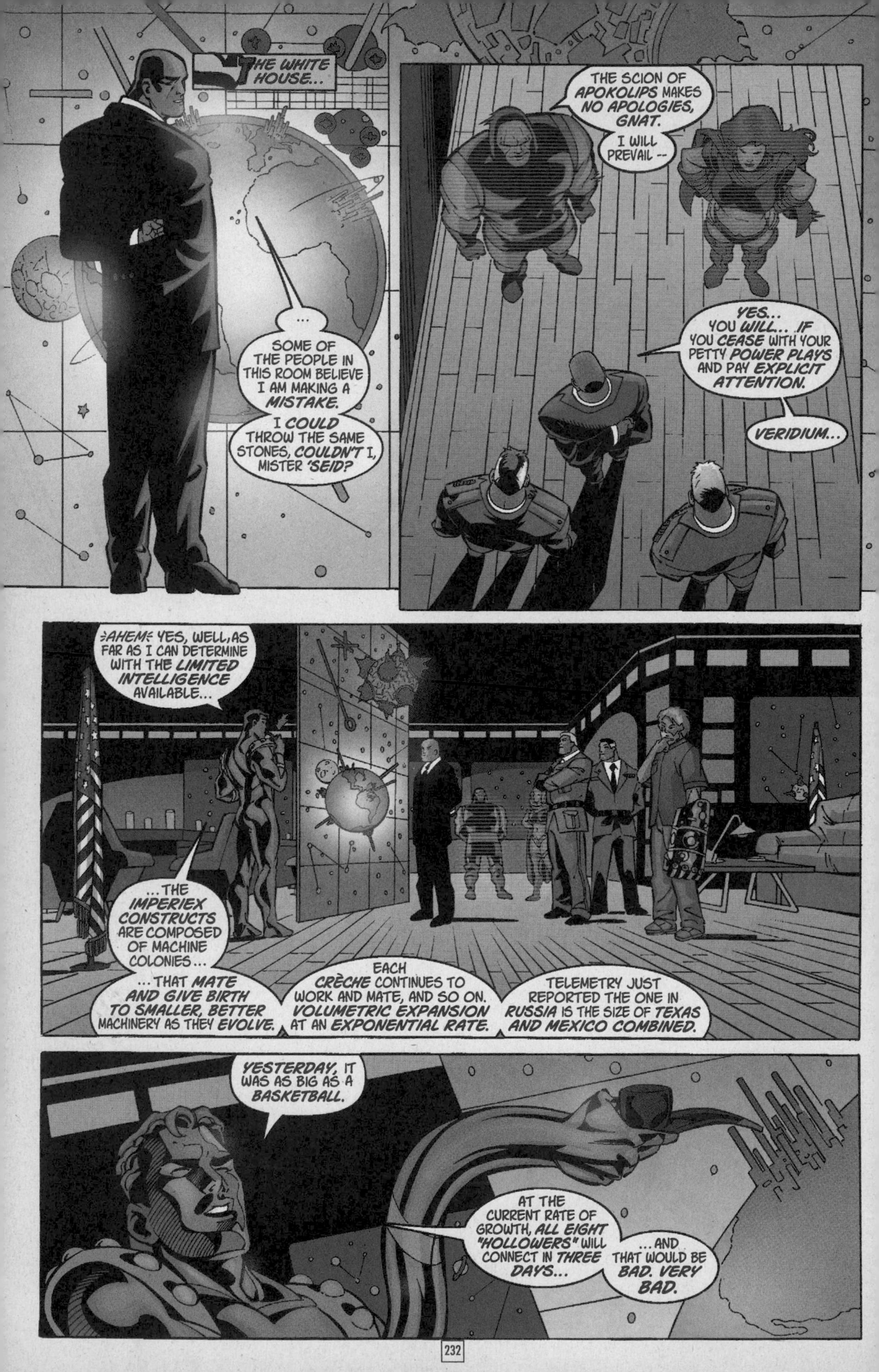
THE WHITE HOUSE...
THE SCION OF APOKOLIPS MAKES NO APOLOGIES, GNAT.
I WILL PREVAIL --
...
SOME OF THE PEOPLE IN THIS ROOM BELIEVE I AM MAKING A MISTAKE.
I COULD THROW THE SAME STONES, COULDN'T I, MISTER 'SEID?
YES... YOU WILL... IF YOU CEASE WITH YOUR PETTY POWER PLAYS AND PAY EXPLICIT ATTENTION.
VERIDIUM...
AHEM YES, WELL, AS FAR AS I CAN DETERMINE WITH THE LIMITED INTELLIGENCE AVAILABLE...
...THE IMPERIEX CONSTRUCTS ARE COMPOSED OF MACHINE COLONIES...
...THAT MATE AND GIVE BIRTH TO SMALLER, BETTER MACHINERY AS THEY EVOLVE.
EACH CRÈCHE CONTINUES TO WORK AND MATE, AND SO ON. VOLUMETRIC EXPANSION AT AN EXPONENTIAL RATE.
TELEMETRY JUST REPORTED THE ONE IN RUSSIA IS THE SIZE OF TEXAS AND MEXICO COMBINED.
YESTERDAY, IT WAS AS BIG AS A BASKETBALL.
AT THE CURRENT RATE OF GROWTH, ALL EIGHT "HOLLOWERS" WILL CONNECT IN THREE DAYS...
...AND THAT WOULD BE BAD. VERY BAD.

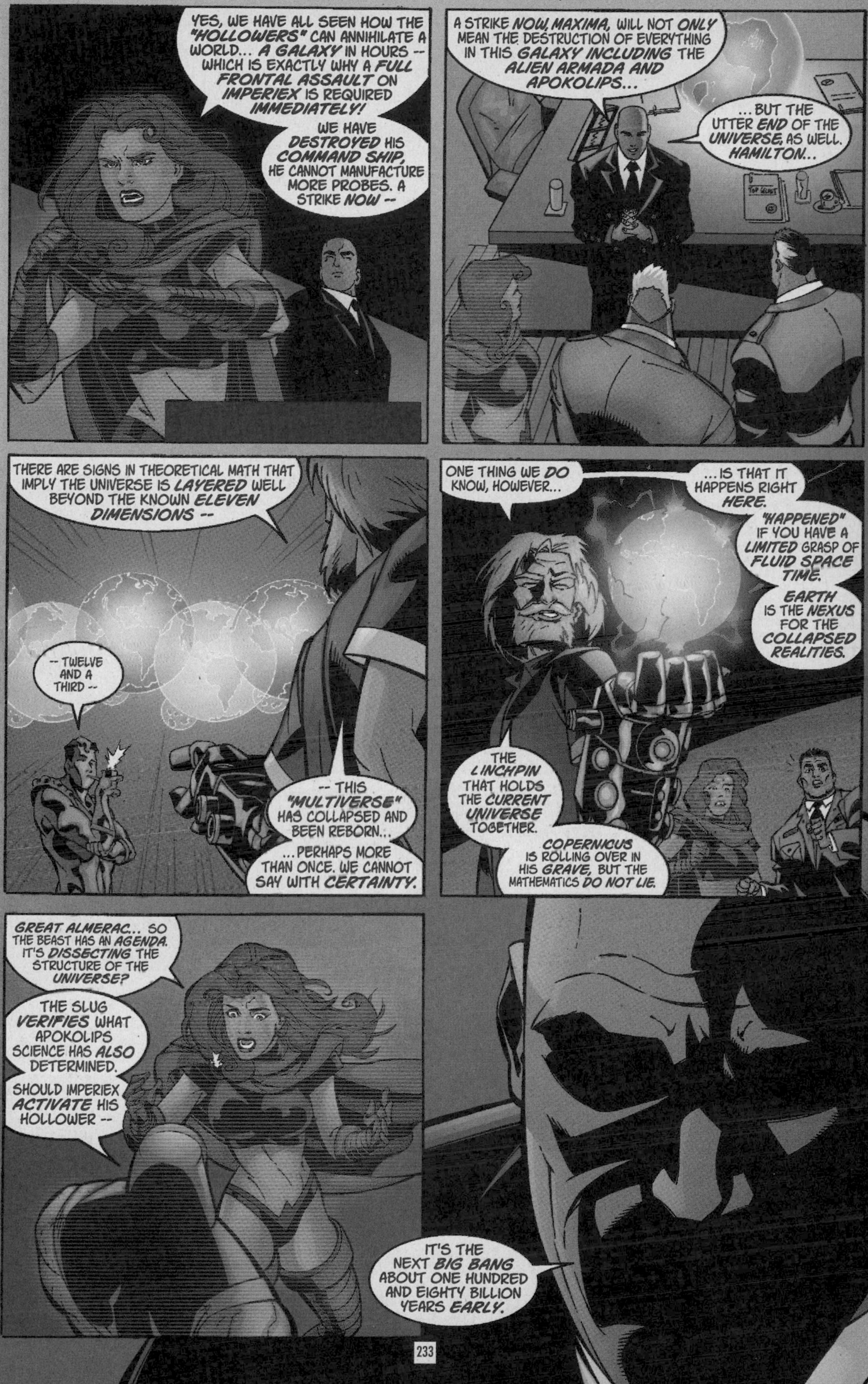

YES, WE HAVE ALL SEEN HOW THE "HOLLOWERS" CAN ANNIHILATE A WORLD... A GALAXY IN HOURS -- WHICH IS EXACTLY WHY A FULL FRONTAL ASSAULT ON IMPERIEX IS REQUIRED IMMEDIATELY!
WE HAVE DESTROYED HIS COMMAND SHIP, HE CANNOT MANUFACTURE MORE PROBES. A STRIKE NOW --
A STRIKE NOW, MAXIMA, WILL NOT ONLY MEAN THE DESTRUCTION OF EVERYTHING IN THIS GALAXY INCLUDING THE ALIEN ARMADA AND APOKOLIPS...
...BUT THE UTTER END OF THE UNIVERSE, AS WELL. HAMILTON...
THERE ARE SIGNS IN THEORETICAL MATH THAT IMPLY THE UNIVERSE IS LAYERED WELL BEYOND THE KNOWN ELEVEN DIMENSIONS --
-- TWELVE AND A THIRD --
-- THIS "MULTIVERSE" HAS COLLAPSED AND BEEN REBORN...
...PERHAPS MORE THAN ONCE. WE CANNOT SAY WITH CERTAINTY.
ONE THING WE DO KNOW, HOWEVER...
...IS THAT IT HAPPENS RIGHT HERE.
"HAPPENED" IF YOU HAVE A LIMITED GRASP OF FLUID SPACE TIME.
EARTH IS THE NEXUS FOR THE COLLAPSED REALITIES.
THE LINCHPIN THAT HOLDS THE CURRENT UNIVERSE TOGETHER.
COPERNICUS IS ROLLING OVER IN HIS GRAVE, BUT THE MATHEMATICS DO NOT LIE.
GREAT ALMERAC... SO THE BEAST HAS AN AGENDA. IT'S DISSECTING THE STRUCTURE OF THE UNIVERSE?
THE SLUG VERIFIES WHAT APOKOLIPS SCIENCE HAS ALSO DETERMINED.
SHOULD IMPERIEX ACTIVATE HIS HOLLOWER --
IT'S THE NEXT BIG BANG ABOUT ONE HUNDRED AND EIGHTY BILLION YEARS EARLY.

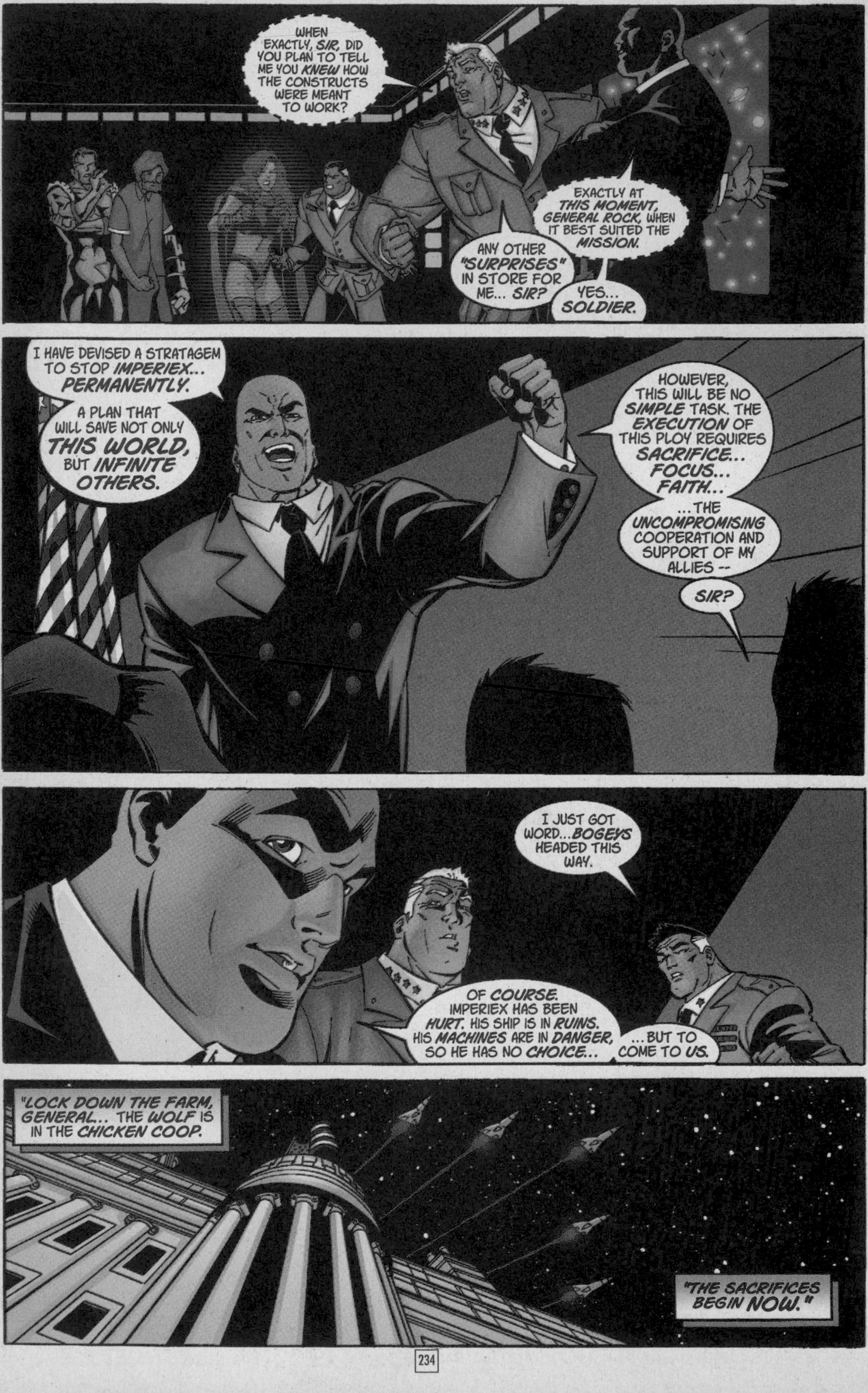
WHEN EXACTLY, SIR, DID YOU PLAN TO TELL ME YOU KNEW HOW THE CONSTRUCTS WERE MEANT TO WORK?
EXACTLY AT THIS MOMENT, GENERAL ROCK, WHEN IT BEST SUITED THE MISSION.
ANY OTHER "SURPRISES" IN STORE FOR ME... SIR?
YES... SOLDIER.
I HAVE DEVISED A STRATAGEM TO STOP IMPERIEX... PERMANENTLY.
A PLAN THAT WILL SAVE NOT ONLY THIS WORLD, BUT INFINITE OTHERS.
HOWEVER, THIS WILL BE NO SIMPLE TASK. THE EXECUTION OF THIS PLOY REQUIRES SACRIFICE... FOCUS... FAITH...
...THE UNCOMPROMISING COOPERATION AND SUPPORT OF MY ALLIES --
SIR?
I JUST GOT WORD...BOGEYS HEADED THIS WAY.
OF COURSE. IMPERIEX HAS BEEN HURT. HIS SHIP IS IN RUINS. HIS MACHINES ARE IN DANGER, SO HE HAS NO CHOICE...
...BUT TO COME TO US.
"LOCK DOWN THE FARM, GENERAL... THE WOLF IS IN THE CHICKEN COOP.
"THE SACRIFICES BEGIN NOW."

MEANWHILE, SPACE...

...WHERE THE BODIES OF FALLEN WARRIORS SEEM TO OUTNUMBER THE STARS.

THE LAST REFUGE OF MILLIONS OF DISPLACED AND WOUNDED, THE PARADOCS...

...BUCKLES UNDER ATTACK!

TWO OF THEM! OH MY GOD!

-- JSA DOWNED THE HOME BASE. WHERE'S HE GOING TO GO --?

-- I NEED NEEDLES THAT PIERCE STEEL --!

-- WHAT CAN I USE FOR VULDARIAN PLASMA --?

WHO'S GOT POWERS?! WEAPONS?!

THEY'VE BREACHED THE HULL. WE'RE GOING TO LOSE OXYGEN UNLESS WE STOP THEM, GREEN LANTERN! WE HAVE TO PROTECT THESE PATIENTS AND --

-- DIANA?

GREAT HERA! NO!

DIANA!

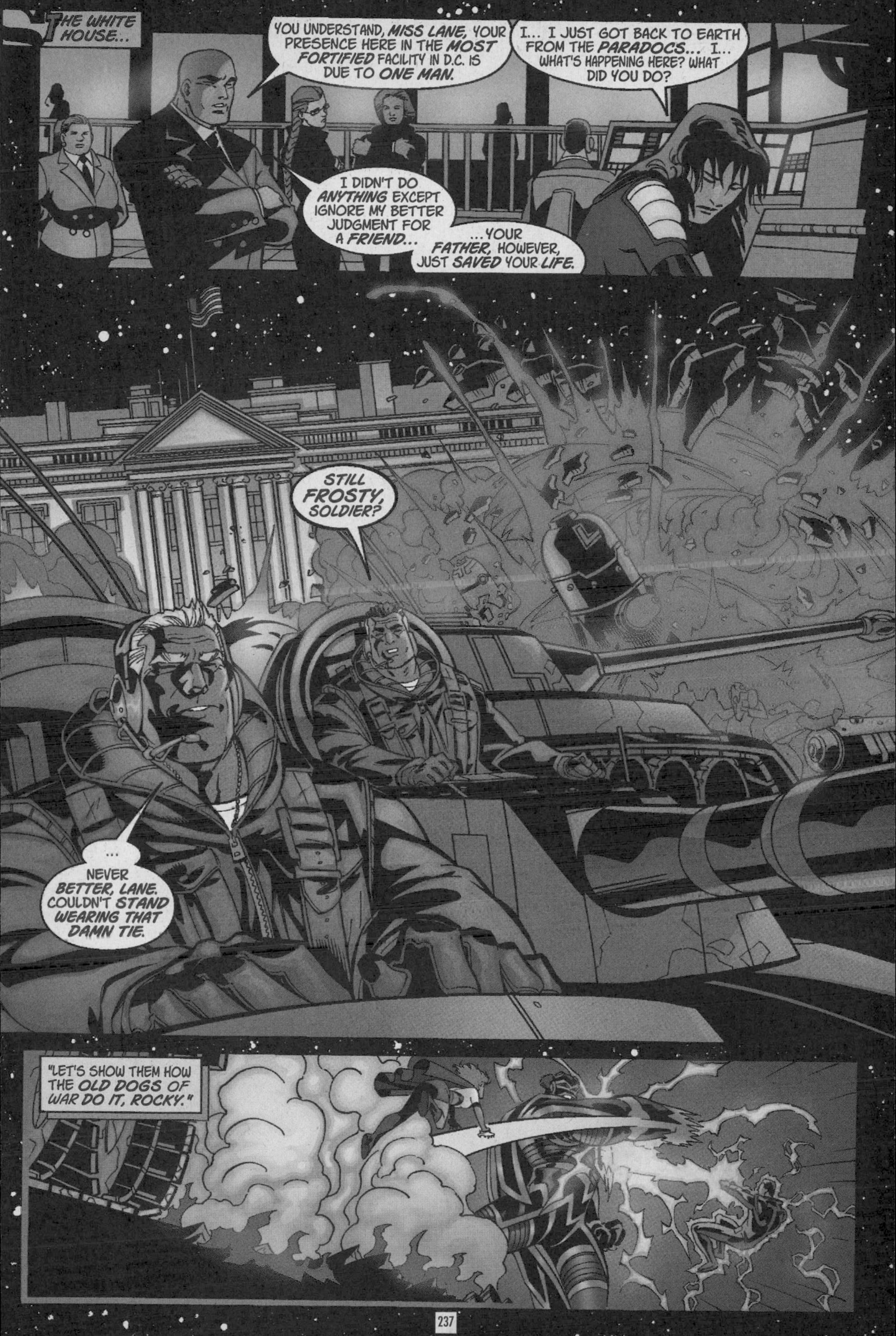
THE WHITE HOUSE...
YOU UNDERSTAND, MISS LANE, YOUR PRESENCE HERE IN THE MOST FORTIFIED FACILITY IN D.C. IS DUE TO ONE MAN.
I... I JUST GOT BACK TO EARTH FROM THE PARADOCS... I... WHAT'S HAPPENING HERE? WHAT DID YOU DO?
I DIDN'T DO ANYTHING EXCEPT IGNORE MY BETTER JUDGMENT FOR A FRIEND...
...YOUR FATHER, HOWEVER, JUST SAVED YOUR LIFE.
STILL FROSTY, SOLDIER?
... NEVER BETTER, LANE. COULDN'T STAND WEARING THAT DAMN TIE.
"LET'S SHOW THEM HOW THE OLD DOGS OF WAR DO IT, ROCKY."

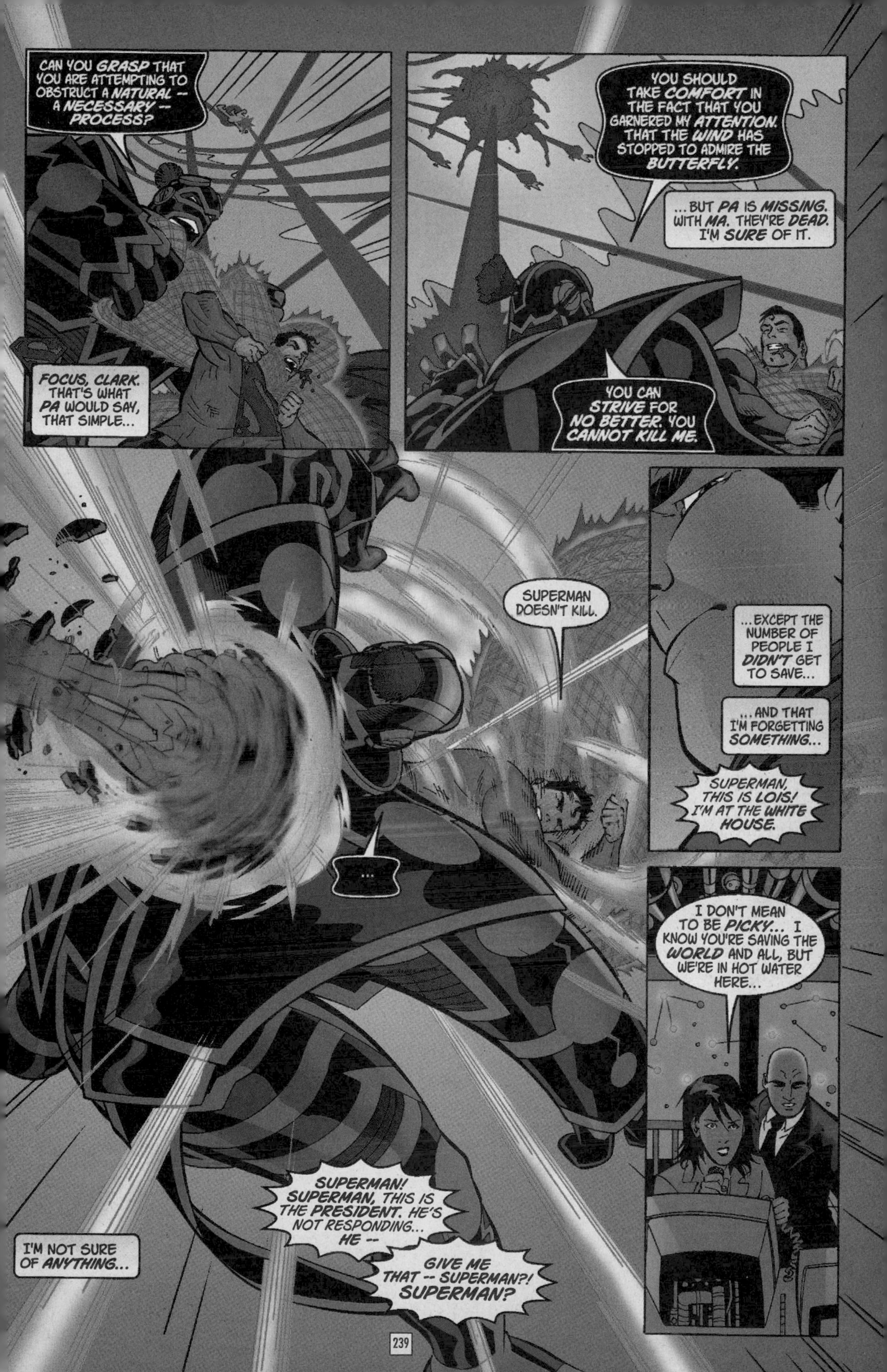
CAN YOU GRASP THAT YOU ARE ATTEMPTING TO OBSTRUCT A NATURAL -- A NECESSARY -- PROCESS?
FOCUS, CLARK. THAT'S WHAT PA WOULD SAY, THAT SIMPLE...
YOU SHOULD TAKE COMFORT IN THE FACT THAT YOU GARNERED MY ATTENTION. THAT THE WIND HAS STOPPED TO ADMIRE THE BUTTERFLY.
...BUT PA IS MISSING. WITH MA. THEY'RE DEAD. I'M SURE OF IT.
YOU CAN STRIVE FOR NO BETTER. YOU CANNOT KILL ME.
SUPERMAN DOESN'T KILL.
...
...EXCEPT THE NUMBER OF PEOPLE I DIDN'T GET TO SAVE...
...AND THAT I'M FORGETTING SOMETHING...
SUPERMAN, THIS IS LOIS! I'M AT THE WHITE HOUSE.
I DON'T MEAN TO BE PICKY... I KNOW YOU'RE SAVING THE WORLD AND ALL, BUT WE'RE IN HOT WATER HERE...
I'M NOT SURE OF ANYTHING...
SUPERMAN! SUPERMAN, THIS IS THE PRESIDENT. HE'S NOT RESPONDING... HE --
GIVE ME THAT -- SUPERMAN?! SUPERMAN?

"PLEASE COME."

COMMAND, I'M HITTING IT WITH *EVERYTHING* I HAVE AND --

NOT *DIANA*... NOT HER *TOO*...

LUTHOR'S ARMAMENTS ARE WORKING, SLOWLY. THEY NEED MORE TIME... MORE POWER...

I CAN'T DO THIS ANYMORE...

DON'T *HAVE* IT. WON'T *GET* IT. BUT THERE *MIGHT* BE SOMETHING -- IT IS *NUCLEAR*, ISN'T IT? THE *ENGINE* IN THIS *HEAP?*

Y-YES, BUT --

SOMEONE *CRACK* THIS THING! I JUST NEED IT *CRACKED* AND I CAN...

I CAN'T...

THAT THING DOES NOT GET PAST US. UNDERSTAND? IT DOES NOT PASS US!

LIGHTNING! LISTEN TO ME --!

GET AWAY FROM HER!

MAJOR LANE! **THAT'S SUICIDE!** FALL BACK! THERE'S NO GUARANTEE...

...SAM, I DON'T EVEN KNOW IF I CAN --

HNNGH!

DO IT SAM! DO IT, **DAMN** YOU!

IT'S FIFTY YARDS FROM THE **PRESIDENT,** SON! YOU CAN AND YOU WILL! BUT YOU -- YOU WILL!

I'M SO LOST.

PLEASE, GOD... TELL ME WHAT TO DO. TELL ME HOW TO *FIGHT ON.*

THANK YOU, SON... ...THANK YOU!

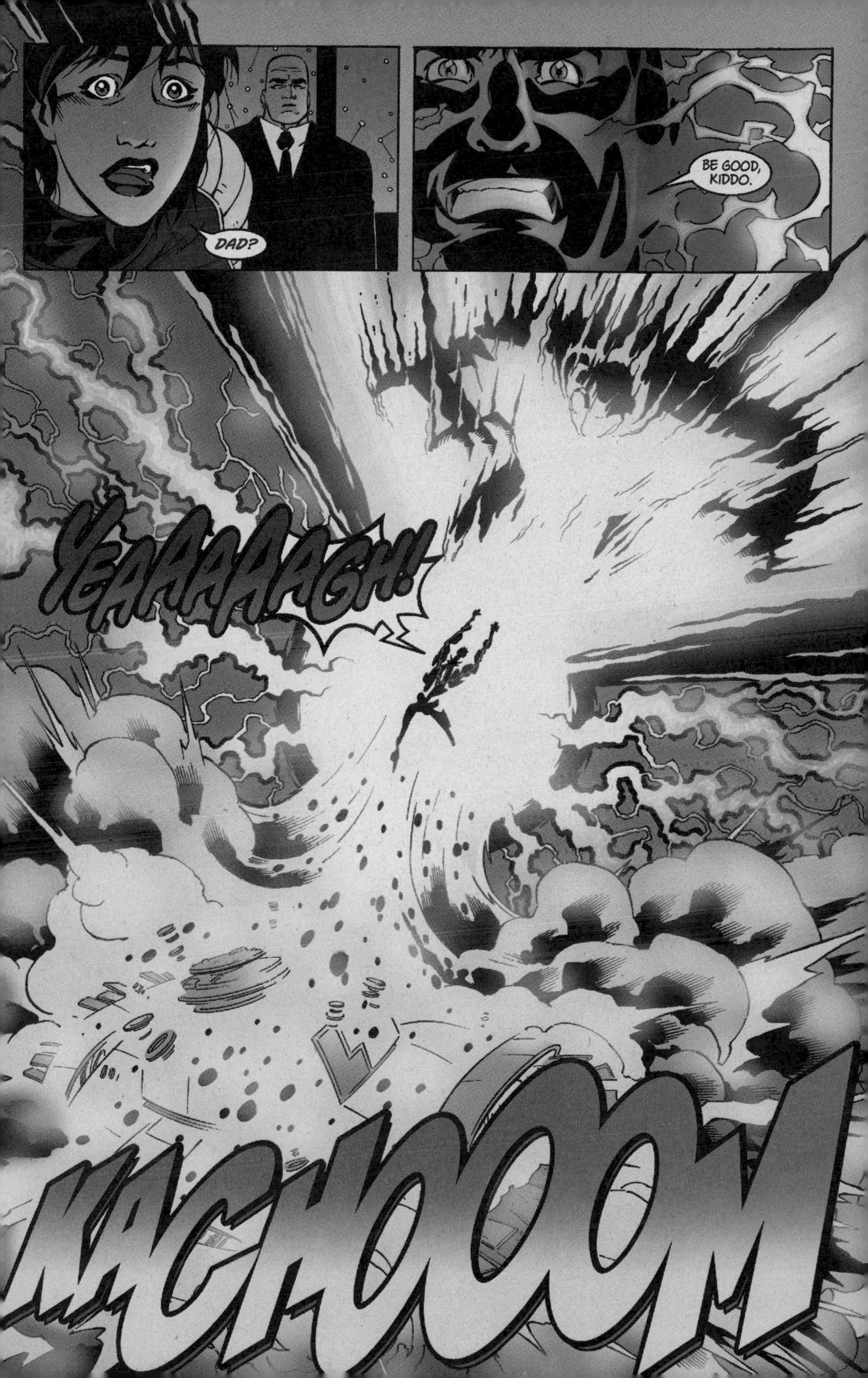
DAD?
BE GOOD, KIDDO.
YEAAAAAAGH!
KACHOOOM

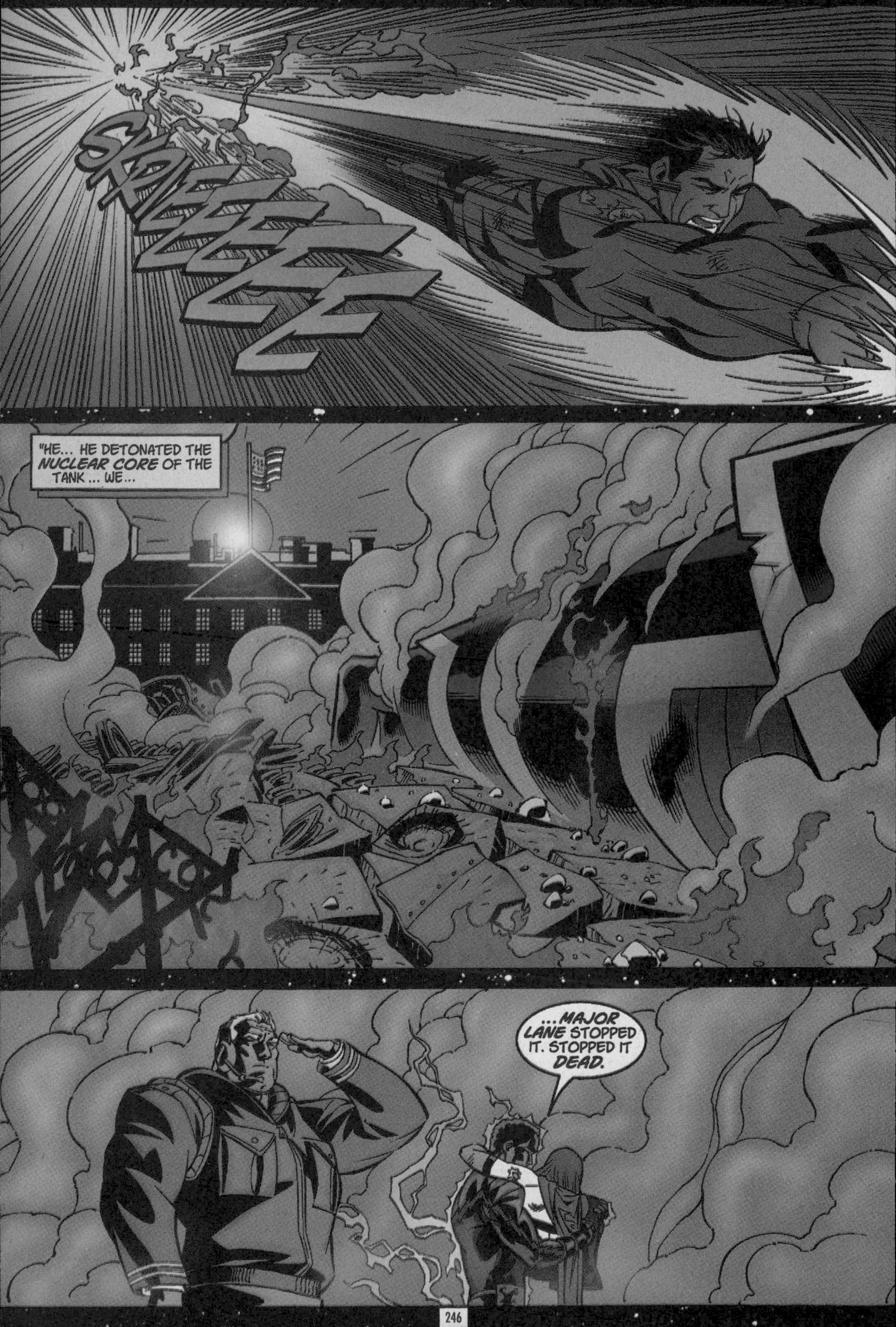
SKREEEEEEE
"HE... HE DETONATED THE NUCLEAR CORE OF THE TANK ... WE...
...MAJOR LANE STOPPED IT. STOPPED IT DEAD.

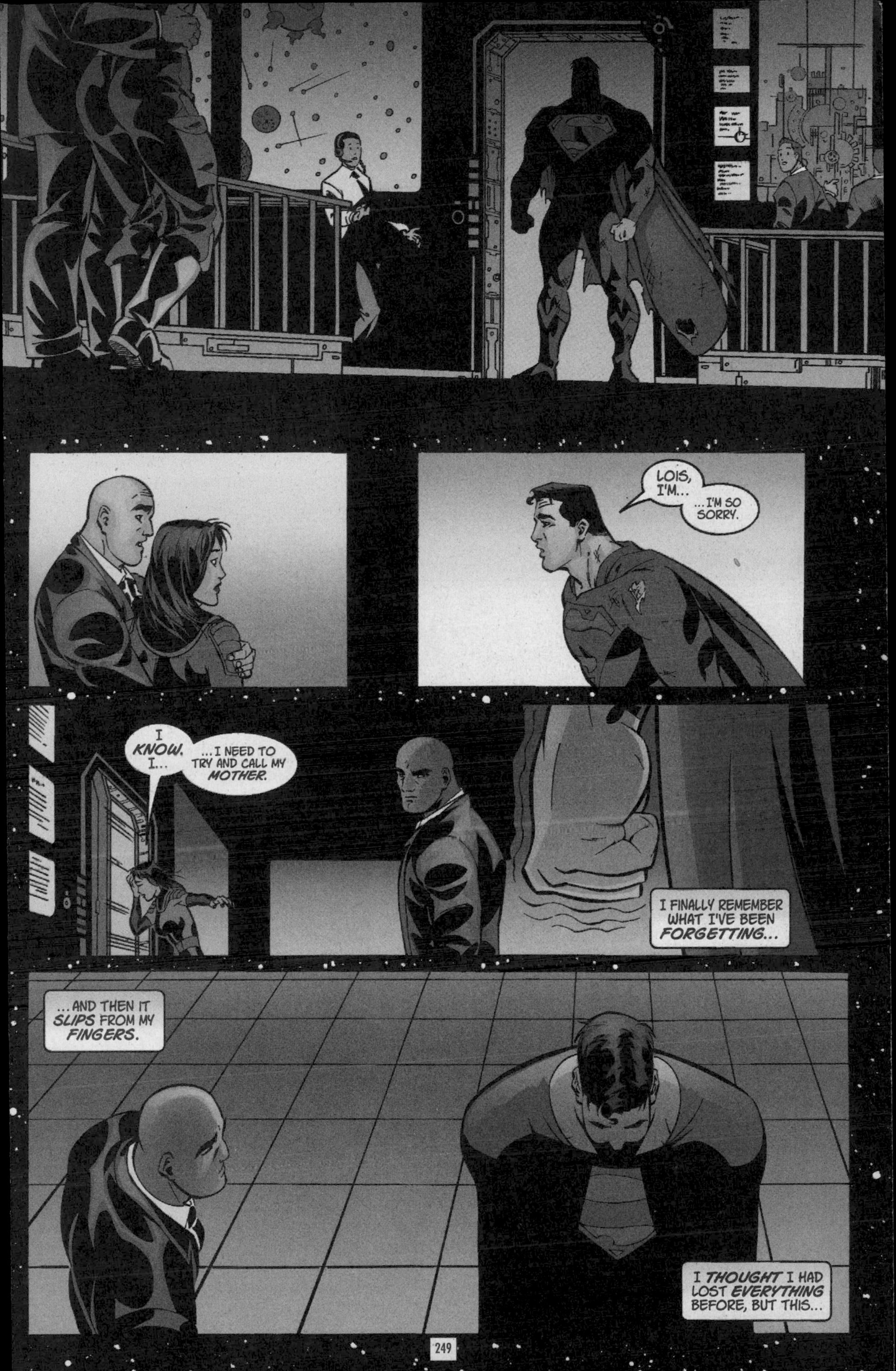
LOIS, I'M...
...I'M SO SORRY.
I KNOW. I...
...I NEED TO TRY AND CALL MY MOTHER.
I FINALLY REMEMBER WHAT I'VE BEEN FORGETTING...
...AND THEN IT SLIPS FROM MY FINGERS.
I THOUGHT I HAD LOST EVERYTHING BEFORE, BUT THIS...

COVER
GALLERY

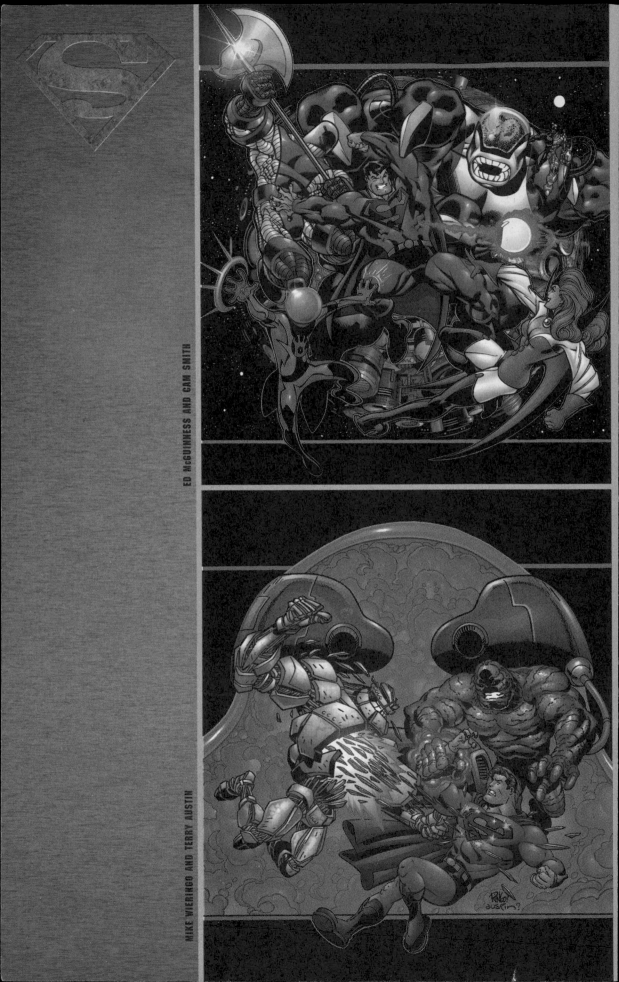

ED McGUINNESS AND CAM SMITH

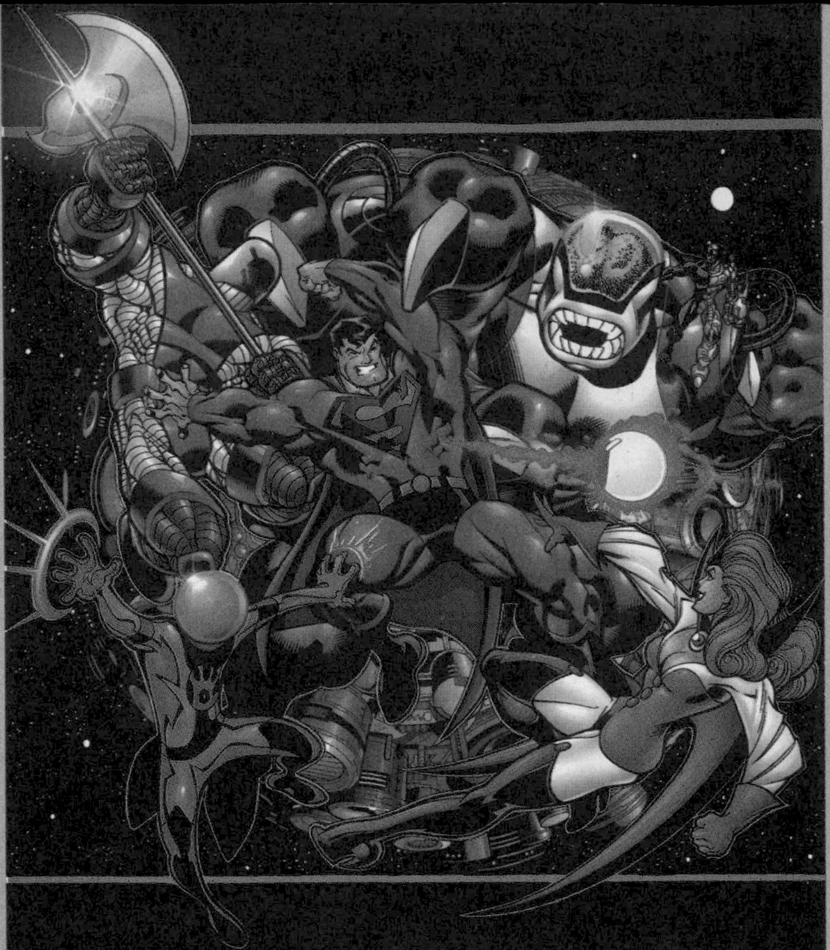

MIKE WIERINGO AND TERRY AUSTIN

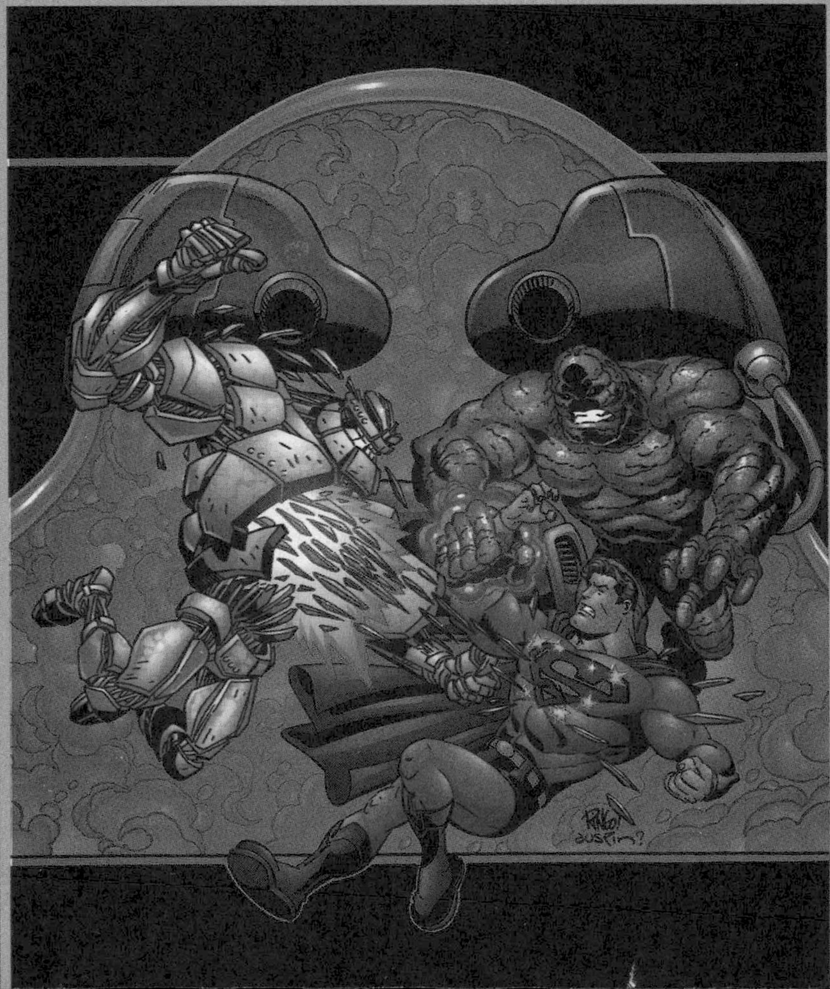

ED McGUINNESS AND CAM SMITH

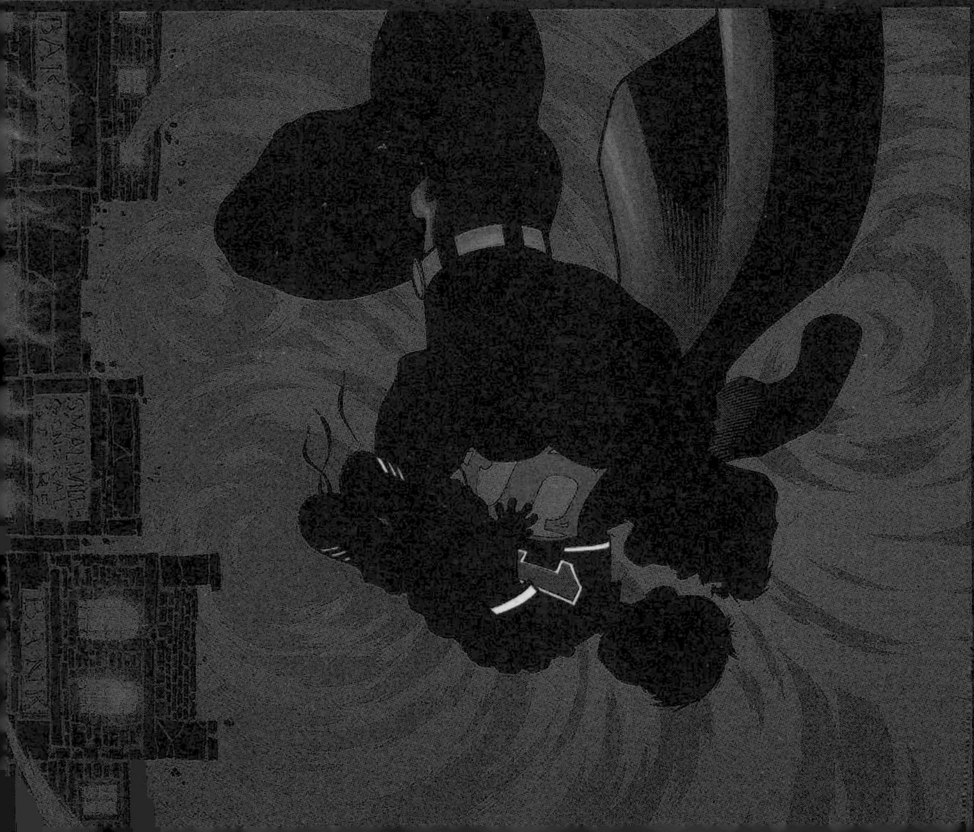
BAKERY
BANK

LEONARD KIRK AND ROBIN RIGGS

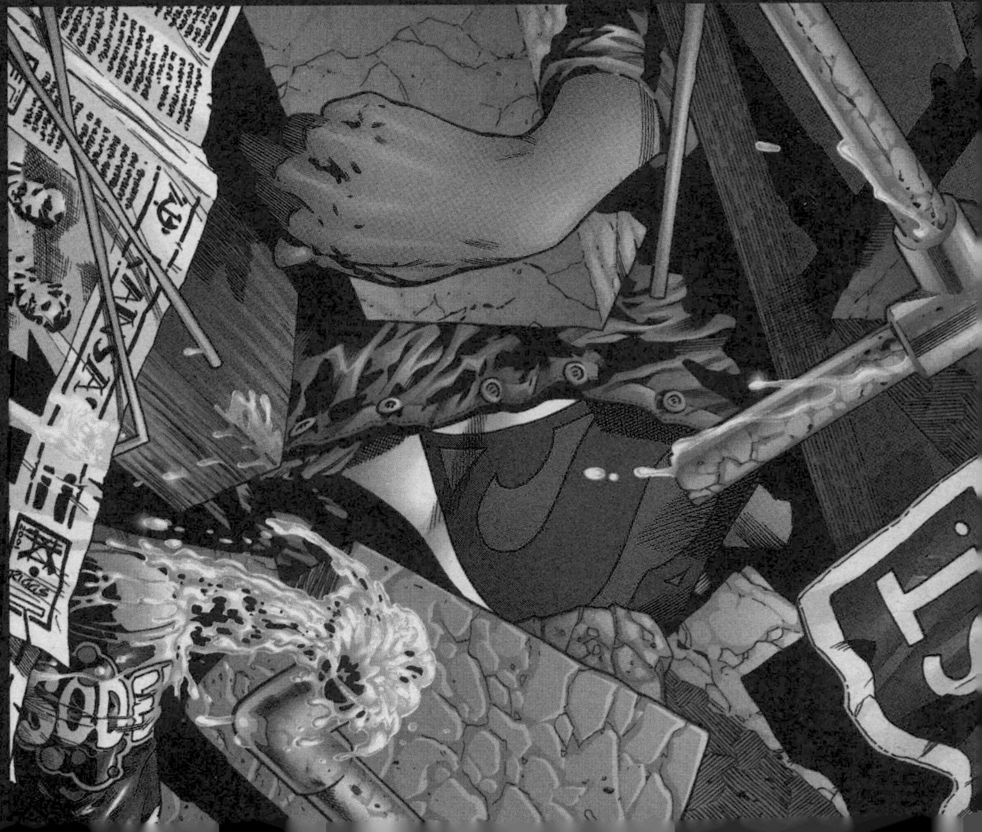

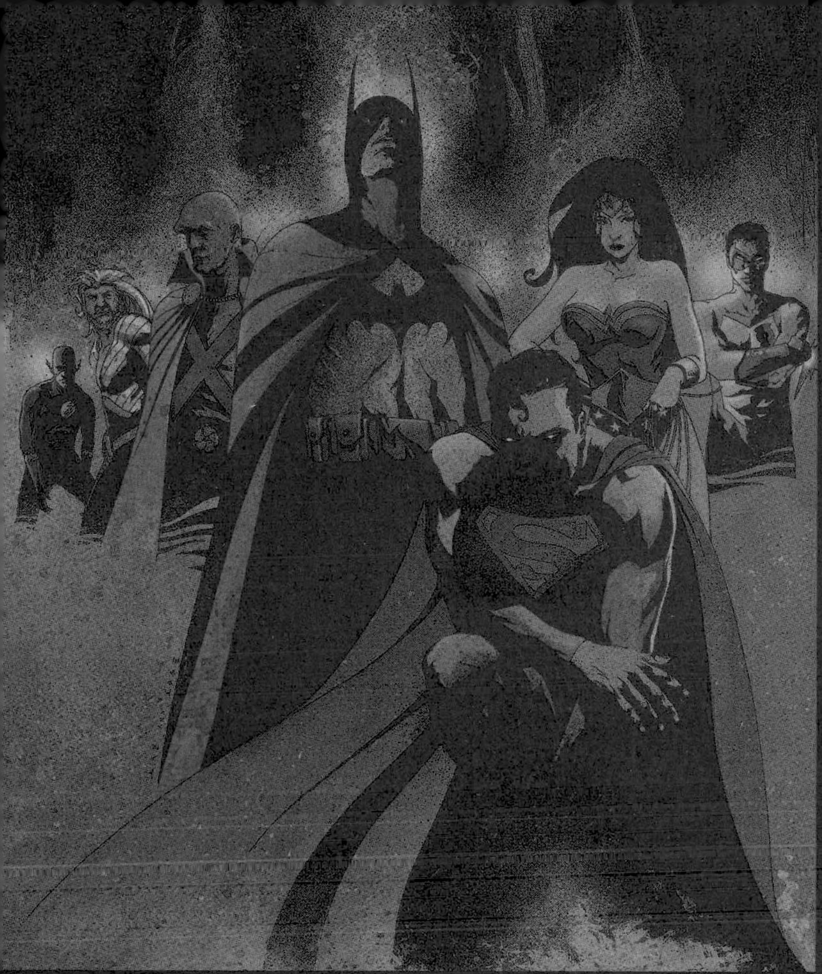

JAE LEE

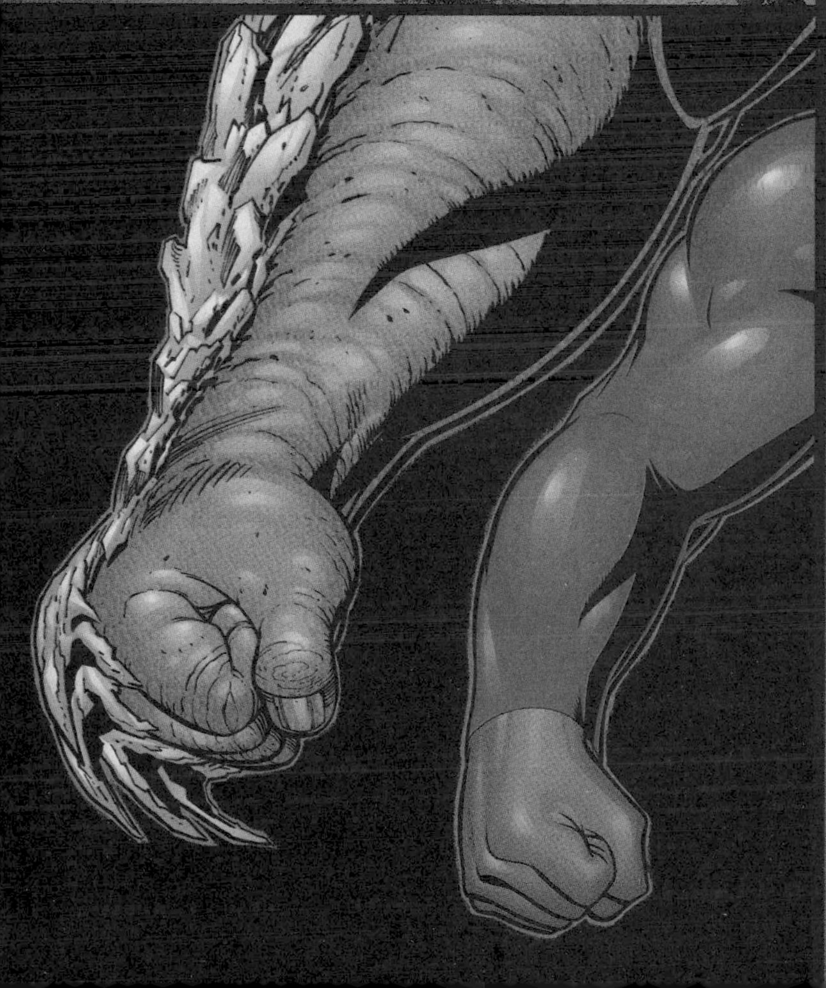

MIKE WIERINGO AND JOSÉ MARZÁN, JR.

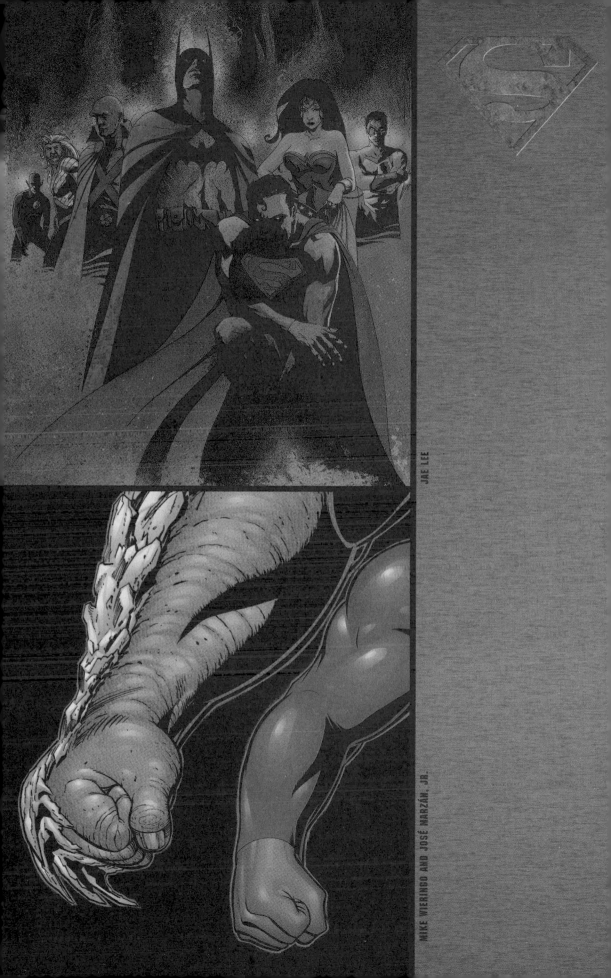

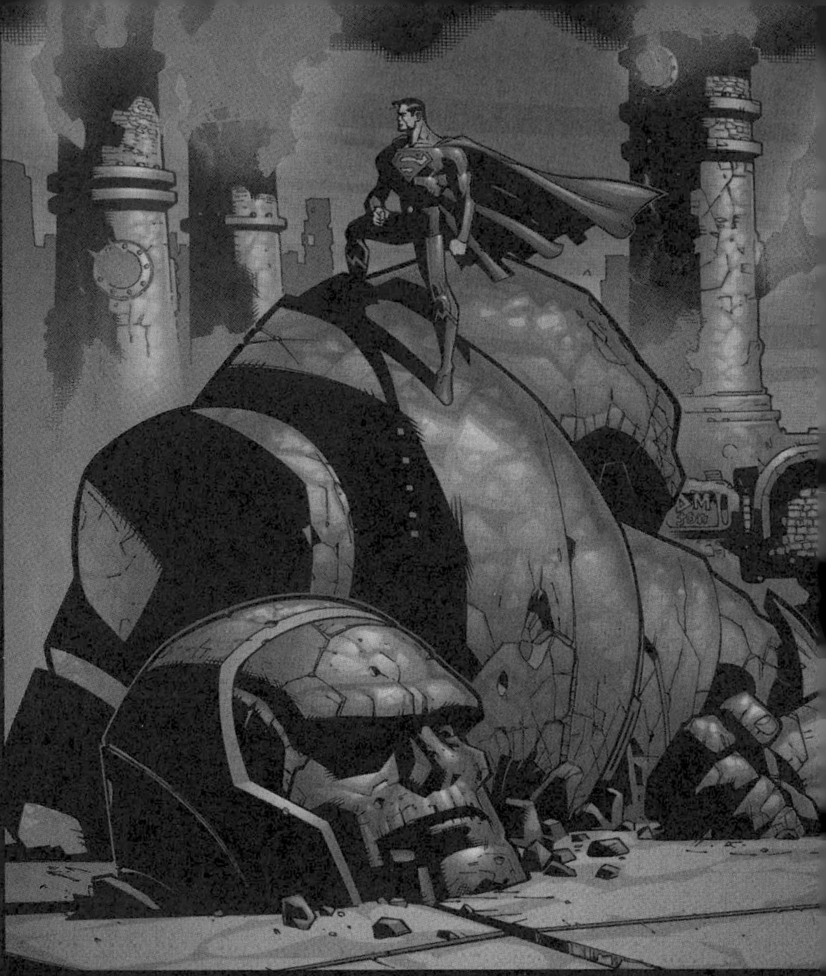

DOUG MAHNKE AND TOM NGUYEN

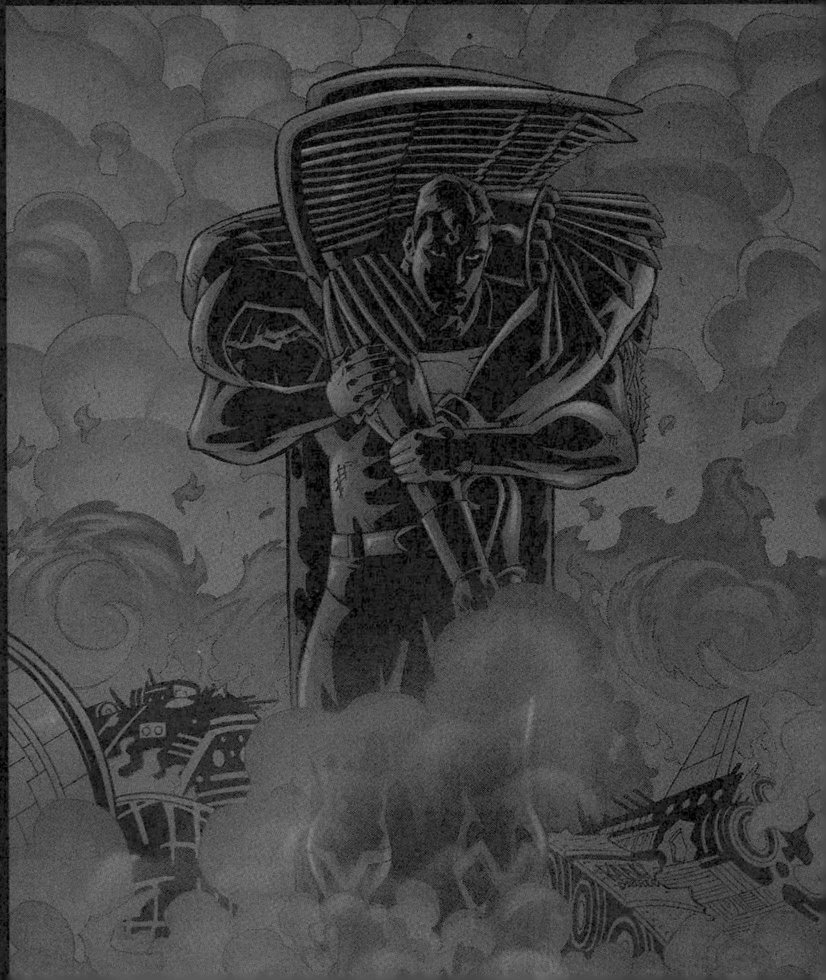

KANO AND MARLO ALQUIZA

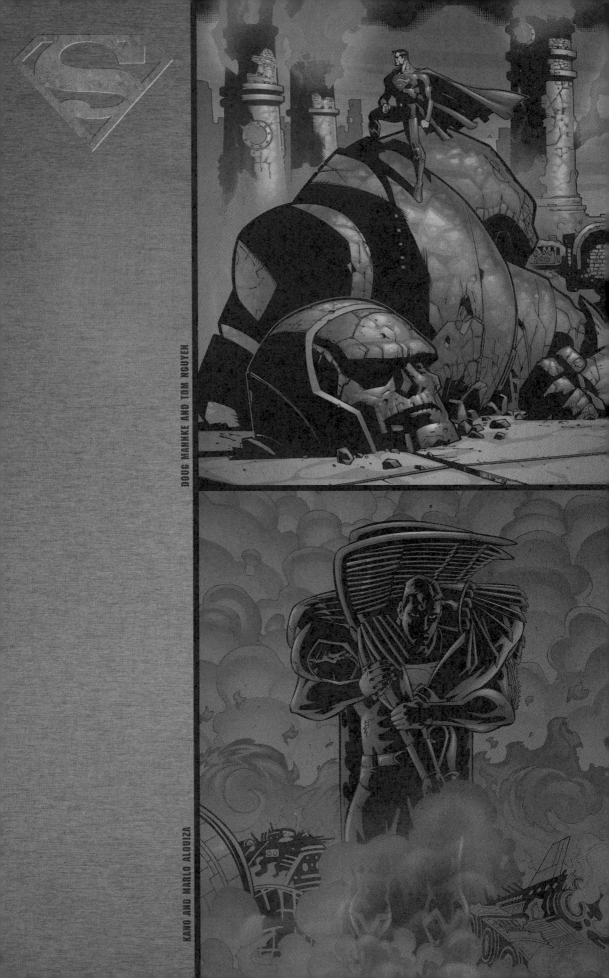

THE ART OF WAR

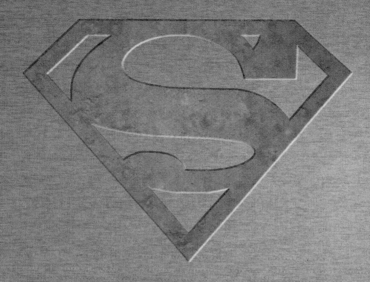

LEXCORP'S FLYING TANKS

Any rumors of Flying Saucers in recent months could have been due to early field tests of LexCorp's FLYING TANKS. With its speed and maneuverability while hovering — as well as a turret that spins 360 degrees — this land vehicle is light-years ahead of any conventional armored tank. These tanks were being readied in preparation for the Pokolistan crisis.

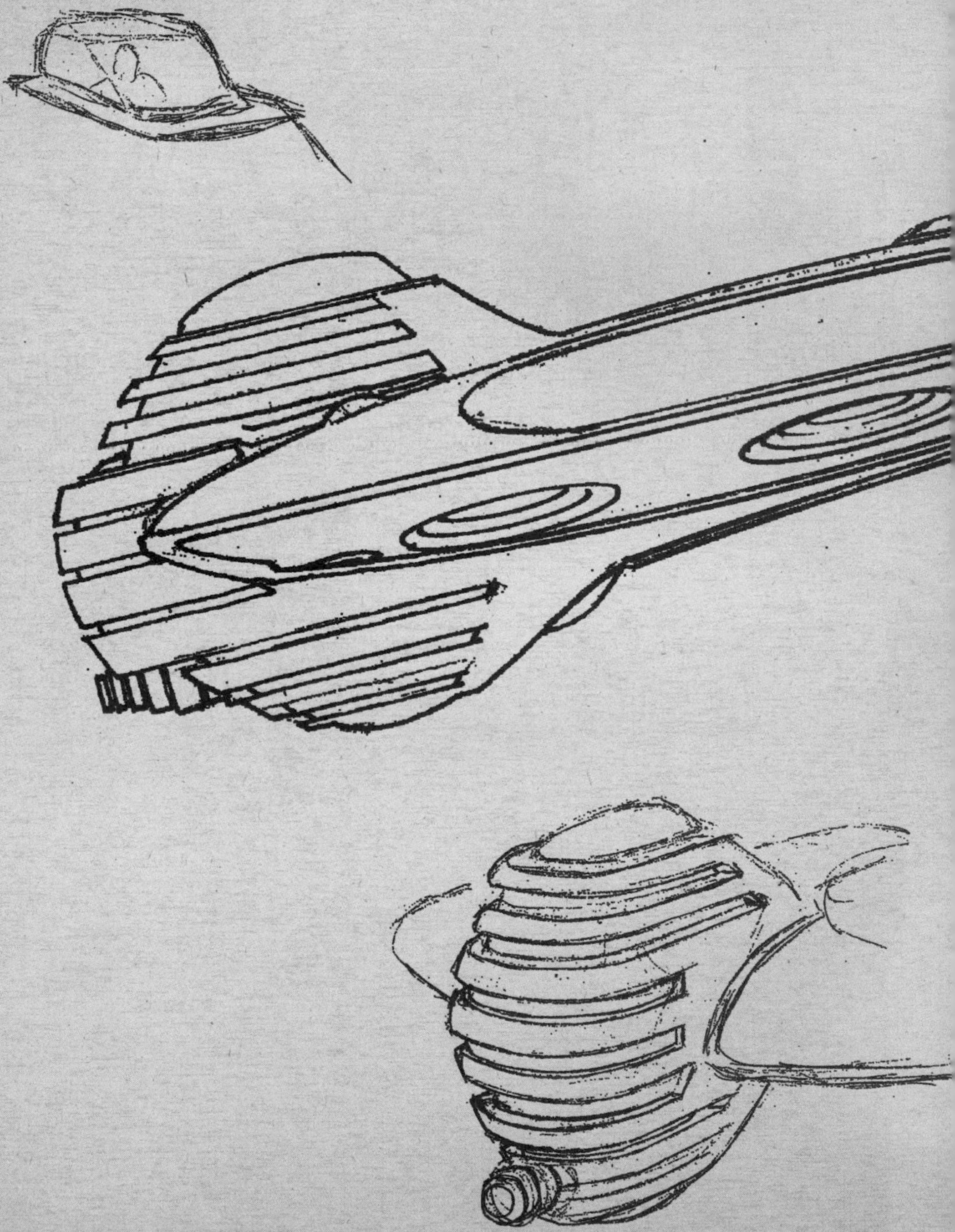

ART BY DUNCAN ROULEAU

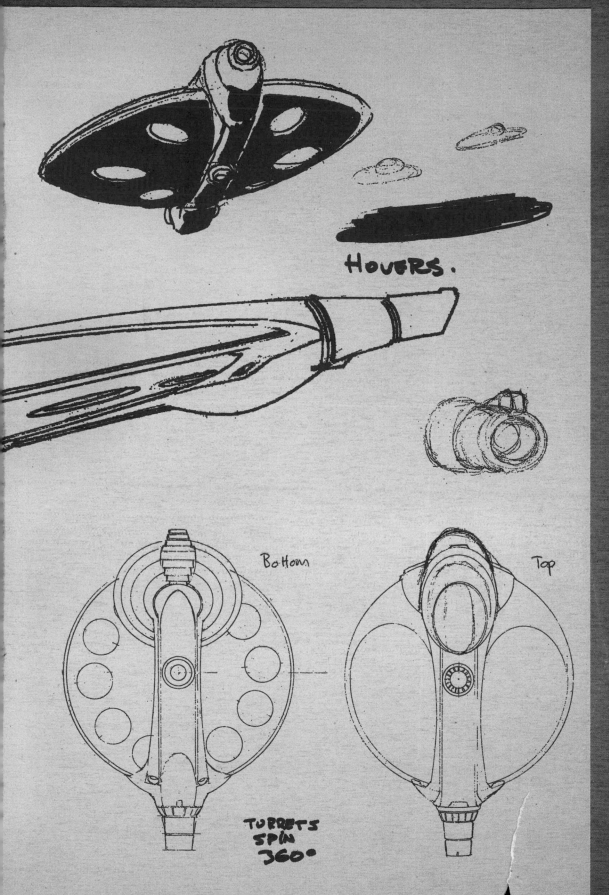

HOVERS.

Bottom

Top

TURRETS
SPIN
360°

SUPERMAN

THE NEVER-ENDING BATTLE CONTINUES IN
THESE BOOKS FROM DC COMICS:

SM0011